HALF
THE SKY

How to Change the World

NICHOLAS D. KRISTOF
AND SHERYL WUDUNN

virago

VIRAGO

First published in Great Britain in 2010 by Virago Press

25

First published in the United States in 2009 by Alfred A. Knopf,
a division of Random House

A CIP catalogue record for this book
is available from the British Library.

ISBN 978-1-84408-682-5

Typeset in Perpetua by M Rules
Printed and bound in Great Britain by
Clays Ltd, St Ives plc

Papers used by Virago are from well-managed forests
and other responsible sources.

MIX
Paper from
responsible sources
FSC
www.fsc.org   FSC® C104740

Nicholas D. Kristof and **Sheryl WuDunn** are the first married couple to win a Pulitzer Prize in journalism, and WuDunn was the first Asian-American to win a Pulitzer. They were foreign correspondents and editors for the *New York Times*, winning their Pulitzer for coverage of China's Tiananmen Square democracy protests. At the *Times*, Sheryl WuDunn worked as a business editor and as a foreign correspondent in Tokyo and Beijing. Nicholas D. Kristof is now an op-ed columnist for the *New York Times* and earned a second Pulitzer for his columns about genocide in Darfur. They live near New York City with their three children.

For our children: Gregory, Geoffrey, and Caroline.
Thanks for your love and patience when research for this book
meant grumpy or absent parents and less cheering at your
soccer games. You've enriched our journeys through
difficult and oppressive countries, and you're
wonderful kids to be arrested with!

And for all those on the front lines around the globe,
saving the world, one woman at a time.

Women hold up half the sky.

– CHINESE PROVERB

CONTENTS

Introduction: The Girl Effect   xi

1   Emancipating Twenty-First-Century Slaves   3
     Fighting Slavery from Seattle   19

2   Prohibition and Prostitution   25
     Rescuing Girls Is the Easy Part   38

3   Learning to Speak Up   51
     The New Abolitionists   60

4   Rule by Rape   68
     Mukhtar's School   79

5   The Shame of 'Honor'   90
     "Study Abroad" – in the Congo   98

6   Maternal Mortality – One Woman a Minute   104
     A Doctor Who Treats Countries, Not Patients   115

7   Why Do Women Die in Childbirth?   121
     Edna's Hospital   137

8   Family Planning and the 'God Gulf'   145
     Jane Roberts and Her 34 Million Friends   162

9   Is Islam Misogynistic?   166
     The Afghan Insurgent   179

10   Investing in Education   184
     Ann and Angeline   198

11   Microcredit: The Financial Revolution   204
     A CARE Package for Goretti   220

12   The Axis of Equality   226
     Tears over *Time* Magazine   239

13   Grassroots vs. Treetops   244
     Girls Helping Girls   254

14   What You Can Do   258
     Four Steps You Can Take in the Next Ten Minutes 279

     Appendix: Organizations Supporting Women   281

     Acknowledgements   285

     Notes   289

     Index   315

who had been promised jobs in the same Thai restaurant. The job agent took the girls deep into Thailand and then handed them to gangsters who took them to Kuala Lumpur, the capital of Malaysia. Rath was dazzled by her first glimpses of the city's clean avenues and gleaming high-rises, including at the time the world's tallest twin buildings; it seemed safe and welcoming. But then thugs sequestered Rath and two other girls inside a karaoke lounge that operated as a brothel. One gangster in his late thirties, a man known as 'the boss,' took charge of the girls and explained that he had paid money for them and that they would now be obliged to repay him. 'You must find money to pay off the debt, and then I will send you back home,' he said, repeatedly reassuring them that if they cooperated they would eventually be released.

Rath was shattered when what was happening dawned on her. The boss locked her up with a customer, who tried to force her to have sex with him. She fought back, enraging the customer. 'So the boss got angry and hit me in the face, first with one hand and then with the other,' she remembers, telling her story with simple resignation. 'The mark stayed on my face for two weeks.' Then the boss and the other gangsters raped her and beat her with their fists.

'You have to serve the customers,' the boss told her as he punched her. 'If not, we will beat you to death. Do you want that?' Rath stopped protesting, but she sobbed and refused to cooperate actively. The boss forced her to take a pill; the gangsters called it 'the happy drug' or 'the shake drug.' She doesn't know exactly what it was, but it made her head shake and induced lethargy, happiness, and compliance for about an hour. When she wasn't drugged, Rath was teary and insufficiently compliant – she was required to beam happily at all customers – so the boss said he would waste no more time on her: She would agree to do as he ordered or he would kill her. Rath then gave in. The girls were forced to work in the brothel seven days a week, fifteen hours a day. They were kept naked to make it more difficult for them to run away or to keep tips or other money, and they were forbidden to ask customers to use condoms. They were battered until they smiled constantly and simulated joy at the sight of customers, because men would not pay as much for sex with girls with reddened eyes and haggard faces. The girls were never allowed out on the street or paid a penny for their work.

'They just gave us food to eat, but they didn't give us much because the customers didn't like fat girls,' Rath says. The girls were bused, under guard, back and forth between the brothel and a tenth-floor apartment where a dozen of them were housed. The door of the apartment was locked from the outside. However, one night, some of the girls went out onto their balcony and pried loose a long, five-inch-wide board from a rack used for drying clothes. They balanced it precariously between their balcony and one on the next building, twelve feet away. The board wobbled badly, but Rath was desperate, so she sat astride the board and gradually inched across.

'There were four of us who did that,' she says. 'The others were too scared, because it was very rickety. I was scared, too, and I couldn't look down, but I was even more scared to stay. We thought that even if we died, it would be better than staying behind. If we stayed, we would die as well.'

Once on the far balcony, the girls pounded on the window and woke the surprised tenant. They could hardly communicate with him because none of them spoke Malay, but the tenant let them into his apartment and then out its front door. The girls took the elevator down and wandered the silent streets until they found a police station and stepped inside. The police first tried to shoo them away, then arrested the girls for illegal immigration. Rath served a year in prison under Malaysia's tough anti-immigrant laws, and then she was supposed to be repatriated. She thought a Malaysian policeman was escorting her home when he drove her to the Thai border – but then he sold her to a trafficker, who peddled her to a Thai brothel.

Rath's saga offers a glimpse of the brutality inflicted routinely on women and girls in much of the world, a malignancy that is slowly gaining recognition as one of the paramount human rights problems of this century.

The issues involved, however, have barely registered on the global agenda. Indeed, when we began reporting about international affairs in the 1980s, we couldn't have imagined writing this book. We assumed that the foreign policy issues that properly furrowed the brow were lofty and complex, like nuclear non-proliferation. It was difficult back then to envision the Council on Foreign Relations fretting about maternal mortality or female genital mutilation. Back then, the oppression of women was a fringe issue, the kind of worthy cause the Girl Scouts might raise money for. We preferred to probe the recondite 'serious issues.'

So this book is the outgrowth of our own journey of awakening as we worked together as journalists for *The New York Times*. The first milestone in that journey came in China. Sheryl is a Chinese-American who grew up in New York City, and Nicholas is an Oregonian who grew up on a sheep and cherry farm near Yamhill, Oregon. After we married, we moved to China, where seven months later we found ourselves standing on the edge af Tianan-men Square watching troops fire their automatic weapons at prodemocracy protesters. The massacre claimed between four hundred and eight hundred lives and transfixed the world. It was the human rights story of the year, and it seemed just about the most shocking violation imaginable.

Then, the following year, we came across an obscure but meticulous demographic study that outlined a human rights violation that had claimed tens of thousands more lives. This study found that thirty-nine thousand baby girls die annually in China because parents don't give them the same medical care and attention that boys receive – and that is just in the first year of life. One Chinese family-planning official, Li Honggui, explained it this way: 'If a boy gets sick, the parents may send him to the hospital at once. But if a girl gets sick, the parents may say to themselves, "Well, let's see how she is tomorrow."' The result is that as many infant girls die unnecessarily *every week* in China as protesters died in the one incident at Tiananmen. Those Chinese girls never received a column inch of news coverage, and we began to wonder if our journalistic priorities were skewed.

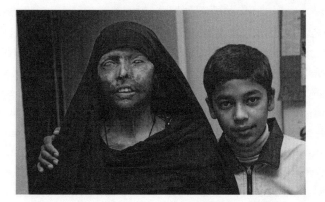

Naeema Azar, a real estate agent, was burned with acid in Rawalpindi,
Pakistan, allegedly by her ex-husband. Since the acid blinded her, her
twelve-year-old son, Ahmed Shah, guides her everywhere.
(Nicholas D. Kristof)

A similar pattern emerged in other countries, particularly in South Asia and the Muslim world. In India, a 'bride burning' – to punish a woman for an inadequate dowry or to eliminate her so a man can remarry – takes place approximately once every two hours, but these rarely constitute news. In the twin cities of Islamabad and Rawalpindi, Pakistan, five thousand women and girls have been doused in kerosene and set alight by family members or in-laws – or, perhaps worse, been seared with acid – for perceived disobedience just in the last nine years. Imagine the outcry if the Pakistani or Indian *governments* were burning women alive at those rates. Yet when the government is not directly involved, people shrug.

When a prominent dissident was arrested in China, we would write a front-page article; when 100,000 girls were routinely kidnapped and trafficked into brothels, we didn't even consider it news. Partly that is because we journalists tend to be good at covering events that happen on a particular day, but we slip at covering events that happen every day – such as the quotidian cruelties inflicted on women and girls. We journalists weren't the only ones who dropped the ball on this subject: A tiny portion of U.S. foreign aid is specifically targeted to women and girls.

Amartya Sen, the ebullient Nobel Prize-winning economist, has developed a gauge of gender inequality that is a striking reminder of the stakes involved. 'More than 100 million women are missing,' Sen wrote in a classic essay in 1990 in *The New York Review of Books*, spurring a new field of research. Sen noted that in normal circumstances women live longer than men, and so there are more females than males in much of the world. Even poor regions like most of Latin America and much of Africa have more females than males. Yet in places where girls have a deeply unequal status, they *vanish*. China has 107 males for every 100 females in its overall population (and an even greater disproportion among newborns), India has 108, and Pakistan has 111. This has nothing to do with biology, and indeed the state of Kerala in the southwest of India, which has championed female education and equality, has the same excess of females that exists in the United States.

The implication of the sex ratios, Professor Sen found, is that about 107 million females are missing from the globe today. Follow-up studies have calculated the number slightly differently, deriving alternative figures for 'missing women' of between 60 million and 101 million. Every year, at least another 2 million girls worldwide disappear because of gender discrimination.

The West has its own gender problems. But discrimination in wealthy countries is often a matter of unequal pay or underfunded sports teams or unwanted touching from a boss. In contrast, in much of the world discrimination is lethal. In India, for example, mothers are less likely to take their daughters to be vaccinated than their sons – that alone accounts for one fifth of India's missing females – while studies have found that, on average, girls are brought to the hospital only when they are sicker than boys taken to the hospital. All told, girls in India from one to five years of age are 50 percent more likely to die than boys the same age. The best estimate is that a little Indian girl dies from discrimination every four minutes.

A big, bearded Afghan named Sedanshah once told us that his wife and son were sick. He wanted both to survive, he said, but his priorities were clear: A son is an indispensable treasure, while a wife is replaceable. He had purchased medication for the boy

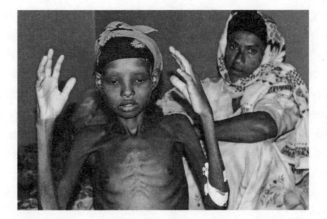

Ummi Ababiya, a thirteen-year-old Ethiopian girl, in an emergency feeding station in southern Ethiopia. Her mother, Zahra, right, said that all the males in the family were well-nourished. Of the dozens of children in the feeding center, almost all were girls, reflecting the way parents typically give priority to boys when food is scarce. Such discrimination kills up to 2 million girls each year worldwide. (Nicholas D. Kristof)

alone. 'She's always sick,' he gruffly said of his wife, 'so it's not worth buying medicine for her.'

Modernization and technology can aggravate the discrimination. Since the 1990s, the spread of ultrasound machines has allowed pregnant women to find out the sex of their fetuses – and then get abortions if they are female. In Fujian Province, China, a peasant raved to us about ultrasound: 'We don't have to have daughters anymore!'

To prevent sex-selective abortion, China and India now bar doctors and ultrasound technicians from telling a pregnant woman the sex of her fetus. Yet that is a flawed solution. Research shows that when parents are banned from selectively aborting female fetuses, more of their daughters die as infants. Mothers do not deliberately dispatch infant girls they are obligated to give birth to, but they are lackadaisical in caring for them. A development economist at Brown University, Nancy Qian, quantified the wrenching trade-off: On average, the deaths of fifteen infant girls can be avoided by allowing one hundred female fetuses to be selectively aborted.

The global statistics on the abuse of girls are numbing. It appears that more girls have been killed in the last fifty years, precisely because they were girls, than men were killed in all the battles of the twentieth century. More girls are killed in this routine 'gendercide' in any one decade than people were slaughtered in all the genocides of the twentieth century.

In the nineteenth century, the central moral challenge was slavery. In the twentieth century, it was the battle against totalitarianism. We believe that in this century the paramount moral challenge will be the struggle for gender equality around the world.

The owners of the Thai brothel to which Rath was sold did not beat her and did not constantly guard her. So two months later, she was able to escape and make her way back to Cambodia.

Upon her return, Rath met a social worker who put her in touch with an aid group that helps girls who have been trafficked start new lives. The group, American Assistance for Cambodia, used $400 in donated funds to buy a small cart and a starter selection of goods so that Rath could become a street peddler. She found a good spot in the open area between the Thai and Cambodian customs offices in the border town of Poipet. Travelers crossing between Thailand and Cambodia walk along this strip, the size of a football field, and it is lined with peddlers selling drinks, snacks, and souvenirs.

Rath outfitted her cart with shirts and hats, costume jewelry, notebooks, pens, and small toys. Now her good looks and outgoing personality began to work in her favor, turning her into an effective saleswoman. She saved and invested in new merchandise, her business thrived, and she was able to support her parents and two younger sisters. She married and had a son, and she began saving for his education.

In 2008, Rath turned her cart into a stall, and then also acquired the stall next door. She also started a 'public phone' business by charging people to use her cell phone. So if you ever cross from Thailand into Cambodia at Poipet, look for a shop on your left, halfway down the strip, where a teenage girl will call out to you,

Srey Rath and her son in front of her shop in Cambodia
(Nichola D. Kristof)

smile, and try to sell you a souvenir cap. She'll laugh and claim she's giving you a special price, and she's so bubbly and appealing that she'll probably make the sale.

Rath's eventual triumph is a reminder that if girls get a chance, in the form of an education or a microloan, they can be more than baubles or slaves; many of them can run businesses. Talk to Rath today – after you've purchased that cap – and you find that she exudes confidence as she earns a solid income that will provide a better future for her sisters and for her young son. Many of the stories in this book are wrenching, but keep in mind this central truth: *Women aren't the problem but the solution. The plight of girls is no more a tragedy than an opportunity.*

That was a lesson we absorbed in Sheryl's ancestral village, at the end of a dirt road amid the rice paddies of southern China. For many years we have regularly trod the mud paths of the Taishan region to Shunshui, the hamlet in which Sheryl's paternal grandfather grew up. China traditionally has been one of the more repressive and smothering places for girls, and we could see hints of this in Sheryl's own family history. Indeed, on our first visit, we accidentally uncovered a family secret: a long-lost stepgrandmother. Sheryl's grandfather had traveled to America with his first wife, but she had given birth only to daughters. So Sheryl's grand-father gave up on her and returned her to Shunshui, where he married a younger woman as a second wife and took her to America. This was Sheryl's grandmother, who duly gave birth to a son – Sheryl's dad. The previous wife and daughters were then wiped out of the family memory.

Something bothered us each time we explored Shunshui and the surrounding villages: Where were the young women? Young men were toiling industriously in the paddies or fanning themselves indolently in the shade, but young women and girls were scarce. We finally discovered them when we stepped into the factories that were then spreading throughout Guangdong Province, the epicenter of China's economic eruption. These factories produced the shoes, toys, and shirts that filled America's shopping malls, generating economic growth rates almost unprecedented in the history of the world – and creating the most effective antipoverty program ever recorded. The factories turned out to be cacopho-nous hives of distaff bees. Eighty percent of the employees on the assembly lines in coastal China are female, and the proportion across the manufacturing belt of East Asia is at least 70 percent. The economic explosion in Asia was, in large part, an outgrowth of the economic empowerment of women. 'They have smaller fin-gers, so they're better at stitching,' the manager of a purse factory explained to us. 'They're obedient and work harder than men,' said the head of a toy factory. 'And we can pay them less.'

Women are indeed a linchpin of the region's development strat-egy. Economists who scrutinized East Asia's success noted a common pattern. These countries took young women who pre-viously had contributed negligibly to gross national product (GNP) and injected them into the formal economy, hugely increasing the labor force. The basic formula was to ease repression, educate girls as well as boys, give the girls the freedom to move to the cities and take factory jobs, and then benefit from a demographic dividend as they delayed marriage and reduced childbearing. The women meanwhile financed the education of younger relatives, and saved enough of their pay to boost national savings rates. This pattern has been called 'the girl effect.' In a nod to the female chromosomes, it could also be called 'the double X solution.'

Evidence has mounted that helping women can be a successful poverty-fighting strategy anywhere in the world, not just in the booming economies of East Asia. The Self Employed Women's Association was founded in India in 1972 and ever since has supported the poorest women in starting businesses – raising living standards in ways that have dazzled scholars and foundations. In Bangladesh, Muhammad Yunus developed microfinance at the Grameen Bank and targeted women borrowers – eventually winning a Nobel Peace Prize for the economic and social impact of his work. Another Bangladeshi group, BRAC, the largest antipoverty organization in the world, worked with the poorest women to save lives and raise incomes – and Grameen and BRAC made the aid world increasingly see women not just as potential beneficiaries of their work, but as agents of it.

In the early 1990s, the United Nations and the World Bank began to appreciate the potential resource that women and girls represent. 'Investment in girls' education may well be the highest-return investment available in the developing world,' Lawrence Summers wrote when he was chief economist of the World Bank. 'The question is not whether countries can afford this investment, but whether countries can afford not to educate more girls.' In 2001 the World Bank produced an influential study, *Engendering Development Through Gender Equality in Rights, Resources, and Voice*, arguing that promoting gender equality is crucial to combat global poverty. UNICEF issued a major report arguing that gender equality yields a 'double dividend' by elevating not only women but also their children and communities. The United Nations Development Programme (UNDP) summed up the mounting research this way: 'Women's empowerment helps raise economic productivity and reduce infant mortality. It contributes to improved health and nutrition. It increases the chances of education for the next generation.'

More and more, the most influential scholars of development and public health – including Sen and Summers, Joseph Stiglitz,

Jeffrey Sachs, and Dr. Paul Farmer – are calling for much greater attention to women in development. Private aid groups and foundations have shifted gears as well. 'Women are the key to ending hunger in Africa,' declared the Hunger Project. French foreign minister Bernard Kouchner, who founded Doctors Without Borders, bluntly declared of development: 'Progress is achieved through women.' The Center for Global Development issued a major report explaining 'why and how to put girls at the center of development.' CARE is taking women and girls as the centerpiece of its antipoverty efforts. The Nike Foundation and the NoVo Foundation are both focusing on building opportunities for girls in the developing world. 'Gender inequality hurts economic growth,' Goldman Sachs concluded in a 2008 research report that emphasized how much developing countries could improve their economic performance by educating girls. Partly as a result of that research, Goldman Sachs committed $100 million to a '10,000 Women' campaign meant to give that many women a business education.

Concerns about terrorism after the 9/11 attacks triggered interest in these issues in an unlikely constituency: the military and counterterrorism agencies. Some security experts noted that the countries that nurture terrorists are disproportionally those where women are marginalized. The reason there are so many Muslim terrorists, they argued, has little to do with the Koran but a great deal to do with the lack of robust female participation in the economy and society of many Islamic countries. As the Pentagon gained a deeper understanding of counterterrorism, and as it found that dropping bombs often didn't do much to help, it became increasingly interested in grassroots projects such as girls' education. Empowering girls, some in the military argued, would disempower terrorists. When the Joint Chiefs of Staff hold discussions of girls' education in Pakistan and Afghanistan, as they did in 2008, you know that gender is a serious topic that fits squarely on the international affairs agenda. That's evident also in the Council on Foreign Relations. The wood-paneled halls that have been used for discussions of MIRV warheads and NATO policy are now employed as well to host well-attended sessions on maternal mortality.

We will try to lay out an agenda for the world's women focusing on three particular abuses: sex trafficking and forced prostitution; gender-based violence, including honor killings and mass rape; and maternal mortality, which still needlessly claims one woman a minute. We will lay out solutions such as girls' education and microfinance, which are working right now.

It's true that there are many injustices in the world, many worthy causes competing for attention and support, and we all have divided allegiances. We focus on this topic because, to us, this kind of oppression feels transcendent – and so does the opportunity. We have seen that outsiders can truly make a significant difference.

Consider Rath once more. We had been so shaken by her story that we wanted to locate that brothel in Malaysia, interview its owners, and try to free the girls still imprisoned there. Unfortunately, we couldn't determine the brothel's name or address. (Rath didn't know English or even the Roman alphabet, so she hadn't been able to read signs when she was there.) When we asked her if she would be willing to return to Kuala Lumpur and help us find the brothel, she turned ashen. 'I don't know,' she said. 'I don't want to face that again.' She wavered, talked it over with her family, and ultimately agreed to go back in the hope of rescuing her girlfriends.

Rath voyaged back to Kuala Lumpur with the protection of an interpreter and a local antitrafficking activist. Nonetheless, she trembled in the red-light districts upon seeing the cheerful neon signs that she associated with so much pain. But since her escape, Malaysia had been embarrassed by public criticism about trafficking, so the police had cracked down on the worst brothels that imprisoned girls against their will. One of those was Rath's. A modest amount of international scolding had led a government to take action, resulting in an observable improvement in the lives of girls at the bottom of the power pyramid. The outcome under-scores that this is a hopeful cause, not a bleak one.

Honor killings, sexual slavery, and genital cutting may seem to Western readers to be tragic but inevitable in a world far, far away. In much the same way, slavery was once widely viewed by many decent Europeans and Americans as a regrettable but ineluctable feature of human life. It was just one more horror that had existed for thousands of years. But then in the 1780s a few indignant Britons, led by William Wilberforce, decided that slavery was so offensive that they had to abolish it. And they did. Today we see the seed of something similar: a global movement to emancipate women and girls.

So let us be clear about this up front: We hope to recruit you to join an incipient movement to emancipate women and fight global poverty by unlocking women's power as economic catalysts. That is the process under way — not a drama of victimization but of empowerment, the kind that transforms bubbly teenage girls from brothel slaves into successful businesswomen.

This is a story of transformation. It is change that is already taking place, and change that can accelerate if you'll just open your heart and join in.

HALF
THE SKY

CHAPTER ONE

Emancipating Twenty-First-Century Slaves

Women might just have something to contribute to
civilization other than their vaginas.

– CHRISTOPHER BUCKLEY, *Florence of Arabia*

The red-light district in the town of Forbesgunge does not actually have any red lights. Indeed, there is no electricity. The brothels are simply mud-walled family compounds along a dirt path, with thatch-roof shacks set aside for customers. Children play and scurry along the dirt paths, and a one-room shop on the corner sells cooking oil, rice, and bits of candy. Here, in the impoverished northern Indian state of Bihar, near the Nepalese border, there's not much else available commercially – except sex.

As Meena Hasina walks down the path, the children pause and stare at her. The adults stop as well, some glowering, and the tension rises. Meena is a lovely, dark-skinned Indian woman in her thirties with warm, crinkly eyes and a stud in her left nostril. She wears a sari and ties her black hair back, and she seems utterly relaxed as she strolls among people who despise her.

Meena is an Indian Muslim who for years was prostituted in a brothel run by the Nutt, a low-caste tribe that controls the local sex trade. The Nutt have traditionally engaged in prostitution and petty crime, and theirs is the world of intergenerational prostitution, in which mothers sell sex and raise their daughters to do the same.

Meena strolls through the brothels to a larger hut that functions

Meena Hasina with her son, Vivek, in Bihar, India (Nicholas D. Kristof)

as a part-time school, sits down, and makes herself comfortable. Behind her, the villagers gradually resume their activities.

'I was eight or nine years old when I was kidnapped and trafficked,' Meena begins. She is from a poor family on the Nepal border and was sold to a Nutt clan, then taken to a rural house where the brothel owner kept prepubescent girls until they were mature enough to attract customers. When she was twelve – she remembers that it was five months before her first period – she was taken to the brothel.

'They brought in the first client, and they'd taken lots of money from him,' Meena recounted, speaking clinically and without emotion. The induction was similar to that endured by Rath in Malaysia, for sex trafficking operates on the same business model worldwide, and the same methods are used to break girls everywhere. 'I started fighting and crying out, so that he couldn't succeed,' Meena said. 'I resisted so much that they had to return the money to him. And they beat me mercilessly, with a belt, with sticks, with iron rods. The beating was tremendous.' She shook her head to clear the memory. 'But even then I resisted. They showed me swords and said they would kill me if I didn't agree. Four or five times, they brought customers in, and I still resisted, and they kept beating me. Finally they drugged me: They gave me wine in

Gangsters in Bihar, India, tried to force this man to sell his daughter into prostitution. When he refused and the girl hid, they destroyed his home. The aid organization Apne Aap Women Worldwide is helping the family.
(Nicholas D. Kristof)

my drink and got me completely drunk.' Then one of the brothel owners raped her. She awoke, hungover and hurting, and realized what had happened. 'Now I am wasted,' she thought, and so she gave in and stopped fighting customers.

In Meena's brothel, the tyrant was the family matriarch, Ainul Bibi. Sometimes Ainul would beat the girls herself, and sometimes she would delegate the task to her daughter-in-law or to her sons, who were brutal in inflicting punishment.

'I wasn't even allowed to cry,' Meena remembers. 'If even one tear fell, they would beat me. I used to think that it was better to die than to live like this. Once I jumped from the balcony, but nothing happened. I didn't even break a leg.'

Meena and the other girls were never allowed out of the brothel and were never paid. They typically had ten or more customers a day, seven days a week. If a girl fell asleep or complained about a stomachache, the issue was resolved with a beating. And when a girl showed any hint of resistance, all the girls would be summoned to watch as the recalcitrant one was tied up and savagely beaten.

'They turned the stereo up loud to cover the screams,' Meena said dryly.

India almost certainly has more modern slaves, in conditions like these, than any other country. There are 2 to 3 million prostitutes in India, and although many of them now sell sex to some degree willingly, and are paid, a significant share of them entered the sex industry unwillingly. One 2008 study of Indian brothels found that of Indian and Nepali prostitutes who started as teenagers, about half said they had been coerced into the brothels; women who began working in their twenties were more likely to have made the choice themselves, often to feed their children. Those who start out enslaved often accept their fate eventually and sell sex willingly, because they know nothing else and are too stigmatized to hold other jobs.

China has more prostitutes than India – some estimates are as high as 10 million or more – but fewer of them are forced into brothels against their will. Indeed, China has few brothels as such. Many of the prostitutes are freelancers working as *ding-dong xiao-jie* (so called because they ring hotel rooms looking for business), and even those working in massage parlors and saunas are typically there on commission and can leave if they want to.

Paradoxically, it is the countries with the most straitlaced and sexually conservative societies, such as India, Pakistan, and Iran, that have disproportionately large numbers of forced prostitutes. Since young men in those societies rarely sleep with their girlfriends, it has become acceptable for them to relieve their sexual frustrations with prostitutes.

The implicit social contract is that upper-class girls will keep their virtue, while young men will find satisfaction in the brothels. And the brothels will be staffed with slave girls trafficked from Nepal or Bangladesh or poor Indian villages. As long as the girls are uneducated, low-caste peasants like Meena, society will look the other way – just as many antebellum Americans turned away from the horrors of slavery because the people being lashed looked different from them.

In Meena's brothel, no one used condoms. Meena is healthy for now, but she has never had an AIDS test. (While HIV prevalence is low in India, prostitutes are at particular risk because of their large number of customers.) Because Meena didn't use condoms, she became pregnant, and this filled her with despair.

'I used to think that I never wanted to be a mother, because my life had been wasted, and I didn't want to waste another life,' Meena said. But Ainul's brothel, like many in India, welcomed the pregnancy as a chance to breed a new generation of victims. Girls are raised to be prostitutes, and boys become servants to do the laundry and cooking.

In the brothel, without medical help, Meena gave birth to a baby girl, whom she named Naina. But soon afterward, Ainul took the baby away from Meena, partly to stop her from breast-feeding – customers dislike prostitutes who are lactating – and partly to keep the baby as a hostage to ensure that Meena would not try to flee.

'We will not let Naina stay with you,' Ainul told her. 'You are a prostitute, and you have no honor. So you might run away.' Later a son, Vivek, followed, and the owners also took him away. So both of Meena's children were raised by others in the brothel, mostly in sections of the compound where she was not allowed to go.

'They held my children captive, so they thought I would never try to escape,' she said. To some degree, the strategy worked. Meena once helped thirteen of the girls escape, but didn't flee her-self because she couldn't bear to leave her children. The penalty for staying behind was a brutal beating for complicity in the escape.

Ainul had herself been a prostitute when she was young, so she was unsympathetic to the younger girls. 'If my own daughters can be prostituted, then you can be, too,' Ainul would tell the girls. And it was true that she had prostituted her own two daughters. ('They had to be beaten up to agree to it,' Meena explained. 'No one wants to go into this.')

Meena estimates that in the dozen years she was in the brothel, she was beaten on average five days a week. Most girls were quickly broken and cowed, but Meena never quite gave in. Her distinguishing characteristic is obstinacy. She can be dogged and mulish, and that is one reason the villagers find her so unpleasant. She breaches the pattern of femininity in rural India by talking back – and fighting back.

The police seemed unlikely saviors to girls in the brothels because police officers regularly visited the brothels and were serviced free. But Meena was so desperate that she once slipped out and went to the police station to demand help.

'I was forced into prostitution by a brothel in town,' Meena told the astonished desk officer at the police station. 'The pimps beat me up, and they're holding my children hostage.' Other policemen came out to see this unusual sight, and they mocked her and told her to go back.

'You have great audacity to come here!' one policeman scolded her. In the end, the police sent her back after extracting a promise from the brothel not to beat her. The brothel owners did not immediately punish her. But a friendly neighbor warned Meena that the brothel owners had decided to murder her. That doesn't happen often in redlight districts, any more than farmers kill producing assets such as good milk cows, but from time to time a prostitute becomes so nettlesome that the owners kill her as a warning to the other girls.

Fearing for her life, Meena abandoned her children and fled the brothel. She traveled several hours by train to Forbesgunge. Someone there told one of Ainul's sons, Manooj, of her whereabouts, and he soon arrived to beat up Meena. Manooj didn't want her causing trouble in his brothel again, so he told her she could live on her own in Forbesgunge and prostitute herself, but she would have to give him money. Not knowing how she could survive otherwise, Meena agreed.

Whenever Manooj returned to Forbesgunge to collect money, he was dissatisfied with the amount Meena gave him and beat her. Once Manooj threw Meena to the ground and was beating her furiously with a belt when a respectable local man intervened.

'You're already pimping her, you're already taking her life-blood,' remonstrated her savior, a pharmacist named Kuduz. 'Why beat her to death as well?'

It wasn't the same as leaping on Manooj to pull him off her, but for a woman like Meena, who was scorned by society, it was star-tling to have anyone speak up for her. Manooj backed off, and Kuduz helped her up. Meena and Kuduz lived near each other in Forbesgunge, and the incident created a bond between them. Soon Kuduz and Meena were chatting regularly, and then he offered to marry her. Thrilled, she accepted.

Manooj was furious when he heard about the marriage, and he offered Kuduz 100,000 rupees ($2,500) to give Meena up – a sum that perhaps reflected his concern that she might use her new respectability as a married woman to cause trouble for the brothel. Kuduz wasn't interested in a deal.

'Even if you offer me two hundred fifty thousand rupees, I will not give her up,' Kuduz said. 'Love has no price.'

After they were married, Meena bore two daughters with Kuduz, and she went back to her native village to look for her par-ents. Her mother had died – neighbors said she had cried constantly after Meena disappeared, then had gone mad – but her father was stunned and thrilled to see his daughter resurrected.

Life was clearly better, but Meena couldn't forget her first two children left behind in the brothel. So she began making journeys back – five hours by bus – to Ainul Bibi's brothel. There she would stand outside and plead for Naina and Vivek.

'As many times as I could, I would go back to fight for my chil-dren,' she remembered. 'I knew they would not let me take my children. I knew they would beat me up. But I thought I had to keep trying.'

It didn't work. Ainul and Manooj didn't let Meena in the brothel; they whipped her and drove her away. The police wouldn't listen to her. The brothel owners not only threatened to kill her, they also threatened to kidnap her two young daughters with Kuduz and sell them to a brothel. Once a couple of gangsters showed up at Meena's house in Forbesgunge to steal the two little girls, but Kuduz grabbed a knife and warned: 'If you even try to steal them, I'll cut you into pieces.'

Meena was terrified for her two younger girls, but she couldn't forget Naina. She knew that Naina was approaching puberty and would soon be put on the market. But what could she do?

Interviewing women like Meena over the years has led us to change our own views on sex trafficking. Growing up in the United States and then living in China and Japan, we thought of prostitution as something that women may turn to opportunistically or out of economic desperation. In Hong Kong, we knew an Australian prostitute who slipped Sheryl into the locker room of her 'men's club' to meet the local girls, who were there because they saw a chance to enrich themselves. We certainly didn't think of prostitutes as slaves, forced to do what they do, for most prostitutes in America, China, and Japan aren't truly enslaved.

Yet it's not hyperbole to say that millions of women and girls *are* actually enslaved today. (The biggest difference from nineteenth-century slavery is that many die of AIDS by their late twenties.) The term that is usually used for this phenomenon, 'sex trafficking,' is a misnomer. The problem isn't sex, nor is it prostitution as such. In many countries – China, Brazil, and most of sub-Saharan Africa – prostitution is widespread but mostly voluntary (in the sense that it is driven by economic pressure rather than physical compulsion). In those places, brothels do not lock up women, and many women work on their own without pimps or brothels. Nor is the problem exactly 'trafficking,' since forced prostitution doesn't always depend on a girl's being transported over a great distance by a middleman. The horror of sex trafficking can more properly be labeled slavery.

The total number of modern slaves is difficult to estimate. The International Labour Organization, a UN agency, estimates that at any one time there are 12.3 million people engaged in forced labor of all kinds, not just sexual servitude. A UN report estimated that 1 million children in Asia alone are held in conditions indistinguishable from slavery. And *The Lancet*, a prominent medical journal in Britain, calculated that '1 million children are forced into prostitution every year and the total number of prostituted children could be as high as 10 million.'

Antitrafficking campaigners tend to use higher numbers, such as 27 million modern slaves. That figure originated in research by Kevin Bales, who runs a fine organization called Free the Slaves. Numbers are difficult to calculate in part because sex workers can't be divided neatly into categories of those working voluntarily and those working involuntarily. Some commentators look at prostitutes and see only sex slaves; others see only entrepreneurs. But in reality there are some in each category and many other women who inhabit a gray zone between freedom and slavery.

An essential part of the brothel business model is to break the spirit of girls, through humiliation, rape, threats, and violence. We met a fifteen-year-old Thai girl whose initiation consisted of being forced to eat dog droppings so as to shatter her self-esteem. Once a girl is broken and terrified, all hope of escape squeezed out of her, force may no longer be necessary to control her. She may smile and laugh at passersby, and try to grab them and tug them into the brothel. Many a foreigner would assume that she is there voluntarily. But in that situation, complying with the will of the brothel owner does not signify consent.

Our own estimate is that there are 3 million women and girls (and a very small number of boys) worldwide who can be fairly termed enslaved in the sex trade. That is a conservative estimate that does not include many others who are manipulated and intimidated into prostitution. Nor does it include millions more who are under eighteen and cannot meaningfully consent to work in brothels. We are talking about 3 million people who in effect are the property of another person and in many cases could be killed by their owner with impunity.

Technically, trafficking is often defined as taking someone (by force or deception) across an international border. The U.S. State Department has estimated that between 600,000 and 800,000 people are trafficked across international borders each year, 80 percent of them women and girls, mostly for sexual exploitation. Since Meena didn't cross a border, she wasn't trafficked in the traditional sense. That's also true of most people who are enslaved in

Long Pross was thirteen when she was kidnapped and sold to a brothel in Cambodia. When she rebelled, the female brothel owner punished her by gouging out her eye with a metal rod. (Nicholas D. Kristof)

brothels. As the U.S. State Department notes, its estimate doesn't include 'millions of victims around the world who are trafficked within their own national borders.'

In contrast, in the peak decade of the transatlantic slave trade, the 1780s, an average of just under eighty thousand slaves were shipped annually across the Atlantic from Africa to the New World. The average then dropped to a bit more than fifty thousand between 1811 and 1850. In other words, far more women and girls are shipped into brothels each year in the early twenty-first century than African slaves were shipped into slave plantations each year in the eighteenth or nineteenth centuries – although the overall population was of course far smaller then. As the journal *Foreign Affairs* observed: 'Whatever the exact number is, it seems almost certain that the modern global slave trade is larger in absolute terms than the Atlantic slave trade in the eighteenth and nineteenth centuries was.'

As on slave plantations two centuries ago, there are few practical restraints on slave owners. In 1791, North Carolina decreed that killing a slave amounted to 'murder,' and Georgia later established that killing or maiming a slave was legally the same as killing or maiming a white person. But these doctrines existed more on paper than on plantations, just as Pakistani laws exist in the statute

12

books but don't impede brothel owners who choose to eliminate troublesome girls.

While there has been progress in addressing many humanitarian issues in the last few decades, sex slavery has actually worsened. One reason for that is the collapse of Communism in Eastern Europe and Indochina. In Romania and other countries, the immediate result was economic distress, and everywhere criminal gangs arose and filled the power vacuum. Capitalism created new markets for rice and potatoes, but also for female flesh.

A second reason for the growth of trafficking is globalization. A generation ago, people stayed at home; now it is easier and cheaper to set out for the city or a distant country. A Nigerian girl whose mother never left her tribal area may now find herself in a brothel in Italy. In rural Moldova, it is possible to drive from village to village and not find a female between the ages of sixteen and thirty.

A third reason for the worsening situation is AIDS. Being sold to a brothel was always a hideous fate, but not usually a death sentence. Now it often is. And because of the fear of AIDS, customers prefer younger girls whom they believe are less likely to be infected. In both Asia and Africa, there is also a legend that AIDS can be cured by sex with a virgin, and that has nurtured demand for young girls kidnapped from their villages.

These factors explain our emphasis on sex slaves as opposed to other kinds of forced labor. Anybody who has spent time in Indian brothels and also, say, at Indian brick kilns knows that it is better to be enslaved working a kiln. Kiln workers most likely live together with their families, and their work does not expose them to the risk of AIDS, so there's always hope of escape down the road.

Inside the brothel, Naina and Vivek were beaten, starved, and abused. They were also confused about their parentage. Naina grew up calling Ainul Grandma, and Ainul's son Vinod, Father. Naina sometimes was told that Vinod's wife, Pinky, was her mother; at other times she was told her mother had died and that

Pinky was her stepmother. But when Naina asked to go to school, Vinod refused and described the relationship in blunter terms.

'You must obey me,' he told Naina, 'because I am your owner.'

The neighbors tried to advise the children. 'People used to say that they could not be my real parents, because they tortured me so much,' Naina recalled. Occasionally, the children heard or even saw Meena coming to the door and calling out to them. Once Meena saw Naina and told her, 'I am your mother.'

'No,' Naina replied. 'Pinky is my mother.'

Vivek remembers Meena's visits as well. 'I used to see her being beaten up and driven away,' he says. 'They told me that my mother was dead, but the neighbors told me that she was my mother after all, and I saw her coming back to try to fight for me.'

Naina and Vivek never went to a day of school, never saw a doctor, and were rarely allowed out. They were assigned chores such as sweeping floors and washing clothes, and they had only rags to wear – and no shoes, for that might encourage them to run away. Then, when Naina was twelve, she was paraded before an older man in a way that left her feeling uncomfortable. 'When I asked "Mother" about the man,' Naina recalled, 'she beat me up and sent me to bed without dinner.'

A couple of days later, 'Mother' told Naina to bathe and took her to the market, where she bought her nice clothes and a nose ring. 'When I asked her why she was buying me all these things, she started scolding me. She told me that I had to listen to everything the man says. She also told me, "Your father has taken money from the man for you." I started crying out loudly.'

Pinky told Naina to wear the clothes, but the girl threw them away, crying inconsolably. Vivek was only eleven, a short boy with a meek manner. But he had inherited his mother's incomprehension of surrender. So he pleaded with his 'parents' and his 'grandma' to let his sister go, or to find a husband for her. Each appeal brought him only another beating – administered with scorn. 'You don't earn any income,' 'Father' told him mockingly, 'so how do you think you can look after your sister?'

Yet Vivek found the courage to confront his tormentors again and again, begging for his sister's freedom. In a town where police officers, government officials, Hindu priests, and respectable middle-class citizens all averted their eyes from forced prostitution, the only audible voice of conscience belonged to an eleven-year-old boy who was battered each time he spoke up. His outspokenness gained him nothing, though. Vinod and Pinky locked him up, forced Naina into the new clothes, and the girl's career as a prostitute began.

'My "mother" was telling me not to get scared, as he is a nice man,' Naina remembered. 'Then they locked me inside the room with the man. The man told me to lock the room from the inside. I slapped him . . . Then that man forced me. He raped me.'

Once a customer gave Naina a tip, and she secretly passed on the money to Vivek. They thought that perhaps Vivek could use a phone, a technology that they had no experience with, to track down the mysterious woman who claimed to be their real mother and seek help from her. But when Vivek tried to use the telephone, the brothel owners found out and both children were flogged.

Ainul thought that Vivek could be distracted with girls, and so he was told to try to have sex with the prostitutes. He was overwhelmed and intimidated at the thought, and when he balked, Pinky beat him up. Seething and fearful of what would become of his sister, Vivek decided that their only hope would be for him to run away and try to find the person who claimed to be their mother. Somewhere Vivek had heard that the woman's name was Meena and that she lived in Forbesgunge, so he fled to the train station one morning and used Naina's tip to buy a ticket.

'I was trembling because I thought that they would come after me and cut me into pieces,' he recalled. After arriving in Forbesgunge, he asked directions to the brothel district. He trudged down the road to the red-light area and then asked one passerby after another: *Where is Meena? Where does she live?*

Finally, after a long walk and many missed turns, he knew he was close to her home, and he called out: *Meena! Meena!* A woman came out of one little home – Vivek's lip quivered as he recounted this part of the story – and looked him over wonderingly. The boy and the woman gazed at each other for a long moment, and then the woman finally said in astonishment: 'Are you Vivek?'

The reunion was sublime. It was a blessed few weeks of giddy, unadulterated joy, the first happiness that Vivek had known in his life. Meena is a warm and emotional woman, and Vivek was thrilled to feel a mother's love for the first time. Yet now that Meena had news about Naina, her doggedness came to the surface again: She was determined to recover her daughter.

'I gave birth to her, and so I can never forget her,' Meena said. 'I must fight for her as long as I breathe. Every day without Naina feels like a year.'

Meena had noticed that Apne Aap Women Worldwide, an organization that fights sex slavery in India, had opened an office in Forbesgunge. Apne Aap is based in Kolkata, the city formerly known as Calcutta, but its founder – a determined former journalist named Ruchira Gupta – grew up partly in Forbesgunge. Other aid groups are reluctant to work in rural Bihar because of the widespread criminality, but Ruchira knew the area and thought it was worth the risk to open a branch office. One of the first people to drop in was Meena. 'Please, please,' Meena begged Ruchira, 'help me get my daughter back!'

There had never been a police raid on a brothel in Bihar State, as far as anyone knew, but Ruchira decided that this could be the first. While Ainul Bibi's brothel had warm ties with the local police, Ruchira had strong connections with national police officials. And Ruchira can be every bit as intimidating as any brothel owner.

So Apne Aap harangued the local police into raiding the brothel to rescue Naina. The police burst in, found Naina, and took her to the police station. But the girl had been so drugged and broken that at the station she looked at Meena and declared numbly: 'I'm not your daughter.' Meena was shattered.

Naina explained later that she had felt alone and terrified, partly because Ainul Bibi had told her that Vivek had died. But after an hour in the police station, Naina began to realize that maybe she

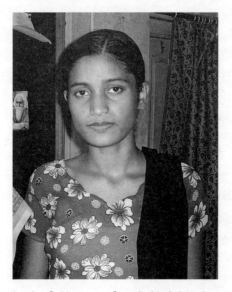

Naina shortly after her rescue from the brothel (Sraboni Sircar)

could escape the brothel, and she finally whispered: 'Yes, you're my mother.'

Apne Aap whisked Naina off to a hospital in Kolkata, where she was treated for severe injuries and a morphine addiction. The brothel had drugged Naina constantly to render her compliant, and the morphine withdrawal was brutal to watch.

In Forbesgunge, life became more difficult and dangerous for Meena and her family. Some of the brothel owners there are related to Ainul and Manooj, and they were furious at Meena. Even those in the Nutt community who didn't like prostitution disapproved of the police raid, and so the townspeople shunned Apne Aap's school and shelter. Meena and her children were stigmatized, and a young man working with Apne Aap was stabbed. Threats were made against Meena's two daughters with Kuduz. Yet Meena was serene as she walked about the streets. She laughed at the idea that she should feel cowed.

'They think that good is bad,' she scoffed, speaking of the local villagers. 'They may not speak to me, but I know what is right and I will stick to it. I will never accept prostitution of myself or my children as long as I breathe.' Meena is working as a community organizer in Forbesgunge, trying to discourage parents from prostituting their daughters and urging them to educate their sons and daughters alike. Over time the resentment against her has diminished a bit, but she is still seen as pushy and unfeminine.

Apne Aap later started a boarding school in Bihar, partly with donations from American supporters, and Meena's children were placed there. The school has a guard and is a much safer place for them. Naina now studies at the boarding school and hopes to become a teacher, and in particular to help disadvantaged children.

One afternoon, Meena was singing to her two young daughters, teaching them a song:

India will not be free,
Until its women are free.
What about the girls in this country?
If girls are insulted and abused and enslaved in this country,
Put your hand on your heart and ask,
Is this country truly independent?

Fighting Slavery from Seattle

People always ask how they can help. Given concerns about corruption, waste, and mismanagement, how can one actually help women like Meena and defeat modern slavery? Is there anything an ordinary person can do?

A starting point is to be brutally realistic about the complexities of achieving change. To be blunt, humanitarians sometimes exaggerate and oversell, eliding pitfalls. They sometimes torture frail data until it yields the demanded 'proof' of success. Partly this is because the causes are worthy and inspiring; those who study education for girls, for example, naturally believe in it. As we'll see, the result is that the research often isn't conducted with the same rigor as is found in, say, examinations of the effectiveness of toothpastes. Aid groups are also reluctant to acknowledge mistakes, partly because frank discussion of blunders is an impediment in soliciting contributions.

The reality is that past efforts to assist girls have sometimes backfired. In 1993, Senator Tom Harkin wanted to help Bangladeshi girls laboring in sweatshops, so he introduced legislation that would have banned imports made by workers under the age of fourteen. Bangladeshi factories promptly fired tens of thousands of these young girls, and many of them ended up in brothels and are presumably now dead of AIDS.

Yet many forms of assistance – particularly in health and education – have an excellent record. Consider the work of Frank Grijalva, the principal of the Overlake School in Redmond, Washington, a fine private school with 450 students in grades five through twelve. Annual tuition hovers around $22,000, and most of the kids are raised in a sheltered upper-middle-class environment. Grijalva was looking for a way to teach his students about how the other half lives.

'It became clear that we, as a very privileged community, needed to be a bigger, more positive force in the world,' Grijalva recalled. Frank heard about Bernard Krisher, a former *Newsweek* correspondent who was so appalled by poverty in Cambodia that he formed an aid group, American Assistance for Cambodia. Rescuing girls from brothels is important, Krisher believes, but the best way to save them is to prevent them from being trafficked in the first place – which means keeping them in school. So American Assistance for Cambodia focuses on educating rural children, especially girls. Bernie Krisher's signature program is the Rural School Project. For $13,000, a donor can establish a school in a Cambodian village. The donation is matched by funds from the World Bank and again by the Asian Development Bank.

Grijalva had a brainstorm: His students could sponsor a school in Cambodia and use it as a way of emphasizing the importance of public service. Initially the response from students and parents was polite but cautious, but then the attacks of 9/11 took place, and suddenly the community was passionately concerned with the larger world and engaged in this project. The students conducted bake sales, car washes, and talent shows, and also educated themselves about Cambodia's history of war and genocide. The school was built in Pailin, a Cambodian town on the Thai border that is notorious for cheap brothels that cater to Thai men.

In February 2003, the school construction was completed, and Grijalva led a delegation of nineteen students from Overlake School to Cambodia for the opening. A cynic might say that the money for the visit would have been better spent building another Cambodian school, but in fact that visit was an essential field trip and learning opportunity for those American students. They lugged along boxes of school supplies, but as they approached Pailin by car, they realized that Cambodia's needs were greater than they ever could have imagined. The dirt-and-gravel road to Pailin was so deeply rutted that it was barely passable, and they saw a bulldozer overturned beside a crater – it had hit a land mine.

When the Americans reached the Cambodian school, they saw a sign declaring it the OVERLAKE SCHOOL in English and Khmer script. At the ribbon cutting, the Americans were welcomed by a sea of excited Cambodians – led by a principal who was missing a leg, a landmine victim himself. Cambodian men then had an average of only 2.6 years of education, and Cambodian women averaged just 1.7 years, so a new school was appreciated in a way the Americans could barely fathom.

The school dedication – and the full week in Cambodia – left an indelible impression on the American students. So Overlake students and parents decided to forge an ongoing relationship with its namesake in Cambodia. The Americans funded an English teacher at the school and arranged for an Internet connection for e-mail. They built a playground and sent books. Then, in 2006, the American school decided to send delegations annually, dispatching students and teachers during spring vacation to teach English and arts to the Cambodian pupils. And in 2007, the group decided to assist a school in Ghana as well, and to send a delegation there.

'This project is simply the most meaningful and worthwhile initiative that I have undertaken in my thirty-six years in education,' Frank Grijalva said. The Overlake School in Cambodia is indeed an extraordinary place. A bridge has washed out, so you have to walk across a stream to reach it, but it looks nothing like the dilapidated buildings that you see in much of the developing world. There are 270 students, ranging in age from six to fifteen. The English teacher is university-educated and speaks good English. Most stunning of all, when we dropped by, the sixth graders were busy sending e-mails from their Yahoo accounts – to the kids at Overlake School in America.

One of those writing an e-mail was Kun Sokkea, a thirteen-year-old girl who would soon be the first in her family ever to graduate from elementary school. Her father had died of AIDS, and her mother was sick with the same disease and needed to be

Kun Sokkea in front of the Overlake School in Cambodia
(Nicholas D. Kristof)

nursed constantly. Kun Sokkea is rail-thin, a bit gangly, with long, stringy black hair. She is reserved, and her shoulders sag with the burdens of poverty.

'My mom encourages me to stay in school, but sometimes I think I should go out and earn money,' Kun Sokkea explained. 'I have no dad to support Mom, so maybe I should provide for her. In one day, I could earn seventy baht [a bit more than two dollars] cutting hay or planting corn.'

To address these financial pressures, American Assistance for Cambodia started a program called Girls Be Ambitious, which in effect bribes families to keep girls in school. If a girl has perfect attendance in school for one month, her family gets $10. A similar approach has been used very effectively and cheaply to increase education for girls in Mexico and other countries. Kun Sokkea's family is now getting the stipend. For donors who can't afford to fund an entire school, it's a way to fight trafficking at a cost of $120 per year per girl. The approach helps because it is typically girls like Kun Sokkea who end up trafficked. Their families are desperate for money, the girls are poorly educated, and a trafficker promises them a great job selling fruit in a distant city.

Kun Sokkea showed us her home, a rickety shack built on

stilts – to guard against flooding and vermin – in a field near the school. The house has no electricity, and her possessions were in one small bag. She never has to worry about choosing what to wear: She has just one shirt, and no shoes other than a pair of flip-flops. Kun Sokkea has never been to a dentist and to a doctor only once, and she gets the family's drinking water from the nearby creek. That's the same creek in which Kun Sokkea washes the family clothes (she borrows someone else's shirt to wear when she has to wash her own). She shares a mattress on the floor with her brother, as three other family members sleep a few feet away. Kun Sokkea has never touched a phone, ridden in a car, or had a soft drink; when she was asked if she ever drank milk, she looked confused and said that as a baby she had drunk her mother's milk.

Yet one thing Kun Sokkea has beside her bed is a photo of the American Overlake students on their campus. In the evenings before she goes to sleep, she sometimes picks up the photo and studies the smiling faces and neat lawns and modern buildings. In her own shack, with her mother sick and often crying, her siblings hungry, it is a window into a magical land where people have plenty to eat and get cured when they fall ill. In such a place, she thinks, everybody must be happy all the time.

Kun Sokkea and her family aren't the only beneficiaries. The Americans themselves have been transformed as much as the Cambodians. And that is something you see routinely: Aid projects have a mixed record in helping people abroad, but a superb record in inspiring and educating the donors. Sometimes the lessons are confusing, as Overlake found when it tried to help Kun Sokkea get to middle school after graduating from the elementary school. She needed transport because the middle school was far away, and young men in the area often harassed girls on their way to the school.

So, at the teachers' suggestion, Overlake bought Kun Sokkea a bicycle, and for several months that worked very well. Then an older woman, a neighbor, asked to borrow Kun Sokkea's bicycle; the girl felt she couldn't say no to an older person. The woman then sold the bicycle and kept the money she received for it. Frank

Grijalva and the American students were beside themselves, but they had learned an important lesson about how defeating poverty is more difficult than it seems at first. The Americans decided they couldn't just buy Kun Sokkea another bicycle, so the girl returned to walking an hour each way to school and back. Perhaps in part because of the distance involved and the risks of getting to school, Kun Sokkea began to miss a fair number of days. Her grades suffered. In early 2009, she dropped out of school.

America's schools rarely convey much understanding of the 2.7 billion people (40 percent of the world's population) who today live on less than $2 a day. So while the primary purpose of a new movement on behalf of women is to stop slavery and honor killings, another is to expose young Americans to life abroad so that they, too, can learn and grow and blossom – and then continue to tackle the problems as adults.

'After going to Cambodia, my plans for the future have changed,' said Natalie Hammerquist, a seventeen-year-old at Overlake who regularly e-mails two Cambodian students. 'This year I'm taking three foreign languages, and I plan on picking up more in college.'

Natalie's Cambodian girlfriend wants to be a doctor but can't afford to go to university. That grates on Natalie: *A girl just like me has to abandon her dreams because they're unaffordable*. Now Natalie plans on a career empowering young people around the world: 'All anyone should do is use their gifts in what way they can, and this is how I can use mine. That is the weight of how valuable seeing Cambodia was for me.'

CHAPTER TWO

Prohibition and Prostitution

> Although volume upon volume is written to prove slavery a
> very good thing, we never hear of the man who wishes to
> take the good of it, by being a slave himself.

– ABRAHAM LINCOLN

After visiting Meena Hasina and Ruchira Gupta in Bihar, Nick crossed from India into Nepal at a border village crowded with stalls selling clothing, snacks, and more sinister wares. That border crossing is the one through which thousands of Nepali girls are trafficked into India on their way to the brothels of Kolkata. There they are valued for their light skin, good looks, docility, and inability to speak the local language, hindering the possibility of escape. As Nick filled out some required paperwork at the border post, Nepalis streamed into India, without filling out a form.

While sitting in the border shack, Nick began talking with one Indian officer who spoke excellent English. The man said he had been dispatched by the intelligence bureau to monitor the border.

'So what exactly are you monitoring?' Nick asked.

'We're looking for terrorists, or terror supplies,' said the man, who wasn't monitoring anything very closely, since one truck after another was driving past. 'After 9/11, we've tightened things up here. And we're also looking for smuggled or pirated goods. If we find them, we'll confiscate them.'

'What about trafficked girls?' Nick asked. 'Are you keeping an eye out for them? There must be a lot.'

'Oh, a lot. But we don't worry about them. There's nothing you can do about them.'

'Well, you could arrest the traffickers. Isn't trafficking girls as important as pirating DVDs?'

The intelligence officer laughed genially and threw up his hands. 'Prostitution is inevitable.' He chuckled. 'There has always been prostitution in every country. And what's a young man going to do from the time when he turns eighteen until when he gets married at thirty?'

'Well, is the best solution really to kidnap Nepali girls and imprison them in Indian brothels?'

The officer shrugged, unperturbed. 'It's unfortunate,' he agreed. 'These girls are sacrificed so that we can have harmony in society. So that good girls can be safe.'

'But many of the Nepali girls being trafficked are good girls, too.'

'Oh, yes, but those are peasant girls. They can't even read. They're from the countryside. The good Indian middle-class girls are safe.'

Nick, who had been gritting his teeth, offered an explosive suggestion: 'I've got it! You know, in the United States we have a lot of problems with harmony in society. So we should start kidnapping Indian middle-class girls and forcing them to work in brothels in the United States! Then young American men could have fun, too, don't you think? That would improve our harmony in society!'

There was an ominous silence, but finally the police officer roared with laughter.

'You are joking!' the officer said, beaming. 'That's very funny!' Nick gave up.

People get away with enslaving village girls for the same reason that people got away with enslaving blacks two hundred years ago: The victims are perceived as discounted humans. India had delegated an intelligence officer to look for pirated goods because it knew that the United States cares about intellectual property. When India feels that the West cares as much about slavery as it does about pirated DVDs, it will dispatch people to the borders to stop traffickers.

A Cambodian teenager, kidnapped and sold to a brothel, in the room where she works (Nicholas D. Kristof)

The tools to crush modern slavery exist, but the political will is lacking. That must be the starting point of any abolitionist movement. We're not arguing that Westerners should take up this cause because it's the fault of the West; Western men do not play a central role in prostitution in most poor countries. True, American and European sex tourists are part of the problem in Thailand, the Philippines, Sri Lanka, and Belize, but they are still only a small percentage of the johns. The vast majority are local men. Moreover, Western men usually go with girls who are more or less voluntary prostitutes, because they want to take the girls back to their hotel rooms, while forced prostitutes are not normally allowed out of the brothels. So this is not a case where we in the West have a responsibility to lead because we're the source of the problem. Rather, we single out the West because, even though we're peripheral to the slavery, our action is necessary to overcome a horrific evil.

One reason the modern abolitionist movement hasn't been more effective is the divisive politics of prostitution. In the 1990s, the American left and right collaborated and achieved the Trafficking Victims Protection Act of 2000, which was a milestone in raising awareness of international trafficking on the global agenda. The antitrafficking movement then was unusually bipartisan, strongly backed by some liberal Democrats, such as the late senator Paul Wellstone, and by some conservative Republicans, such as Senator Sam Brownback. Hillary Rodham Clinton was also a leader on this issue, and no one has been a greater champion than Carolyn Maloney, a Democratic congresswoman from New York. Likewise, one of George W. Bush's few positive international legacies was a big push against trafficking. Vital Voices and other liberal groups were stalwart on sex trafficking, as were International Justice Mission and other conservative evangelical groups. Yet while the left and the right each do important work fighting trafficking, they mostly do it separately. The abolitionist movement would be far more effective if it forged unity in its own ranks.

One reason for discord is a dispute about how to regard prostitution. The left often refers nonjudgmentally to 'sex workers' and tends to be tolerant of transactions among consenting adults. The right, joined by some feminists, refers to 'prostitutes' or 'prostituted women' and argues that prostitution is inherently demeaning and offensive. The result of this bickering is a lack of cooperation in combatting what *everybody* believes is abhorrent: forced prostitution and child prostitution.

'The debate is being carried on in a theoretical framework at universities,' Ruchira Gupta of Apne Aap said, rolling her eyes, as she sat in her old family home in Bihar after a day in the red-light district. 'Very few of those theorists come to the grassroots and see what is going on. The whole debate about what we should call the problem is irrelevant. What is relevant is that children are being enslaved.'

What policy should we pursue to try to eliminate that slavery? Originally, we sympathized with the view that a prohibition won't work any better against prostitution today than it did against alcohol in America in the 1920s. Instead of trying fruitlessly to ban prostitution, we believed it would be preferable to legalize and regulate it. That pragmatic 'harm reduction' model is preferred by many aid groups, because it allows health workers to pass out condoms and curb the spread of AIDS, and it permits access to brothels so that they can more easily be checked for underage girls.

Over time, we've changed our minds. That legalize-and-regulate model simply hasn't worked very well in countries where prostitution is often coerced. Partly that's because governance is often poor, so the regulation is ineffective, and partly it's that the legal brothels tend to attract a parallel illegal business in young girls and forced prostitution. In contrast, there's empirical evidence that crackdowns can succeed, when combined with social services such as job retraining and drug rehabilitation, and that's the approach we've come to favor. In countries with widespread trafficking, we favor a law enforcement strategy that pushes for fundamental change in police attitudes and regular police inspections to check for underage girls or anyone being held against their will. That means holding governments accountable not just to pass laws but also to enforce them, and monitoring how many brothels are raided and pimps are arrested. Jail-like brothels should be closed down, sting operations should be mounted against buyers of virgin girls, and national police chiefs must be under pressure to crack down on corruption as it relates to trafficking. The idea is to reduce the brothel owners' profits.

We won't eliminate prostitution. In Iran, brothels are strictly banned, and the mayor of Tehran was a law-and-order hard-liner until, according to Iranian news accounts, he was arrested in a police raid on a brothel where he was in the company of six naked prostitutes. So crackdowns don't work perfectly, but they tend to lead nervous police to demand higher bribes, which reduces profitability for the pimps. Or the police will close down at least those brothels that aren't managed by other police officers. With such methods, we can almost certainly reduce the number of fourteen-year-old girls who are held in cages until they die of AIDS.

'It's pretty doable,' says Gary Haugen, who runs International Justice Mission. 'You don't have to arrest everybody. You just have to get enough that it sends a ripple effect and changes the calculations. That changes the pimps' behavior. You can drive traffickers of virgin village girls to fence stolen radios instead.'

Many liberals and feminists are taken aback by the big stick approach we advocate, arguing that it just drives sex establishments underground. They argue instead for a legalize-and-regulate model based on empowerment of sex workers, and they cite a success: the Sonagachi Project.

Sonagachi, which means 'golden tree,' is a sprawling red-light district in Kolkata. In the 1700s and 1800s, it had been a legendary locale for concubines. Today it has hundreds of multistory brothels built along narrow alleys, housing more than six thousand prostitutes. In the early 1990s, health experts were deeply concerned by the spread of AIDS in India, and in 1992 they started the Sonagachi Project with the backing of the World Health Organization (WHO). A key element was to nurture a union of sex workers, Durbar Mahila Samanwaya Committee (DMSC), which would encourage condom use and thus reduce the spread of HIV through prostitution.

DMSC seemed successful in encouraging the use of condoms. It publicized its role as a pragmatic solution to the public health problems of prostitution. One study found that the Sonagachi Project increased consistent condom use by 25 percent. A 2005 study found that only 9.6 percent of Sonagachi sex workers were infected with HIV, compared to about 50 percent in Mumbai (the city formerly known as Bombay), where there was no sex workers' union. DMSC became media-savvy and offered tours of Sonagachi, emphasizing that its members block the arrival of underage or unwilling girls, and that selling sex is at least a way for unskilled female laborers to earn a decent income. The Sonagachi model has also had the indirect support of both CARE and the Bill & Melinda Gates Foundation, two organizations that we greatly respect. And many development experts have applauded the model.

As we probed the numbers, however, we saw that they were flimsier than they at first appeared. HIV prevalence was inexplicably high among new arrivals to Sonagachi – 27.7 percent among sex workers aged twenty or younger. Research had also shown that, initially, all sex workers interviewed in Sonagachi claimed to use condoms nearly all the time. But when pressed, they admitted lower rates: Only 56 percent said they had used condoms consistently with their last three customers. Moreover, the contrast with Mumbai was misleading, because southern and western India had always had far higher HIV rates than northern and eastern India. Indeed, at the time the Sonagachi Project began in Kolkata, HIV prevalence among sex workers in Mumbai was already 51 percent and in Kolkata 1 percent, according to a study by the Harvard School of Public Health. DMSC may well have encouraged the use of condoms, but the public health benefits seem more modest than supporters claim.

Nick criticized DMSC on his blog, and an Indian responded:

It never ceases to amaze me how supposedly feminist, progressive thinkers like you often get weak-kneed at the prospect of women actually owning decisions about sex and work . . . It is highly unsavory of you to exploit the difficult stories of sex workers as an argument against sex work as a profession at a time when sex workers are finally making some headway in creating safety for themselves. Your stance . . . smacks of the Western missionary position of rescuing brown savages from their fate.

Many Indian liberals agree with that perspective. But we heard contrary views from women with long experience fighting trafficking in the red-light districts of Kolkata. One is Ruchira Gupta. Another is Urmi Basu, who runs a foundation called New Light that fights for current and former prostitutes. Both Ruchira and Urmi say that DMSC has become a front for the brothel owners, and that well-meaning Western support for DMSC has provided cover for traffickers.

Urmi introduced us to Geeta Ghosh, who portrayed a very different Sonagachi than the one seen on DMSC tours. Geeta grew up in a poor village in Bangladesh and fled from abusive parents when she was eleven. A friend's 'aunt' offered to help Geeta and took her to Sonagachi, where the aunt turned out to be a brothel owner. Geeta never saw any hint that DMSC was blocking the trafficking of girls like her.

At first, the aunt treated Geeta well. But when Geeta was twelve, the aunt dolled her up with a new hairstyle, gave her a skimpy dress, and locked her in a room with an Arab customer.

'I was terrified to see this huge man in front of me,' she said. 'I cried a lot and fell to his feet, pleading. But I couldn't make him understand me. He pulled off my dress, and the rapes went on for a month like that. He made me sleep naked beside him, and he drank a lot . . . It was a very painful experience. I had lots of bleeding.'

During her first three years as a prostitute in Sonagachi, Geeta was not allowed outside and had none of the freedoms that DMSC claims exist. She was beaten regularly with sticks and threatened with a butcher's knife.

'There was a big drain in the house for sewage,' Geeta recalled. 'The madam said, "If you ever try to run away, we'll chop you up and throw the pieces down this drain."' As far as Geeta could see, the supposed campaign by DMSC to prevent trafficking was simply an illusion peddled to outsiders. Even when she was finally allowed to stand on the street outside the brothel to wave to customers, she was closely watched. Contradicting the notion that the girls get a decent income, Geeta was never paid a single rupee for her work. It was slave labor, performed under threat of execution. Other women who worked in Sonagachi after DMSC took control offered similar stories.

Anybody can walk through Sonagachi in the evening and see the underage girls. Nick toured Sonagachi several times, entering the brothels seemingly as a potential customer. He saw many young girls but wasn't allowed to take them off the premises, presumably for fear that that they would flee. And because they spoke only Bengali, Nepali, or Hindi, and he speaks none of those languages, he couldn't interview them. But Anup Patel, a Hindi-speaking medical student at Yale University, conducted research on condom use in Kolkata in 2005. He found that not only is the price of sex in Sonagachi negotiated between the customer and the brothel owner (rather than with the girl herself), but the customer can pay the brothel owner a few extra rupees for the right not to use a condom. The girl has no say in that.

Anup joined a DMSC tour and listened as a madam boasted how almost all of the prostitutes come to Sonagachi on their own to enter 'the noble profession of sex work.' In one brothel, Anup and two others sat on a bed in the back, near a prostitute who was listening mutely as the madam claimed that the girls chose voluntarily to earn the quick money and human rights that DMSC can assure them. He explained:

While the madam spoke with others in the room, gushing about the group's success, the three of us on the bed asked the prostitute in Hindi to tell us if those things were true. Afraid and timid, the prostitute remained silent until we assured her that we wouldn't get her in trouble. Barely audible, she told us that almost none of the prostitutes in Sonagachi came with aspirations of becoming a sex worker. Most of them, like herself, were trafficked . . . When I asked her if she wanted to leave Sonagachi, her eyes lit up; before she could say anything, the DMSC official put her hand on my back and said that it was time to move on . . .

We continued to the next brothel on the tour, passing hundreds of prostitutes along the way. A person in our group asked if we could visit Neel Kamal, the brothel that was rumored to still prostitute minors. The DMSC official quickly rejected the idea, suggesting that the DMSC had not asked for prior permission and didn't want to violate the prostitutes' rights before warning them. Big talk goes far in India — faced with a stern threat to 'make the appropriate phone calls' if the terrified-looking DMSC official did not cooperate, she took us in the direction of the notorious Neel Kamal.

Five pimps guarded the locked gate that marked the entrance to the multistory brothel. While one pimp unlocked the gate, the four others ran inside with a clarion call: 'Visitors are here!' Our group rushed in, climbing the staircase to the first floor, but stopped dead in our tracks: Dozens of girls, no older than sixteen, with bright red lipstick, began running down the dingy hallways, disappearing into hidden rooms.

The pimps kept shouting as the DMSC official told us to remain still. Everywhere I looked, girls were fleeing. In the meantime, I had managed to block a doorway where two teenage girls, no more than fourteen years old, were sprawled on the bed with their legs wide open, their genitals visible through denim miniskirts.

While the Sonagachi Project enjoyed some success in curbing AIDS, there is an intriguing contrast with the big-stick approach taken in Mumbai. Mumbai's brothels historically were worse than Kolkata's, and they are famous for the 'cage girls' who were held behind bars in brothels. Yet as a result of crackdowns, in part because of American pressure, the number of prostitutes in central Mumbai fell sharply over several years. The central red-light district of Mumbai may have just six thousand prostitutes today, down from thirty-five thousand a decade ago. The number in Sonagachi remained unchanged.

It's true that the crackdown in Mumbai drove some brothels underground. That made it hard to determine how successful the crackdown truly was, and also harder to provide condoms and medical services to prostitutes. It's possible that HIV prevalence among them rose, although it's impossible to be sure because there is no way to test girls in clandestine brothels. But the crackdown also made prostitution less profitable for brothel owners, and so the price of a girl bought or sold among Mumbai's brothels tumbled. Thus traffickers instead began shipping young flesh to Kolkata, where they could get a better price. That suggests that there is now less trafficking into Mumbai, which represents at least some success.

The Netherlands and Sweden highlight the differences between the big-stick approach and the legalize-and-regulate model. In

2000, the Netherlands formally legalized prostitution (which had always been tolerated) in the belief that it would then be easier to provide health and labor checks to prostitutes, and to keep minors and trafficking victims from taking up the trade. In 1999, Sweden took the opposite approach, criminalizing the purchase of sexual services, but not the sale of them by prostitutes; a man caught paying for sex is fined (in theory, he can be imprisoned for up to six months), while the prostitute is not punished. This reflected the view that the prostitute is more a victim than a criminal.

A decade later, Sweden's crackdown seems to have been more successful in reducing trafficking and forced prostitution. The number of prostitutes in Sweden dropped by 41 percent in the first five years, according to one count, and the price of sex dropped, too – a pretty good indication that demand was down. Swedish prostitutes are unhappy with the change, because of the falling prices, but that decline has made Sweden a less attractive destination for traffickers. Indeed, some traffickers believe that trafficking girls into Sweden is no longer profitable and that girls should be taken to Holland instead. Swedes themselves believe the measure has been a success, although it was controversial at the time it was instituted; one poll showed that 81 percent of Swedes approved of the law.

In the Netherlands, legalization has facilitated health checkups for women in the legal brothels, but there's no evidence that sexually transmitted diseases (STDs) or HIV has declined. Pimps in the Netherlands still offer underage girls, and trafficking and forced prostitution continue. At least initially, the number of illegal prostitutes increased, apparently because Amsterdam became a center for sex tourism. The Amsterdam City Council found the sex tourism and criminality so vexing that in 2003 it ended its experiment with 'tolerance zones' for street prostitution, although it retained legal brothels. The bottom line? Customers can easily find an underage Eastern European girl working as a prostitute in Amsterdam, but not in Stockholm.

Other European countries have concluded that Sweden's experiment has been more successful and are now moving toward that model. We would also like to see some American states try to determine if it is feasible in the United States as well.

In the developing world, however, this difficult, polarizing debate is mostly just a distraction. In India, for example, brothels are technically illegal – but, as we said earlier, they are ubiquitous; the same is true in Cambodia. In poor countries, the law is often irrelevant, particularly outside the capital. Our focus has to be on changing reality, not changing laws.

Congress took an important step in that direction in 2000 by requiring the State Department to put out an annual Trafficking in Persons Report – the TIP report. The report ranks countries according to how they tackle trafficking, and those in the lowest tier are sanctioned. This meant that for the first time U.S. embassies abroad had to gather information on trafficking. American diplomats began holding discussions with their foreign ministry counterparts, who then had to add trafficking to the list of major concerns such as proliferation and terrorism. As a result, the foreign ministries made inquiries of the national police agencies.

Simply asking questions put the issue on the agenda. Countries began passing laws, staging crackdowns, and compiling fact sheets. Pimps found that the cost of bribing police went up, eroding their profit margins.

This approach can be taken further. Within the State Department, the trafficking office has been marginalized, even relegated to another building. If the secretary of state publicly and actively embraced the trafficking office, taking its director along on relevant trips, for instance, that would elevate the issue's profile. The president could visit a shelter like Apne Aap's on a state visit to India. Europe should have made trafficking an issue in negotiating the accession of Eastern European countries wishing to enter the European Union, and it can still make this an issue for Turkey in that regard.

The big-stick approach should focus in particular on the sale of virgins. Such transactions, particularly in Asia, account for a disproportionate share of trafficker profits and kidnappings of young teenagers. And the girls, once raped, frequently resign themselves to being prostitutes until they die. It is often rich Asians, particularly overseas Chinese, who are doing the buying – put a few of them in jail, and good things will happen: The market for virgins will quickly shrink, their price will drop, gangs will shift to less risky or more profitable lines of business, the average age of prostitutes will rise somewhat, and the degree of compulsion in prostitution will diminish as well.

We saw such a shift in Svay Pak, a Cambodian village that used to be one of the most notorious places in the world for sex slavery. On Nick's first visit, brothels there had seven- and eight-year-old girls for sale. Nick was taken for a prospective customer and was allowed to talk to a thirteen-year-old girl who had been sold to the brothel and was waiting in terror for the sale of her virginity. But then the State Department began putting out the TIP report and severely criticized Cambodia, media reports put a spotlight on Cambodian slavery of girls, and the International Justice Mission opened an office there. Svay Pak became a symbol of sexual slavery, and the Cambodian government decided that the bribes paid by the brothel owners weren't worth the hassle and embarrassment. So the police cracked down.

The last couple of times Nick visited Svay Pak, girls were not openly on display and the front gates of the brothels were chained. Brothel Owners, imagining him to be a customer, nervously whisked him inside the back entrances and brought out a few prostitutes, but there seemed to be at most only one tenth as many as there had been. And when Nick asked to see young girls or virgins, the owners said they were out of stock and would have to make arrangements to bring one in for an appointment a day or two later. This is a sign that meaningful progress is possible. Some degree of prostitution will probably always be with us, but we need not acquiesce to widespread sexual slavery.

Rescuing Girls Is the Easy Part

We became slave owners in the twenty-first century the old-fashioned way: We paid cash in exchange for two slave girls and a couple of receipts. The girls were then ours to do with as we liked.

Rescuing girls from brothels is the easy part, however. The challenge is keeping them from returning. The stigma that the girls feel in their communities after being freed, coupled with drug dependencies or threats from pimps, often lead them to return to the red-light district. It's enormously dispiriting for well-meaning aid workers who oversee a brothel raid to take the girls back to a shelter and give them food and medical care, only to see the girls climb over the back wall.

Our unusual purchase came about when Nick traveled with Naka Nathaniel, then a *New York Times* videographer, to an area in north-western Cambodia notorious for its criminality. Nick and Naka arrived in the town of Poipet and checked in to an $8-a-night guesthouse that doubled as a brothel. They focused their interviews on two teenage girls, Srey Neth and Srey Momm, each in a different brothel.

Neth was very pretty, short and light-skinned. She looked fourteen or fifteen, but she thought she was older than that; she had no idea of her actual birth date. A woman pimp brought her to Nick's room, and she sat on the bed, quivering with fear. She had been in the brothel only a month, and Nick would have been her first foreign customer. Nick needed his interpreter present in the room as well, and this puzzled the pimp, who nevertheless accommodated.

Srey Neth at the entrance to her home, right after we took her back to her family from the brothel (Nicholas D. Kristof)

Black hair fell over Neth's shoulders and onto her tight pink T-shirt. Below, she wore equally tight blue jeans, and sandals. Neth had plump cheeks, but the rest of her was thin and fragile; thick makeup caked her face in a way that seemed incongruous, as if she were a child who had played with her mother's cosmetics.

After some awkward conversation through the interpreter, as Nick asked Neth about how she had grown up and about her family, she began to calm down. She stopped trembling and mostly looked in the direction of the television in the corner of the room, which Nick had put on to muffle the sound of their voices. She responded to questions briefly and without interest.

For the first five minutes, Neth claimed that she was selling her body of her own volition. She insisted that she was free to come and go as she pleased. But when it became clear that this wasn't some sort of test by her pimp, and that she wouldn't be beaten for telling the truth, she recounted her story in a dull monotone.

A female cousin had taken Neth from their village, telling the family that Neth would be selling fruit in Poipet. Once in Poipet, Neth was sold to the brothel and closely guarded. After a check by a doctor confirmed that her hymen was intact, the brothel auctioned her virginity to a Thai casino manager, who locked her up in a hotel room for several days and slept with her three times (he later died of AIDS). Now Neth was confined to the guesthouse and was young enough and light-skinned enough to rent for top rates.

'I can walk around in Poipet, but only with a close relative of the owner,' Neth explained. 'They keep me under close watch. They do not let me go out alone. They're afraid I would run away.'

'So why not escape at night?' Nick asked.

'They would get me back, and something bad would happen. Maybe a beating. I heard that when a group of girls tried to escape, they locked them in the rooms and beat them up.'

What about the police? Could the girls go to the police for help?

Neth shrugged uninterestedly. 'The police wouldn't help me because they get bribes from the brothel owners,' she said in her robotic way, still staring at the television.

'Would you want to leave here? If you were set free, what would you do?'

Neth suddenly looked away from the television, a flash of interest in her eyes.

'I'd go back home,' she said, and she seemed to be gauging whether the question was serious. 'Back to my family. I'd like to try to open a little shop to make money.'

'Do you really want to leave?' Nick asked. 'If I were to buy you from the brothel and take you back to your village, are you absolutely sure that you wouldn't come back to this?'

Neth's listlessness abruptly disappeared. She turned completely away from the television, and the glaze slipped away from her eyes. 'This is a hell,' she snorted, speaking with passion for the first time. 'You think I want to do this?'

So, quietly and carefully, Nick schemed with Neth to buy her from the brothel owners and take her back to her family. After some dickering, Neth's owner sold her for $150 and gave Nick a receipt.

In a different brothel, we met Momm, a frail girl with oversized eyes who had been pimped for five years and seemed near to cracking from the strain. One moment Momm would laugh and tell jokes, and the next she would dissolve into sobs and rage, but she pleaded to be purchased, freed, and taken back to her home. We negotiated with Momm's owner, who eventually sold her for $203 and filled out the receipt.

We took the girls out of town and back to their families. Neth's home was closer, and we left her money to open a little grocery store in her village. Initially it thrived. American Assistance for Cambodia agreed to look after her and help her. Neth had been away for only six weeks, and her family accepted her story that she had been selling vegetables and welcomed her home without suspicion.

Momm lived all the way across Cambodia, and with every passing mile of our long drive, she became more anxious about whether her family would accept or reject her. It had been five years since she had run away and then been sold into a brothel, and she had had no communication with her family. Momm was bouncing up and down nervously as we finally approached her village. Suddenly she screamed and, although the car was still

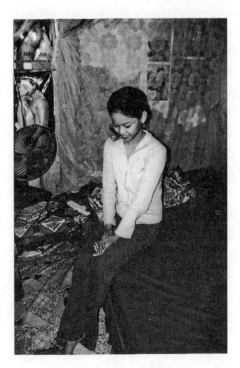

Momm in her room in the brothel in Poipet (Nicholas D. Kristof)

moving, yanked open the door and leaped out. She hurtled over to a middle-aged woman who was staring wonderingly at the vehicle, and then the woman, Momm's aunt, was screaming as well and they were embracing and crying.

A moment later, it seemed as if everybody in the village was shrieking and running up to Momm. Momm's mother was at her stall in the market a mile away when a child ran up to tell her that Momm had returned. Her mother started sprinting back to the village, tears streaming down her cheeks. She embraced her daughter, who was trying to drop to the ground to beg forgiveness, and they both tumbled down. It was ninety minutes before the shouting died away and the eyes dried, and then there was an impromptu feast. Family members may have suspected that Momm had been trafficked, but they didn't press her when she said vaguely that she had been working in western Cambodia. The family decided that Momm would sell meat in a stall in the market right next to her mother, and Nick left some money to finance the project. American Assistance for Cambodia agreed to monitor Momm and assist her transition, and in the next few days Momm phoned repeatedly with updates.

'We've rented the stall right next to my mom's, and I'll be working there tomorrow,' she told us. 'Everything is going great. I'll never go back to Poipet.'

A week later, an excruciating e-mail arrived from Lor Chandara, our interpreter:

> Very bad, bad news. Srey Momm has voluntarily gone back to the Poipet brothel, according to her father. I asked the father if anyone beat or blamed her but he told me that nothing bad had happened to her. She left the village at 8 a.m. on Monday without telling her family. Srey Momm left her phone with the family, and she called them last night to tell them that she is in Poipet.

Momm, like many brothel girls, had become addicted to methamphetamines. Often the brothel owners give girls meth to keep them compliant and dependent. In her village, the craving had overwhelmed her, and she was consumed by the need to go back to the brothel and get some meth.

As soon as she had gotten her fix, Momm wanted to leave the brothel. Bernie Krisher of American Assistance for Cambodia set her up in Phnom Penh twice more, but each time she ran away after a few days, desperate to get back to her meth supply. Momm is by no means a 'hard woman' – she's sweet, even a bit cloying, and is always buying gifts for her friends and praying at the Buddhist altar for divine intervention on their behalf. She yearned to leave the brothel behind, but she could not overcome her addiction.

The next time we visited Poipet, a full year had passed. When Nick walked into Momm's brothel, she saw him and dashed away in tears. After she had composed herself, she came out and kneeled on the floor and begged forgiveness.

'I never lie to people, but I lied to you,' she said forlornly. 'I said I would not come back, and I did. I didn't want to return, but I did.'

Neth and Momm underscore that many prostitutes are neither acting freely nor enslaved, but living in a world etched in ambiguities somewhere between those two extremes. After her return, Momm was bound to the brothel by drugs and debts, but the owner let her leave freely with customers, and Momm could easily have escaped if she had wanted to do so.

Over the years, as she grew older, Momm's price to customers dropped to just $1.50 per session. She was assigned a roommate to share her cubicle in the brothel, except when either was entertaining a man. The new roommate, Wen Lok, was a sixteen-year-old who had run away from home after the family's motorcycle was stolen from her; she couldn't bear to face her father's wrath and fled. A trafficker promised her a job as a hotel maid in Poipet and then sold her to Momm's brothel, where she was beaten until she accepted customers. Momm became the new girl's minder, ensuring that she did not escape.

Momm had been brutalized for years in the brothels, but now she seemed to be slipping into a managerial role; if that continued, she would be breaking young girls into the business – or beating them, just as she herself had been beaten. The slave was becoming the overseer.

Yet that fate did not come to pass – and it was a crackdown on the brothels that ended Momm's managerial trajectory. Momm's brothel was owned by a middle-aged woman named Sok Khorn, who was always complaining about the business. 'It's only barely profitable, and it's a huge amount of work,' she would moan as she sat in the foyer of the brothel (which was also her family home). 'Plus those drunken men – they're often so unpleasant – and the cops always have their hands out.' Sok Khorn's disillusionment arose in part because her husband never did any chores in the brothel but constantly had sex with the girls, outraging her; they finally divorced. In addition, her daughter had reached the age of thirteen, and Sok Khorn worried about her as she did her homework in the foyer, with drunken men barging in and reaching out for anything female. The final straw came in 2008, when the Cambodian authorities reacted to growing Western pressure by cracking down on sex trafficking. That raised the cost of new girls, and the police began to demand larger bribes from the brothel owners. Any cop in the neighborhood would drop by and demand $5. At that point, about half the brothels in Poipet folded. Sok Khorn announced in disgust that she would try something else as well. 'It wasn't making money, so I gave up and thought I'd open a little grocery shop,' she said.

None of the other brothels was buying girls, so Momm suddenly found herself free. It was a giddy but scary feeling. She hurriedly married one of her customers, a policeman, and they settled down together in his house. Over Christmas vacation 2008, we took our family to Cambodia – including our three children – and had a joyous meeting with Momm in Poipet. 'I'm a housewife now,' she told us, beaming with pride. 'I don't have any customers now. I've left that life forever.'

*

As for Neth, her new grocery shop initially did a booming business, since there was no other store in the village. She and her family were thrilled. But when other villagers saw Neth's business flourishing, they opened their own shops. Soon the village had a half-dozen stores. Neth found her sales faltering.

Worse, Neth's family continued to regard her as a foolish little girl with no rights. So any man in the family who needed something took it from Neth's store – sometimes paying, sometimes not. When a Cambodian festival rolled around, the men in Neth's family didn't have enough money to buy food for a feast, so they came to raid her shop. Neth protested.

Her mother recalled later: 'Neth got mad. She said we [the family] had to stay away, or everything would be gone. She said she had to have money to buy new things.' But in a Cambodian village, nobody listens to an uneducated teenage girl. The feast went ahead, the store was emptied. Afterward, Neth had no money to replenish her inventory. Four months after the shop had opened, her business plan had collapsed.

Mortified that her capital was gone, Neth began to discuss with a few girlfriends the idea of seeking jobs in a city. A trafficker promised to get the girls jobs as dishwashers in Thailand. But the girls would have to pay $100 to be smuggled there, money they didn't have, so they would have to go into debt to the trafficker. That's a classic means of gaining leverage over girls: The debts mount with exorbitant interest rates, and when girls can't repay the loans, the trafficker sells them to a brothel.

Neth fretted about the risks but was desperate to make money. Her father had tuberculosis and was coughing up blood, and there was no money for treatment. So she decided to brave the risk and go to Thailand. Just as Neth and her girlfriends were about to leave, an aid worker from American Assistance for Cambodia dropped by to see how she was getting on. The aid worker, wary of the trafficker's enticements, persuaded Neth not to take the risk. But what could Neth do instead?

Bernie Krisher of American Assistance for Cambodia tried another approach. He arranged for Neth to move to Phnom Penh and study hairdressing at Sapor's, the best beauty shop in the city. Neth lived in the American Assistance compound and studied English on the side, while working full-time in the beauty shop, learning to cut hair and give manicures. She placed third in a competition to apply makeup, and she lived sedately and quietly, pouring all her energy into her studies.

'I'm happy with Srey Neth,' the owner, Sapor Rendall, said at the time. 'She studies hard.' Sapor said she had just one problem with Neth: 'She doesn't want to do massage. I've talked to her about it many times, but she's very reluctant.' Neth never dared explain to Sapor the reason for her timidity about massages. In a respectable beauty shop like Sapor's, they are not sexual, but for a girl with Neth's past, the notion of administering any kind of massage conjured horrible memories.

Over time, Neth mellowed. She had always been very thin and a bit somber, but she put on a bit of weight and became relaxed, sometimes even vivacious and giggly. She was acting the way a teenager should, and boys noticed. They flirted with her. She ignored them.

'I stay away from them,' she explained dryly. 'I don't want to play around with boys. I just want to learn hairdressing, so that I can open my own salon.'

Neth decided that after completing her course she would work as a beautician in a small beauty shop, to get experience in managing a business. Then, after a year or so, she would open her own shop in the provincial town of Battambang, near her village. That way she could look after her father, as well as raise money to get him medical treatment.

Then Neth's health began to decline. She suffered inexplicable fevers and headaches that persisted for months, and she lost some of the weight she had recently put on. She went to a clinic in Battambang, and the staff gave her a routine AIDS test. Half an hour later, they handed her a slip of paper: The test was positive for HIV.

Neth was shattered. She walked out of the clinic with the paper scrunched up in her hand. In rural Cambodia, an HIV diagnosis felt like a death sentence, and Neth didn't think she had long to live. She spent days crying, and she couldn't sleep at night. Neth was not one to confide in others or to express emotion, but the pressure built inside her, and she finally shared her bad news with us. American Assistance for Cambodia tried to get her medical treatment, but Neth thought it was hopeless. She was taut with denial and rage, and she drifted back to her village so she could die near her family. A young man named Sothea began courting her. He was a catch for a peasant girl like her: a college-educated man who spoke some English. Tall and scholarly, he was older and more mature, but thrilled to have found such a beautiful woman. She curtly fended him off, but he wouldn't listen.

'When I fell in love with Srey Neth, she discouraged me,' Sothea said. 'She told me: "I am poor. I live near Battambang [he is from Phnom Penh]. Don't love me." But I told her that I still loved her and would love her to the end.'

Neth found herself falling for him. Soon he asked her to marry him. She agreed. Neth told him that she had worked in Poipet and was friends with an American journalist, but she balked at acknowledging that she had been a prostitute – or that she had tested positive for HIV. Her secret nagged at her constantly, but she never dared confide.

Soon after the wedding, Neth became pregnant. If a pregnant woman takes a drug called nevirapine before childbirth and does not breast-feed afterward, she can drastically reduce the risk of infecting her child with HIV. But to take that route, Neth would have to tell Sothea that she was HIV positive and had contracted the disease as a prostitute. It was wrenching to watch Neth and Sothea during the pregnancy, because Sothea was so much in love with a woman who was secretly endangering his life and their child's life.

One afternoon we were sitting outside their house as Sothea told us how his parents had looked down on Neth, because she had worked for a time in a restaurant. They considered that low-class behavior for a young woman. 'My parents are mad at me, but I promised Srey Neth that I would love her forever,' Sothea said.

'My parents said they would never allow me to go home. They said: "If you choose Srey Neth, we don't care about you anymore." My parents tried to separate us by sending me to Malaysia, but even though I was there with good food, living in a nice place, I missed Srey Neth so much that I had to go back to her. Even if I run into problems, I will never leave her – even if I starve, I want to be with her.'

Neth looked uncomfortable with this public pronouncement of love, but they caught each other's eyes and dissolved into giggles. This should have been a high point in Neth's life, but she was scrawny and looked sickly. She seemed already to have contracted full-blown AIDS.

'She's become weaker and weaker,' Sothea fretted. 'Normally pregnant women want to eat, but she's not so hungry.'

When Sothea stepped away for a few minutes, Neth turned toward us, looking haggard.

'I know, I know,' she whispered, sounding anguished. 'I want to tell him. I try to tell him. But he loves me so much, how will he take it?' She shook her head and her voice broke: 'For the first time, somebody really loves me. It's so hard to tell him what happened to me.'

We told her that if she loved Sothea, she had to tell him. When Sothea returned, we tried to direct the conversation to the subject of Neth's health. 'You should both check your HIV status before the birth,' Nick suggested, in what he hoped was a casual tone. 'People get it in all kinds of ways, and it's a good time to check.'

Sothea smiled indulgently and scoffed. 'I'm sure my wife doesn't have HIV,' he said dismissively. 'I never go with other girls, or to brothels. So how could she get it?'

On several occasions, we visited Neth and gave her bags of food and powdered milk for her pregnancy, and each time we saw her was heartbreaking. Her brief time in the brothel seemed to have left her with a disease that would kill her, her husband, and their unborn child. Just when her life seemed to be coming together, it was being torn apart.

Then, as the time for delivery approached, Neth agreed to be tested again. And this time, incredibly, the result came back: HIV *negative*. This test was more modern and reliable than the previous one. Neth had definitely been sickly and gaunt, but perhaps that had been from tuberculosis, parasites, or exhaustion. In any case, she didn't have AIDS.

Once she knew this, Neth began to feel better. She put on weight and soon looked healthier. The prospect of a grandchild led Sothea's parents to forgive the couple, and the family was reunited.

In 2007, Neth gave birth to a son. The baby was strong, healthy, and pudgy. Neth radiated joy as she cuddled him in the courtyard of her home. When our family dropped in on Neth and her husband at the end of 2008, she showed the boy to our children and giggled as he tottered about. She had returned to school for her final classes in hairdressing, and her mother-in-law was planning to buy a small shop where Neth could set up a little business as a beautician and hairdresser. 'I know what I'm going to call the shop,' she said. 'Nick and Bernie's.' After so many twists and setbacks, she had put her life together again; the young girl who had quivered in fear in the brothel had been buried forever.

For us, there were three lessons in this story. The first is that rescuing girls from brothels is complicated and uncertain. Indeed, it's sometimes impossible, and that's why it is most productive to focus efforts on prevention and putting brothels out of business. The second lesson is to never give up. Helping people is difficult and unpredictable, and our interventions don't always work, but successes are possible, and these victories are incredibly important.

The third lesson is that even when a social problem is so vast as to be insoluble in its entirety, it's still worth mitigating. We may not succeed in educating *all* the girls in poor countries, or in preventing *all* women from dying in childbirth, or in saving *all* the girls who are imprisoned in brothels. But we think of Neth and remember a Hawaiian parable taught to us by Naka Nathaniel, the former *Times* videographer, himself a Hawaiian:

A man goes out on the beach and sees that it is covered with starfish that have washed up in the tide. A little boy is walking along, picking them up and throwing them back into the water.

'What are you doing, son?' the man asks. 'You see how many starfish there are? You'll never make a difference.'

The boy paused thoughtfully, and picked up another starfish and threw it into the ocean.

'It sure made a difference to that one,' he said.

CHAPTER THREE

Learning to Speak Up

Reasonable people adapt themselves to the world.
Unreasonable people attempt to adapt the world to
themselves. All progress, therefore, depends on
unreasonable people.

– GEORGE BERNARD SHAW

One of the reasons that so many women and girls are kidnapped, trafficked, raped, and otherwise abused is that they grin and bear it. Stoic docility – in particular, acceptance of any decree by a man – is drilled into girls in much of the world from the time they are babies, and so they often do as they are instructed, even when the instruction is to smile while being raped twenty times a day.

This is not to blame the victims. There are good practical as well as cultural reasons for women to accept abuse rather than fight back and risk being killed. But the reality is that as long as women and girls allow themselves to be prostituted and beaten, the abuse will continue. When more girls scream and protest, when they run away from the brothels, then the business model of trafficking will be undermined. The traffickers know that, and they tend to prey on uneducated peasant girls precisely because they are the ones most likely to obey orders and resign themselves to their fate. As Martin Luther King Jr. put it during the American civil rights struggle: 'We must straighten our backs and work for our freedom. A man can't ride you unless your back is bent.'

Of course, this is a delicate matter, and it's dangerous for

Usha Narayane in her slum neighborhood in India (Naka Nathaniel)

foreign cheerleaders to urge local girls to assume undue risks. But it's also essential to help young women find their voices. Education and empowerment training can show girls that femininity does not entail docility, and can nurture assertiveness so that girls and women stand up for themselves. This is exactly what has happened in the slum of Kasturba Nagar, outside the central Indian city of Nagpur.

The fetid ditches of Kasturba Nagar ooze sewage, stink, and hopelessness. The inhabitants are Dalits – Untouchables. Most of them have dark complexions and signal in their clothing and bearing that they are poor. They live in shacks on winding dirt lanes, which turn to a stew of sewage and mud whenever it rains. The men of Kasturba Nagar drive rickshaws or work in menial or dirty jobs, and the women work as housemaids, or they stay home and raise the children.

In this improbable setting, a young woman named Usha Narayane shook off despair and thrived despite the odds. Usha is a self-assured woman of twenty-eight: short, with long black hair, a round face, and thick eyebrows. In a land like India that has long suffered from malnutrition, pounds can be prestigious, and Usha has just enough weight to hint at her own success. She talks non-stop.

Her father, Madhukar Narayane, is a Dalit, too, but he is also a high school graduate with a good job at the telephone company. Usha's mother, Alka, is also unusually well-educated: Although she married at age fifteen, she has a ninth-grade education and is literate. Both parents were determined that their children get a solid education as an escape route from Kasturba Nagar. So they lived frugally and saved every rupee to educate their children – and they accomplished something heroic. In a slum where no other person had ever gone to college, all five Narayane children, including Usha, graduated from university.

Usha's mother is delighted and a bit horrified at what this education has wrought in her daughter. 'She's fearless,' Alka said. 'She doesn't get frightened by anyone.' Usha graduated with a degree in hotel management and seemed destined to manage a fine hotel somewhere in India. She had already escaped Kasturba Nagar and was preparing to take a hotel job when she came back for a visit – and collided with the ambitions and self-assurance of Akku Yadav.

Akku Yadav was, in a sense, the other 'success' of Kasturba Nagar. He was a higher-caste man who had turned an apprenticeship as a small-time thug into a role as a mobster and king of the slum. He ruled a gang of hoodlums who controlled Kasturba Nagar and who robbed, murdered, and tortured with impunity. The Indian authorities would have prevented a gangster from preying so ruthlessly on a middle-class neighborhood. But in slums with Dalits or low-caste residents, the authorities rarely intervene except to accept cash bribes, and so gangsters sometimes emerge in such places as absolute rulers.

For fifteen years, Akku Yadav had terrorized Kasturba Nagar while shrewdly building a small business empire. One of his specialties was the threat of rape to terrorize anyone who might stand up to him. Murder left inconvenient piles of bodies, requiring bribes to keep the police at bay, while rape is so stigmatizing that the victims could usually be counted on to stay silent. Sexual

humiliation was thus an effective and low-risk strategy to intimi-
date challengers and to control the community.

According to neighbors in the slum, Akku Yadav once raped a
woman right after her wedding. Another time he stripped a man
naked and burned him with cigarettes, then forced him to dance
in front of his sixteen-year-old daughter. They say he took one
woman, Asho Bhagat, and tortured her in front of her daughter
and several neighbors by cutting off her breasts. Then he sliced her
into pieces on the street. One of the neighbors, Avinash Tiwari,
was horrified by Asho's killing and planned to go to the police, so
Akku Yadav butchered him as well.

Akku Yadav continued his assaults. He and his men gang-raped
a woman named Kalma just ten days after she gave birth, and she
was so mortified that she doused herself with kerosene and burned
herself to death. The gang pulled another woman out of her house
when she was seven months pregnant, stripped her naked, and
raped her on the road in public view. The more barbaric the behavior, the more the population was cowed into acquiescence.

Twenty-five families moved away from Kasturba Nagar, but
most Dalits had no choice. They adjusted by pulling their daughters out of school and keeping them locked up inside their homes
where no one could see them. Vegetable vendors steered clear of
Kasturba Nagar, so housewives had to trek to distant markets to
buy food. And as long as Akku Yadav targeted only the Dalits, the
police didn't interfere.

'The police were very class conscious,' Usha noted. 'So if you
were lighter-skinned, then they thought you were higher class and
they might help. But they would swoop down on anyone darker-
skinned or unshaven. Often, people went to the police to
complain, and then the police arrested them,' Usha said. One
woman went to the police to report that she had been gang-raped
by Akku Yadav and his thugs; the police responded by gang-raping
her themselves.

Usha's family was the only one that Akku Yadav didn't torment.
He gave the Narayanes a wide berth, wary that their education
might give them power to complain effectively. In developing

countries, tormenting the illiterate is usually risk-free; preying on the educated is more perilous. But finally, when Usha was back for her visit, the two families met head-on.

Akku Yadav had just raped a thirteen-year-old girl. He was feeling cocky. He and his men went to the next-door neighbor of the Narayanes, Ratna Dungiri, to demand money. The thugs smashed her furniture and threatened to kill her family. When Usha arrived afterward, she told Ratna to go to the police. Ratna wouldn't, so Usha herself went to the police and filed a complaint. The police informed Akku Yadav of Usha's action, and he was enraged. So he and forty of his thugs showed up at the Narayane house and surrounded it. Akku Yadav carried a bottle of acid and shouted through the door for Usha to back down. *You withdraw the complaint and I won't harm you*, he said.

Usha barricaded the door and shouted back that she would never give in. Then she frantically telephoned the police. They said that they would come, but they never did. Meanwhile, Akku Yadav was pounding on the door.

I'll throw acid on your face, and you won't be in a position to file any more complaints, he roared. *If we ever meet you, you don't know what we'll do to you. Gang rape is nothing. You can't imagine what we'll do to you.*

Usha shouted back insults, and Akku Yadav replied with vivid descriptions of how he would rape her, burn her with acid, slaughter her. He and his men tried to batter the door down. So Usha turned on the cylinder of gas the family used for cooking and grabbed a match.

If you break into the house, I'll light the match and blow us all up, she shouted wildly. The thugs could smell the gas, and they hesitated. *Back off or you'll get blown up*, Usha shouted again. The attackers stepped back.

Meanwhile, word of the confrontation had rushed around the neighborhood. The Dalits were deeply proud of Usha's schooling and success, and the thought that Akku Yadav would destroy her was agonizing. The neighbors gathered at a distance, not knowing quite what to do. But when they saw Usha fighting back and hurling abuse at Akku Yadav, finally forcing his gang to retreat, they found courage. Soon there were a hundred angry Dalits on the street, and they began picking up sticks and stones.

'People realized that if he could do this to Usha, there was just no hope,' one neighbor explained. Stones began to fly toward Akku Yadav's men, who saw the crowd's ugly mood and fled. The mood in the slum became giddy. For the first time, the people had won a confrontation. The Dalits marched through the slum, celebrating. Then they went down the street to Akku Yadav's house and burned it to the ground.

Akku Yadav went to the police, who arrested him for his own protection. Apparently the police officers planned to keep him in custody until the mood cooled and then to let him go. A bail hearing for Akku Yadav was scheduled, and rumors spread that the police were planning to release him as part of a corrupt bargain. The bail hearing was to take place miles away in the center of Nagpur. Hundreds of women marched there from Kasturba Nagar and filed into the high-ceilinged grand courtroom with its marble floor and faded British grandeur. The Dalit women were uneasy there in their sandals and faded saris, but they took seats near the front. Akku Yadav strutted in, confident and unrepentant, sensing that the women were disoriented in the grand setting of the courtroom. Spotting one woman he had raped, he mocked her as a prostitute and shouted that he would rape her again. She rushed forward and hit him on the head with a slipper.

'This time, either I will kill you, or you will kill me,' she shrieked. At that, the dam burst, apparently by prearrangement. All the women from Kasturba Nagar pressed forward and surrounded Akku Yadav, screaming and shouting. Some pulled chili powder from under their clothes and threw it in the faces of Akku Yadav and the two police officers guarding him. The police, blinded and overwhelmed, fled at once. Then the women pulled out knives from their clothing and began stabbing Akku Yadav.

'Forgive me,' he shouted, in terror now. 'Forgive me! I won't do it again.' The women passed their knives around and kept stabbing him. Each woman had agreed to stab him at least once. Then, in a macabre retaliation for his having cut off Asho Bhagat's breasts, the women hacked off Akku Yadav's penis. By the end, he was mincemeat. When we visited, the courtroom walls were still stained with his blood.

The bloodied women marched triumphantly back to Kasturba Nagar to tell their husbands and fathers that they had destroyed the monster. The slum erupted in celebration. Families put on music and danced in the streets. They dug into their savings to buy lamb and sweets, and they handed out fruit to their friends. Throughout Kasturba Nagar, the festivities resembled a giant wedding.

It was clear that the attack on Akku Yadav had been carefully planned, and Usha was the obvious leader. So even though Usha could conveniently prove that she was not in the courtroom that day, the police arrested her. However, the killing had focused public attention on the plight of Kasturba Nagar, and there was an outcry. A retired high court judge, Bhau Vahane, publicly sided with the women, saying: 'In the circumstances they underwent, they were left with no alternative but to finish Akku. The women repeatedly pleaded with the police for their security. But the police failed to protect them.'

Then the hundreds of women in the slum decided among themselves that if they all claimed responsibility, no one person would be culpable for the murder. They reasoned that if several hundred women each had stabbed Akku Yadav once, then no single stab wound would have been the fatal one. Across Kasturba Nagar, there was a single refrain among the women: *We all killed him. Arrest us all!*

'We all take responsibility for what happened,' said Rajashri Rangdale, a shy young mother. Jija More, a prim housewife of forty-five, added: 'I'm proud of what we did . . . If anybody has to be punished, we'll all be punished.' With considerable satisfaction, Jija asserted: 'We women have become fearless. We were protecting the men.'

The police, grim and frustrated, released Usha after two weeks, but only on the condition that she stay in the area. Her career as a hotel manager is probably over, and she is sure that members of

Akku Yadav's gang will seek revenge by raping her or throwing acid on her face. 'I don't care about that,' she says dismissively, with a confident toss of her head. 'I'm not worried about them.' She began a new life as a community organizer, using her management skills to bring the Dalits together to make pickles, clothing, and other products to sell in the markets. She wants the Dalits to start businesses to raise their incomes, so that they can afford more education.

Now Usha is struggling to make ends meet, but she is the galvanic new boss of Kasturba Nagar, the heroine of the slum. When we went to visit her, our taxi driver had trouble finding her home. He stopped periodically in Kasturba Nagar to ask for directions, but each person the driver asked insisted that there was no such person – or else directed the vehicle away from the neighborhood. Finally, we called Usha to report our difficulties, and she came out onto the main street to flag us down and show us the way, explaining that each of the people who had misdirected us had sent a child running over to her, warning her that a stranger was looking for her. 'They're trying to protect me,' Usha explained, laughing. 'The whole community is looking out for me.'

The saga of Kasturba Nagar is unsettling, with no easy moral. After years of watching women quietly accept abuse, it is cathartic to see someone like Usha lead a countercharge – even if we're uncomfortable with the bloody denouement and cannot condone murder.

'Empowerment' is a cliché in the aid community, but it is truly what is needed. The first step toward greater justice is to transform that culture of female docility and subservience, so that women themselves become more assertive and demanding. As we said earlier, that is, of course, easy for outsiders like us to say: We're not the ones who run horrible risks for speaking up. But when a woman does stand up, it's imperative that outsiders champion her; we also must nurture institutions to protect such people. Sometimes we may even need to provide asylum for those whose lives are in danger. More broadly, the single most important way to encourage women and girls to stand up for their rights is education, and we can do far more to promote universal education in poor countries.

Ultimately, women like those in Kasturba Nagar need to join the human rights revolution themselves. They constitute part of the answer to the problem: There will be less trafficking and less rape if more women stop turning the other cheek and begin slapping back.

The New Abolitionists

Zach Hunter was twelve years old and living with his family in Atlanta when he heard in school that forms of slavery still exist in the world today. He was flabbergasted and began reading up on the subject. The more he read, the more horrified he was, and although he was only a seventh grader he thought he could raise money to fight forced labor. So he formed a group called Loose Change to Loosen Chains, nicknamed LC2LC, a student-run campaign against modern slavery. In his first year, he raised $8,500. Since then, his campaign has ballooned.

Zach, now in high school, travels around the country constantly, speaking to school and church groups about human trafficking. His MySpace page describes his occupation as 'abolitionist/student,' and his hero is William Wilberforce. In 2007, Zach presented to the White House a petition with 100,000 signatures seeking more action on trafficking. He also published a book for teenagers, *Be the Change: Your Guide to Ending Slavery and Changing the World*, and he is nurturing other LC2LC chapters in schools and churches across the country.

Zach is part of an exploding movement of 'social entrepreneurs' who offer new approaches to supporting women in the developing world. Aid workers function in the context of an aid bureaucracy, while social entrepreneurs create their own context by starting a new organization, company, or movement to address a social problem in a creative way. Social entrepreneurs tend not to have the traditional liberal suspicion of capitalism, and many charge for services and use a business model to achieve sustainability.

'Social entrepreneurs are not content just to give a fish or to teach how to fish,' says Bill Drayton, a former management consultant and government official who popularized the idea of social entrepreneurship. 'They will not rest until they have revolutionized the fishing industry.' Drayton is the founder of Ashoka, an organization that supports and trains social entrepreneurs around the world. They are called Ashoka Fellows, and there are now more than two thousand of them – many involved in women's rights campaigns. Drayton's brief history of the rise of social entrepreneurs goes like this:

The agricultural revolution produced only a small surplus, so only a small elite could move into the towns to create culture and conscious history. This pattern persisted ever since: Only a few have held the monopoly on initiative because they alone have had the social tools. That is one reason that per capita income in the West remained flat from the fall of the Roman Empire until about 1700. By 1700, however, a new, more open architecture was beginning to develop in northern Europe: entrepreneurial/competitive business facilitated by more tolerant, open politics . . . One result: the West broke out from 1,200 years of stagnation and soon soared past anything the world had seen before. Average per capita income rose 20 percent in the 1700s, 200 percent in the 1800s, and 740 percent in the last century . . . However, until about 1980, this transformation bypassed the social half of the world's operations . . . It was only about 1980 that the ice began to crack and the social arena as a whole made the structural leap to this new entrepreneurial competitive architecture. However, once the ice broke, catch-up change came in a rush. And it did so pretty much all across the world, the chief exceptions being areas where governments were afraid. Because it has the advantage of not having to be the pioneer, but rather of following business, this second great transformation has been able steadily to compound productivity growth at a very fast rate. In this respect, it resembles successful developing countries like Thailand. Ashoka's best estimate is that the citizen sector is halving the gap between its productivity level and that of business every ten to twelve years.

Think how much more effective a women's rights movement could be if backed by an army of social entrepreneurs. The United Nations and the aid bureaucracies have undertaken a relentless search for technical solutions – including improved vaccines and new processes for boring wells – and those are important. But progress also depends on political and cultural remedies, and, frankly, on charisma. Often the key is a person with a knack for leadership: Martin Luther King Jr. in the United States, Mahatma Gandhi in India, and William Wilberforce in Britain. It's important to invest in these emerging leaders as well as in processes, and aid organizations have largely missed the boat that Drayton launched with Ashoka.

'It does seem to be a major blind spot in development and government efforts,' notes David Bornstein, who wrote an excellent book about social entrepreneurs called *How to Change the World*. The big donors, whether government aid groups or large philanthropic organizations, want to make systematic interventions that are scalable, and there are good reasons for that. But as a result they miss opportunities to bring about social change by failing to set up networks to identify and support individual leaders who can make a difference in the trenches. Donors typically aren't set up to make small, targeted grants at the community level – but such grants can become an important tool to achieve change. A few groups have operated as venture capital providers to support small-scale programs abroad, and in fact that is precisely what Ashoka does with its support of Ashoka Fellows. Likewise, the Global Fund for Women, run by a former graduate school classmate of Sheryl's, Kavita Ramdas, since 1987 has supported more than 3,800 women's organizations in 167 countries. The International Women's Health Coalition, based in New York, is best known for advocacy, but it also awards grants to small organizations around the globe that support women.

Sunitha talking with children in her shelter in India (Nicholas D. Kristof)

Zach is a brilliant social entrepreneur. So are Ruchira Gupta and Usha Narayane. While women worldwide have generally not risen far in the ranks of political leaders, they often dominate the ranks of social entrepreneurs. Even in countries where men monopolize political power, women have formed their own influential organizations and have enjoyed considerable success in bringing about change. In particular, many women have risen as social entrepreneurs to provide leadership in the new abolitionist movement against sex traffickers. One of these is Sunitha Krishnan, an Ashoka Fellow from India who is legendary among those fighting trafficking. We had heard so much about her that when we finally met it was a surprise to see how tiny she is. And her diminutive stature, at four and a half feet tall, is accentuated by a congenital cleft foot that causes her to limp.

When Sunitha was a middle-class child in kindergarten, she took a slate and went to teach a group of poor children what she had learned in school that day. She was so moved by that experience that she decided to become a social worker. She studied social work in college and graduate school in India; her focus was on literacy. Then, one day, she was with a group of fellow students trying to organize poor people in a village, and a gang of men resented the interference.

'They didn't like it, and they decided to teach us a lesson,' Sunitha recalls. She was telling us her story in her small, bare office in the shelter she runs in the city of Hyderabad, nearly one thousand miles southwest of the village in Bihar where Ruchira Gupta is fighting to keep Meena alive. Sunitha speaks in polished, upper-class Indian English, sounding more like a university professor than an activist. She is detached and analytical, but still quietly furious when she explains what happened next: The gang of men opposed to her efforts raped her. Sunitha didn't go to the police. 'I recognized the futility of it,' she says. But Sunitha found herself blamed and her family stigmatized. 'The rape per se didn't impact me so much,' she says. 'What affected me more was the way society treated me, the way people looked at me. Nobody questioned why those guys did it. They questioned why I went there, why my parents gave me freedom. And I realized that what happened to me was a one-time thing. But for many people it was a daily thing.'

That was when Sunitha decided to switch her career focus from literacy to sex trafficking. She traveled around the country talking to as many prostitutes as possible, trying to understand the world of commercial sex. She settled in Hyderabad, shortly before the police launched a crackdown there on one red-light district – perhaps the brothel owners hadn't paid enough bribes and needed a nudge. The crackdown was a catastrophe. Overnight the brothels in that area were closed, with no provision for the girls working there; the prostitutes were so stigmatized that there was no place they could go and no way for them to earn money.

'Many of the women started committing suicide,' Sunitha remembers. 'I was helping cremate dead bodies. Death was binding people together. I went back to the women and said, "Tell me exactly what you want us to do" And they said, "Don't do anything for us, do something for our children."'

Sunitha worked closely with a Catholic missionary, Brother Joe Vetticatil. He has died, but a picture of him hangs in her office, and his faith left a powerful impression on her. 'I'm a staunch Hindu,' she says, 'though the way of Christ inspires me.' Sunitha and Brother Joe started a school in a former brothel. At first, out of five thousand children of prostitutes who were eligible to attend, just five enrolled. But the school grew, and soon Sunitha started shelters as well, for the children and also for girls and women who were rescued from the brothels. She called her organization Prajwala, which means an eternal flame (www.prajwalaindia.org).

Although one red-light district had been closed, there were others in Hyderabad, and Sunitha began to organize rescues from those brothels. She prowled the foulest, most sordid neighborhoods of the city, fearlessly talking to prostitutes and trying to galvanize them to work together and inform on the pimps. She confronted pimps and brothel owners and gathered evidence that she took to the police, browbeating them to mount raids. All this infuriated the brothel owners, who couldn't understand why a sparrow-sized woman – a *girl!* – was standing up to them and making business so unprofitable. The brothel owners organized and began to fight back. Thugs attacked Sunitha and those working with her; she says her right eardrum was ruptured, leaving her deaf in that ear, and one arm was broken.

Sunitha's first employee was Akbar, a former pimp who had developed a conscience. He worked valiantly to help girls who were imprisoned in the red-light district. But the brothel owners retaliated by stabbing Akbar to death. When Sunitha had to tell his family that he had been killed, she acknowledged that she had to be more cautious.

'We realized over time that it was not sustainable,' she says of her early approach. 'I realized that if I'm going to be here for a long time, I have to be accountable to my team, to their families. I can't expect everyone to be a mad person like me.'

Prajwala increasingly began to work with the government and aid groups to provide rehabilitation, counseling, and other services. Sunitha trained the former prostitutes not only to make crafts or bind books – the kind of thing that other rescue organizations do – but also to be welders or carpenters. So far, Prajwala has rehabilitated some fifteen hundred young women by moving them through six to eight months of job training that will help them start new careers. The rehabilitation centers are a curious sight in India:

They are alive with the sounds of hammering and shouts, with young women pounding nails, lugging steel bars, and operating machinery. Prajwala also helps some women return to their families, or get married, or live on their own. So far, Sunitha says, 85 percent of the women have been able to stay out of prostitution, while 15 percent have returned.

Sunitha herself plays down the success. 'There's more prostitution now than when we started,' she confided grimly at one point. 'I'd say we failed. We rescue ten people and twenty come into the brothels.' But that is far too bleak an evaluation.

One warm and sunny day in Hyderabad, Sunitha's brisk efficiency evaporates as she leaves her office. The stern ferocity that she displays toward government officials melts and is replaced by tenderness as children at her school gather round, laughing and shouting. She greets them by name and asks them about their schoolwork.

A simple lunch of dal and chapati is served on battered tin plates to everyone in the compound. While nibbling on her chapati, Sunitha catches up with one of her volunteers, Abbas Be, a young woman with black hair, light chocolate skin, and white teeth. Abbas had been taken to Delhi as a young teenager to work as a maid, but instead she found herself sold to a brothel and beaten with a cricket bat to induce obedience. Three days later, Abbas and all seventy girls in the brothel were made to gather round and watch as the pimps made an example of another teenage girl, who had fought customers and tried to lead the other girls into a rebellion. The troublesome girl was stripped naked, hog-tied, humiliated and mocked, beaten savagely, and then stabbed in the stomach until she bled to death in front of Abbas and the others.

After Abbas was eventually freed in a brothel raid, Sunitha encouraged her to come to Prajwala to learn a vocational skill. Today, Abbas is learning to be a bookbinder and also counsels other girls about how to avoid being trafficked. Sunitha arranged for Abbas to be tested for HIV; she tested positive, so Sunitha is trying to find her an HIV-positive man to marry.

Sunitha and Abbas both want all brothels closed down, not just

Abbas now works in this shelter and is trying to find a man who is HIV positive, as she is, to marry. (Nicholas D. Kristof)

regulated, and Sunitha's voice carries growing weight in the region. A dozen years ago, it would have been absurd to think that a young female social worker, small in stature and with a club foot, could have any impact on the mobs that run the brothels in Hyderabad. Aid groups were too sensible to tackle the problem. Yet Sunitha brazenly marched into the red-light districts and started her own organization, in a way emblematic of social entrepreneurs. They can be difficult, seemingly unreasonable people, but these very qualities are sometimes precisely what allow them to succeed.

On her own, Sunitha would have lacked the resources to wage her campaigns against the brothels, but American donors have supported her and multiplied her impact. Catholic Relief Services in particular has been a stalwart supporter of Sunitha and the Prajwala programs. The networks and introductions that Bill Drayton made for her, as an Ashoka Fellow, also magnified her voice. It's a prototype of the kind of alliance between first world and third that the abolitionist movement needs.

CHAPTER FOUR

Rule by Rape

The mechanism of violence is what destroys women,
controls women, diminishes women and keeps women in
their so-called place.

— EVE ENSLER, *A Memory, a Monologue,
a Rant, and a Prayer*

Rape has become endemic in South Africa, so a medical technician named Sonette Ehlers developed a product that immediately grabbed national attention there. Ehlers had never forgotten a rape victim telling her forlornly: 'If only I had teeth down there.' Some time afterward, a man came into the hospital where Ehlers works in excruciating pain because his penis was stuck in his pants zipper. Ehlers merged those images and came up with a product she called Rapex. It resembles a tube, with barbs inside. The woman inserts it like a tampon, with an applicator, and any man who tries to rape the woman impales himself on the barbs and must go to an emergency room to have the Rapex removed. When critics complained that it was a medieval punishment, Ehlers responded tersely: 'A medieval device for a medieval deed.'

The Rapex is a reflection of the gender-based violence that is ubiquitous in much of the developing world, inflicting far more casualties than any war. Surveys suggest that about one third of all women worldwide face beatings in the home. Women aged fifteen through forty-four are more likely to be maimed or die from male violence than from cancer, malaria, traffic accidents, and war combined. A major study by the World Health Organization found that in most countries, between 30 percent and 60 percent of women had experienced physical or sexual violence by a husband or boyfriend. 'Violence against women by an intimate partner is a major contributor to the ill health of women,' said the former director-general of WHO, Lee Jong-wook.

Rape is so stigmatizing that many women do not report it, and thus researchers have difficulty tabulating accurate figures. Yet some evidence suggests that it is very widespread: 21 percent of Ghanaian women reported in one survey that their sexual initiation was by rape; 17 percent of Nigerian women said that they had endured rape or attempted rape by the age of nineteen; and 21 percent of South African women reported that they had been raped by the age of fifteen.

Violence against women is also constantly mutating into new forms. The first documented acid attack occurred in 1967, in what is now Bangladesh. Now it is increasingly common for men in South Asia or Southeast Asia to take sulfuric acid and hurl it in the faces of girls or women who have spurned them. The acid melts the skin and sometimes the bones underneath; if it strikes the eyes, the woman is blinded. In the world of misogyny, that is techno-logical innovation.

Such violence often functions to keep women down. One impediment for women planning to run for political office in Kenya is the cost of round-the-clock security. That protection is needed to prevent political enemies from having them raped; gangsters calculate that female candidates can be uniquely humil-iated and discredited that way. The result is that Kenyan women candidates routinely carry knives and wear multiple sets of tights to deter, complicate, and delay any attempted rape.

In many poor countries, the problem is not so much individual thugs and rapists but an entire culture of sexual predation. That's the world of Woineshet Zebene.

Woineshet, a light-skinned black girl in Ethiopia, keeps her long hair brushed back, letting it frame a face that is almost always serious, determined, studious. She grew up in a rural area where

Woineshet with her father, Zebene, in Addis Ababa (Nicholas D. Kristof)

kidnapping and raping girls is a time-honored tradition. In the Ethiopian countryside, if a young man has an eye on a girl but doesn't have a bride price (the equivalent of a dowry, but paid by the man), or if he doubts that the girl's family will accept him, then he and several friends kidnap the girl, and he rapes her. That immediately improves his bargaining position, because she is ruined and will have difficulty marrying anyone else. The risks to the boy are minimal, since the girl's parents never prosecute the rapist – that would aggravate the harm to their daughter's reputation and would be resented in the community as a breach of tradition. Indeed, at the time of Woineshet's rape, Ethiopian law explicitly provided that a man could not be prosecuted for violating a woman or girl he later married.

'There were many cases like this in our village,' said Woineshet's father, Zebene, who left years ago to work as a peddler in the Ethiopian capital, Addis Ababa, returning regularly to visit his family. 'I knew it was very bad for the girl, but there was nothing to do. They all married the man . . . When he goes free, people see that, and they do it again and again.'

Woineshet and her father were sitting in his shack, trying to explain what had happened. The shack is on the edge of Addis Ababa, and the traffic noise from beeping cars and buses without mufflers provided a steady background clamor. Neighbors were on all sides, separated by thin walls, and Woineshet and her father spoke in low voices so no one would hear of the girl's rape. Woineshet was reserved, looking at her hands and occasionally at her father as he attempted to explain that the villagers are not bad people. 'Stealing is a very shameful act in the villages,' he said. 'If someone steals a goat, the people would beat him up.'

But kidnapping a girl is okay?

'More weight is still given to the crime of stealing a thing than to the crime of stealing a person,' Zebene said sadly. He looked over at Woineshet and added, 'I never thought this would happen to my family.'

Then Woineshet took over the story. Continuing to look mostly downward, she sat in the dim hut and with quiet dignity told what had happened when she was still living in the village, as a thirteen-year-old seventh grader.

'We were deep asleep when they came,' she said calmly. 'Maybe it was eleven thirty at night. I think there were more than four of them. There was no electricity, but they had a flashlight with them. They broke down the door and took me. We were shouting, but nobody heard us. Or at least nobody came.'

Woineshet didn't know her kidnapper, Aberew Jemma, and had never spoken to him, but Aberew had noticed her. For two days the kidnappers casually battered and raped Woineshet. Her family and a teacher went to the police and demanded that they rescue her. As the police approached, Woineshet escaped – hurtling down the village path, screaming, covered in blood and bruises.

Zebene returned to the village from the capital as soon as he heard of his daughter's kidnapping, and he was not inclined to have his loving, studious daughter marry the man who had raped her. In Addis Ababa, he had often heard radio commercials about women's rights aired by the Ethiopian Women Lawyers Association. He had seen women in the capital working confidently, holding meaningful jobs, enjoying rights and a measure of equality. So Zebene talked to Woineshet, and they decided that she would refuse to marry Aberew. Both Zebene and Woineshet are quiet and unassuming but possess steel spines; both are disinclined to back down. They were appalled by what had happened and refused to be mollified as tradition demanded. They decided that Woineshet would report the rape as a crime.

She walked five miles to the nearest bus stop, waited two days for a bus, then endured the grueling journey to a town with a health center. There she underwent a pelvic exam by a nurse, who wrote in her health record: 'She is no longer a virgin . . . Many bruises and scratches.'

When Woineshet returned to the village, the elders encouraged her family to settle the dispute with Aberew. Seeking to avoid a blood feud, they repeatedly pressured Zebene to accept a couple of cows for allowing Woineshet to marry Aberew. Zebene refused to even discuss such a transaction. As the stalemate persisted, Aberew and his family became increasingly concerned that they might be prosecuted, so they devised a solution: Aberew kidnapped Woineshet again, took her far away, and then resumed the beatings and rapes, demanding that she consent to marriage.

Woineshet managed to escape, but she was recaptured during what was for her a three-day hike back home. Remarkably, Aberew even took her to the local court after kidnapping her, so that she could be bullied into telling court officials that she wanted to marry him. Instead, Woineshet – a battered, pint-sized girl surrounded by men who were threatening her – told the court official that she had been abducted, and she pleaded to be allowed to go home. The official, a man, didn't want to listen to a girl and told Woineshet to get it over with and marry Aberew.

'Even if you go home, Aberew will go after you again,' the official told her. 'So there's no point in resisting.'

Woineshet was determined not to marry anyone yet, let alone her kidnapper. 'I wanted to stay in school,' she recalled, speaking softly but with utter determination. Aberew was keeping her inside a house in a walled compound, but one time she was able to scale the wall and flee. Everyone saw her and heard her scream, yet no one helped.

'People were saying I broke tradition,' Woineshet said bitterly, and she looked up from her hands for a moment. 'They were criticizing me, saying I had escaped. I was furious with that attitude.' In the hope of staying alive, Woineshet moved to the police station and was housed in a jail cell – so the rape victim was in a cell and the rapist was free. The police belatedly gathered evidence, including the broken door to Woineshet's home and her torn and bloody clothing. They also collected statements from witnesses, who included a great many people in the village. But the judges to whom the case was presented thought that prosecution of Aberew was a mistake. At a court hearing, the judge told Woineshet: 'He wants to marry you. Why are you refusing?'

Finally, the judge sentenced Aberew to ten years in prison. But a month later, for reasons that are unclear, the judge released him. Woineshet fled to Addis Ababa, where she moved into her father's shack and resumed her studies.

'I decided to leave and go someplace where no one would recognize me,' she said. Then she added slowly and firmly: 'I will never marry anyone. I don't want to deal with any man.'

Such a culture in rural Ethiopia might seem impervious to change. But Woineshet found support in an unlikely corner: indignant Americans, mostly women, who wrote angry letters demanding change in the Ethiopian legal code. They couldn't undo the trauma Woineshet suffered, but the moral support was important to her and her father – reassurance when virtually everyone around them condemned the family for breaching tradition. Americans also provided financial support and a stipend to help Woineshet pursue her education in Addis Ababa.

The letter writers were mobilized by Equality Now, an advocacy organization based in New York that tackles abuses of women around the world. Its founder, Jessica Neuwirth, had worked at Amnesty International and had seen how letter-writing campaigns could help free political prisoners. So in 1992, she founded Equality Now. It has been an uphill struggle to get enough donations to sustain the effort, but Jessica has kept Equality Now going with the support of guardian angels, including Gloria Steinem and Meryl Streep. Today it has a staff of fifteen in New York, London, and Nairobi, with an annual budget of $2 million – pocket change in the world of philanthropy.

Equality Now launched appeals on behalf of Woineshet, but it seems unlikely that Aberew will go to prison again. However, Equality Now's army of letter writers did shine enough of a spotlight on Ethiopia that it was shamed into changing its laws. Today, a man is liable for rape even if the victim later agrees to marry him.

Of course, that's only the law, and in poor countries laws rarely matter much outside the capital. We sometimes think that Westerners invest too much effort in changing unjust laws and not enough in changing culture, by building schools or assisting grassroots movements. Even in the United States, after all, what brought equal rights to blacks wasn't the Thirteenth, Fourteenth, and Fifteenth Amendments passed after the Civil War, but rather the grassroots civil rights movement nearly one hundred years later. Laws matter, but typically changing the law by itself accomplishes little. Mahdere Paulos, the dynamic woman who runs the Ethiopian Women Lawyers Association, agrees. The association does much of its work by filing suits or otherwise lobbying to change laws, but Mahdere acknowledges that change has to be felt in the culture as well as the legal code.

'Empowering women begins with education,' she said. She sees the cadre of educated women growing. Some twelve thousand women a year now volunteer with the Ethiopian Women Lawyers Association, giving it political as well as legal weight. Equality Now works closely with the Ethiopian Women Lawyers Association, and that is a useful model: We in the West can best help by playing supporting roles to local people. And the Ethiopian Women Lawyers Association may soon have another volunteer. Woineshet is now in high school, getting good grades and planning to go to university and study law.

'I would like, God willing, to take on cases of abduction,' she said simply. 'If I can't get justice for myself, I'll get justice for others.'

*

Behind the rapes and other abuse heaped on women in much of the world, it's hard not to see something more sinister than just libido and prurient opportunism. Namely: sexism and misogyny.

How else to explain why so many more witches were burned than wizards? Why is acid thrown in women's faces, but not in men's? Why are women so much more likely to be stripped naked and sexually humiliated than men? Why is it that in many cultures, old men are respected as patriarchs, while old women are taken outside the village to die of thirst or to be eaten by wild animals? Granted, in the societies where these abuses take place, men also suffer more violence than males do in America – but the brutality inflicted on women is particularly widespread, cruel, and lethal.

These attitudes are embedded in culture and will change only with education and local leadership. But outsiders have their supporting role to play, too, in part by shining a spotlight on these regressive attitudes in an effort to break the taboo that often surrounds them. In 2007, senators Joseph Biden and Richard Lugar first introduced the International Violence Against Women Act, which will be reintroduced annually until it becomes law. The bill provides for $175 million a year in foreign aid to try to prevent honor killings, bride burnings, genital cutting, acid attacks, mass rapes, and domestic violence. The bill would also create an Office of Women's Global Initiatives in the immediate office of the secretary of state, and a Women's Global Development Office in the United States Agency for International Development (USAID). Both offices would press to make gender-based violence a diplomatic priority. For all our skepticism about laws, this one, like the landmark 2000 legislation that required annual reports about human trafficking abroad, would have a real if incremental impact around the world. It won't solve any problem completely, but it could make a difference to girls like Woineshet.

In talking about misogyny and gender-based violence, it would be easy to slip into the conceit that men are the villains. But it's not true. Granted, men are often brutal to women. Yet it is women who routinely manage brothels in poor countries, who ensure that their daughters' genitals are cut, who feed sons before daughters, who take their sons but not their daughters to clinics for vaccination. One study suggests that women perpetrators were involved, along with men, in one quarter of the gang rapes in the Sierra Leone civil war. Typically, women fighters would lure a victim to the rape site, and then restrain her as she was raped by male fighters. 'We would help capture her and hold her down,' one woman ex-combatant explained. The author of the study, Dara Kay Cohen, cites evidence from Haiti, Iraq, and Rwanda to suggest that female participation in Sierra Leone's sexual violence was not an anomaly. She argues that ubiquitous gang rape in civil wars isn't about sexual gratification, but rather is a way for military units – including their female members – to bond, by engaging in sometimes brutally misogynistic violence.

Female infanticide persists in many countries, and often it is mothers who kill their own daughters. Dr. Michael H. Stone, a professor of clinical psychiatry at Columbia University and expert on infanticide, obtained data on Pakistani women who killed their daughters. He found that they usually did so because their husbands threatened to divorce them if they kept the girl. For example, a woman named Shahnaz poisoned her daughter to avoid being divorced by her husband. Perveen poisoned her daughter after her father-in-law beat her for giving birth to a girl. Yet sometimes women in Pakistan or China kill their newborn daughters simply because daughters are less prestigious than sons. Rehana drowned her daughter because 'girls are unlucky.'

As for wife beating, one survey found support for it from 62 percent of Indian village women themselves. And no group systematically abuses young women more cruelly than mothers-in-law, who serve as household matriarchs in much of the world and take charge of disciplining the younger women. The experience of Zoya Najabi, a twenty-one-year-old woman from a middle-class family in Kabul, Afghanistan, illustrates the point. She came to our interview wearing blue jeans with embroidered flowers and looked more like an American than an Afghan. She went to school up to the eighth grade, but then, after her marriage at

Zoya Najabi in a shelter in Afghanistan, after fleeing her husband's family
(Nicholas D. Kristof)

age twelve to a sixteen-year-old boy, she was subjected to constant corporal punishment.

'Not only my husband, but his brother, his mother, and his sister – they all beat me,' Zoya recalled indignantly, speaking at a shelter in Kabul. Even worse, they would punish her for faulty housework by tying her to a bucket and dunking her in the well, leaving her freezing, gasping, and half drowned. The worst moment came when Zoya's mother-in-law was beating her and Zoya unthinkingly kicked back. Resisting a mother-in-law is an outrageous sin. First, Zoya's husband dug out an electrical cable and flogged his wife until she fell unconscious. Then, the next day, her father-in-law strapped Zoya's feet together, tied her down, and gave a stick to the mother-in-law, who whipped the soles of Zoya's feet.

'My feet were beaten until they were like yogurt,' Zoya said. 'All my days there were unhappy, but that was the worst.

'Mostly those kinds of beatings happen because the husbands are illiterate and uneducated,' she added. 'But it also happens that the wife is not taking care of her husband or is not obedient. Then it is appropriate to beat the wife.'

Zoya smiled a bit when she saw the shock on our faces. She

explained patiently: 'I should not have been beaten, because I was always obedient and did what my husband said. But if the wife is truly disobedient, then of course her husband has to beat her.'

In short, women themselves absorb and transmit misogynistic values, just as men do. This is not a tidy world of tyrannical men and victimized women, but a messier realm of oppressive social customs adhered to by men and women alike. As we said, laws can help, but the greatest challenge is to change these ways of thinking. And perhaps the very best means of combating suffocating traditions is education – through schools like one of our favorites, in a remote nook of the Pakistani Punjab, run by one of the world's most extraordinary women.

Mukhtar's School

The most effective change agents aren't foreigners but local women (and sometimes men) who galvanize a movement – women like Mukhtar Mai.

Mukhtar grew up in a peasant family in the village of Meerwala in southern Punjab. When people ask her age, she tosses out one number or another, but the truth is that she doesn't have a clue as to when she was born. Mukhtar never attended school, because there was no school for girls in Meerwala, and she spent her days helping out around the house.

Then, in July 2002, her younger brother, Shakur, was kidnapped and gang-raped by members of a higher-status clan, the Mastoi. (In Pakistan, rapes of boys by heterosexual men are not uncommon and are less stigmatized than the rapes of girls.) Shakur was twelve or thirteen at the time, and after raping him the Mastoi became nervous that they might be punished. So they refused to release Shakur and covered up their crime by accusing him of having had sex with a Mastoi girl, Salma. Because the Mastoi had accused Shakur of illicit sex, the village tribal assembly, dominated by the Mastoi, held a meeting. Mukhtar attended on behalf of her family to apologize and try to soothe feelings. A crowd gathered around Mukhtar, including several Mastoi men armed with guns, and the tribal council concluded that an apology from Mukhtar would not be enough. To punish Shakur and his family, the council sentenced Mukhtar to be gang-raped. Four men dragged her, screaming and pleading, into an empty stable next to the meeting area and, as the crowd waited outside, they stripped her and raped her on the dirt floor, one after the other.

Mukhtar Mai when we first met her, with students at her school
(Nicholas D. Kristof)

'They know that a woman humiliated in that way has no other recourse except suicide,' Mukhtar wrote later. 'They don't even need to use their weapons. Rape kills her.'

After administering the sentence, the rapists pushed Mukhtar out of the stable and forced her to stagger home, almost naked, before a jeering crowd. Once home, she prepared to do what any Pakistani peasant woman would normally do in that situation: kill herself. Suicide is the expected way for a woman to cleanse herself and her family of the shame. But Mukhtar's mother and father kept watch over her and prevented that option; then a local Muslim leader – one of the heroes in this story – spoke up for her at Friday prayers and denounced the rape as an outrage against Islam.

As the days passed, Mukhtar's attitude mutated from humiliation to rage. Finally, she did something revolutionary: She went to the police and reported the rape, demanding prosecution. The police, somewhat surprisingly, then arrested the attackers. President Pervez Musharraf heard about the case and sympathized, sending Mukhtar the equivalent of $8,300 in compensation. But instead of taking the money for herself, Mukhtar decided to invest it in what her village needed most – schools.

'Why should I have spent the money on myself?' she told Nick on his first visit to Meerwala. 'This way the money is helping all the girls, all the children.' During that first visit, Mukhtar was hard to get to know. When her father greeted Nick and invited him into the house, it took Nick a while to figure out who Mukhtar was. Mukhtar's father and brothers did all the talking, and Mukhtar was simply one of several women who listened in the back. She covered her face with a scarf, and all he could see were her eyes, burning with intensity. Time after time, when Nick would ask Mukhtar a question, her older brother would answer.

'So, Mukhtar, why did you use your money to start a school?'

'She started a school because she believes in education.'

After a couple of hours, the novelty of having an American in the house wore off, and the men became fidgety and wandered off to do errands. Finally, Mukhtar herself began to speak, her voice muffled by the scarf. She spoke passionately of her belief in the redemptive quality of education, in her hope that men and women in the villages could live together in harmony if only they had an education. The best way to overcome the attitudes that led to her rape, she said, was to spread education.

The police were stationed in Mukhtar's home, nominally to protect her, and they listened to the entire interview. Afterward, Mukhtar steered Nick aside to plead for help. 'The police are just stealing from my family,' she said angrily. 'They're not helping us. And the government has forgotten about me. It made promises to help my school, but it does nothing.' The new Mukhtar Mai School for Girls stood next to her house, and Mukhtar had enrolled in her own school, sitting beside the littlest girls and learning to read and write with them. But the school was unfinished and running out of operating funds.

Nick's columns about Mukhtar (who at the time went by a variant of her name, Mukhtaran Bibi) brought her $430,000 in contributions from readers, channeled through Mercy Corps, an aid group that does work in Pakistan. But it also brought harassment from the government. President Musharraf initially admired Mukhtar's courage, but he wanted Pakistan to be renowned for a sizzling economy, not notorious for barbaric rapes. Mukhtar's public comments – including her insistence that rape of poor women was a systemic problem – embarrassed him. So the intelligence services began to lean on Mukhtar to keep quiet. She refused to do so, and the government fired a warning shot: Officials ordered the release of the men who had been convicted of raping her. Mukhtar collapsed in tears.

'I'm afraid for my life,' she told us by phone that night. Still, she wouldn't back down, and her response was to call on the Pakistani government to pay more attention to women's rights. Mukhtar went ahead with plans to visit the United States and speak at a conference on women. So President Musharraf, by his own account, put her on the 'exit control list,' a blacklist of Pakistanis barred from leaving the country. Mukhtar denounced the Pakistani government for doing so and refused to be intimidated. So then the intelligence services put her under house arrest and cut off her telephone land line. But she could still go up on her roof and get a weak cell phone connection, so she used it to describe to us how the police who supposedly were protecting her were now pointing their guns at her.

Enraged at Mukhtar's continued defiance and outspokenness, Musharraf ordered her to be kidnapped (or, as he euphemistically put it, brought to the capital). Intelligence agents bustled Mukhtar into a car and a convoy drove her to Islamabad, where she was furiously berated.

'You have betrayed your country and helped our enemies!' an official told her. 'You have shamed Pakistan before the world.' Then the intelligence officers led Mukhtar, sobbing bitterly, off to a safe house, where she was prevented from contacting anyone. As all this was transpiring, Pakistan's foreign minister was visiting the White House and hearing President George W. Bush publicly praise Musharraf's 'bold leadership.'

Publicity about Pakistan's harassment of Mukhtar was embarrassing to the Bush administration, so Secretary of State Condoleezza Rice called the Pakistani foreign minister and told him it had to stop. The authorities released Mukhtar. Musharraf's aides proposed that, when the tempest died down, Pakistani officials accompany Mukhtar on a tightly chaperoned visit to the United States, where she would emphasize what a fine job the Pakistani government was doing. Mukhtar refused. 'I only want to go of my own free will,' she said. Mukhtar also complained publicly that her passport had been seized. Soon Musharraf returned the passport and allowed her to visit the United States on her own.

By now, Musharraf had turned Mukhtar into a celebrity. She was invited to the White House and the State Department, and the French foreign minister discussed international affairs with her. *Glamour* magazine flew Mukhtar first class to New York to honor her as a 'woman of the year' at a banquet where she was introduced by someone she had never heard of – Brooke Shields. Laura Bush offered a video tribute, noting, 'Please don't assume that it's only a tale of heartbreak. Mukhtaran proves that one woman really can change the world.'

On that visit, Mukhtar sat in her palatial hotel suite on Central Park West, dizzied by the attention and luxury and deeply home-sick for Meerwala. She worried about what would happen to the girls in her school during her absence. She found the interviews tiresome, partly because reporters weren't interested in her school but only in the rape. That's all they asked: *So what was it like being gang-raped?* Mukhtar had a disastrous live interview on the CBS morning news in which she was asked about it. Mukhtar indignantly replied: *I don't really want to talk about that* . . . There was an awkward silence.

During her American visit, Mukhtar was repeatedly invited by important people to dine in fancy restaurants; she kept asking for Pakistani takeout. Officials would tell Mukhtar how active their governments or aid groups were in Pakistan, and she would ask: 'Where in Pakistan do you operate?' And the answer would come: Islamabad, Karachi, Lahore. Mukhtar would shake her head and say, 'Where we need help is the countryside. Please, go to the villages and do your work there.'

Mukhtar herself lived by that credo. Sympathetic aid workers constantly urged her to move to Islamabad, where she could be safe. But she refused to discuss it. 'My work is in my village,' she said when we brought it up. 'That is where the needs are. I am afraid, but I will meet my fate; It is in God's hands.'

Visitors to events where Mukhtar was honored saw a shy woman with a head scarf getting one standing ovation after another (when she appeared in *Glamour*, she set the magazine's all-time record for clothing-to-skin ratio). But Mukhtar's passion was always her school and her village, and most of her work was not at all glamorous.

Nick has twice been a commencement speaker at Mukhtar's school, and the ceremony is quite a sight. More than one thousand students, parents, and relatives gather in a huge tent erected in a field, and they watch the students sing and perform skits warning against wife beating or early marriage. The mood is festive, and even some of the children of Mukhtar's imprisoned rapists take part. The girls incongruously break into spasms of laughter when pretending to be beaten by their husbands. Yet the constant message is for parents to keep girls in school, and that is an obsession for Mukhtar.

She was particularly determined to save one of her fourth-grade students, Halima Amir, from being pulled out of school to be married. Halima was twelve, tall and thin with long black hair, and she had been engaged at age seven to a boy five years older.

'I saw him once,' Halima said of her fiancé, As-Salam. 'I never talked to him. I wouldn't recognize him if I saw him again. I don't want to get married now.' Halima had been first in her class the previous year, and her favorite subject was English. Her fiancé was illiterate. But her parents worried that she would soon hit puberty, and they wanted her to be married off before she might develop a crush on someone else and start people gossiping – or damage her most valuable possession of all, her hymen. Time and again, Mukhtar went to Halima's home, pleading with her parents to keep her in school. The drama was unfolding during one of Nick's visits to the school, and so on his next trip he asked about Halima.

'She's not here anymore,' another student explained. 'Her parents arranged a marriage for her. They waited until Mukhtar was away on trip, and then they pulled Halima out of school and married her off. Now she's living a long way away.' Not every battle ends in victory.

With the help of the contributions people sent her, Mukhtar expanded her activities. She built a girls' high school and began operating a school for boys as well. She obtained a herd of dairy cows to provide income to sustain the schools. She bought a school van that doubles as an ambulance, to take pregnant women to a hospital when they are ready to deliver. She built another school in a nearby gangster-ridden area, where even the government didn't dare operate – and the gangsters, rather than rob the school, enrolled their own children in it. She persuaded the province to build a women's college to absorb her high school's graduates.

Mukhtar welcomes volunteers to teach English in her schools and will give them free room and board as long as they commit to staying a few months. We can't imagine a richer learning experience.

Mukhtar also started her own aid group, the Mukhtar Mai Women's Welfare Organization, which operates a twenty-four-hour hotline for battered women, a free legal clinic, a public library, and a shelter for victims of violence. That was necessary because as Mukhtar's fame spread – partly through a weekly television show she launched – women from around the country started showing up at her home. They arrived by bus, foot, taxi, or rickshaw – and often they didn't even have money to pay the driver. The rickshaw drivers came to realize that if they showed up at Mukhtar's home with a sobbing woman, Mukhtar would pay the fare. Then Mukhtar used her prominence to nudge police, journalists, and lawyers to help the victims. Mukhtar didn't speak with sophistication or learning, but she was relentless and effective. And when women came to her with their faces destroyed by acid attacks or with their noses chopped off – a traditional punishment for 'bad' or 'loose' women – Mukhtar arranged plastic surgery.

Mukhtar herself changed with time. She learned Urdu and became fluent. When we first visited Meerwala, she asked permission from her father or older brother every time she left the house. That became less tenable when she was hosting ambassadors, so she began going out without permission. This offended her older brother (her father and younger brother admire her too much to be bothered) and put a strain on the family. At one point, her older brother threatened to kill her unless she was more obedient. It didn't help that the forlorn women who were arriving at Mukhtar's doorstep were devouring the family's food and monopolizing the outhouse. But her older brother mellowed, for he is also moved by the stories of the visitors; a bit grudgingly, he admits that his sister is doing extraordinary work, and that times are changing.

Mukhtar always used to cover her face and hair entirely, with just her eyes peeking through a slit. At the banquets where she was being honored in the United States, men had to be warned not to try to shake hands with her, to hug her, or – most scandalous – to peck her on the cheek. Yet after a year or so, Mukhtar became less finicky about her head scarf and began to shake hands with men. Her faith is still enormously important to her, but she realizes that the world will not end if her scarf drops.

As Mukhtar's fame grew, the government began to push back. President Musharraf was still aggrieved at her for 'embarrassing' Pakistan, so his intelligence services harried her and her supporters. An arrest warrant was issued against one of Mukhtar's brothers on manifestly bogus charges. For a time, the Pakistani government denied us visas because we had championed her case and were close to her. The intelligence apparatus planted articles in Urdu-language newspapers accusing Mukhtar of extravagance (totally untrue) or of being a stooge for Indians and for Nick in their supposed efforts to harm Pakistan. Some upper-class Pakistanis, while originally sympathetic to Mukhtar, scorned her as an uneducated peasant and were uncomfortable with the way she was lionized abroad. They unskeptically accepted the slander that she was a money-hungry publicity hound, and they urged us to focus not on Mukhtar but on the work of doctors and lawyers in the cities. 'Mukhtar means well, but she's just a peasant,' one Pakistani told us scornfully. All the slanders left Mukhtar deeply wounded.

Mukhtar today in her steadily expanding school
(Nicholas D. Kristof)

'My life and death is in God's hands,' she said, as she had before. 'That doesn't bother me. But why does the government keep treating me as if I were a liar and a criminal?

'For the first time, I feel that the government has a plan to deal with me,' Mukhtar added. The plan, she said, was to kill or imprison her or to fake a scandal to discredit her.

Sure enough, a senior police official warned that if she was uncooperative, the government would imprison her for fornication. Fornication? On any given night there were about a dozen other women taking shelter alongside Mukhtar on the floor of her bedroom (she gave the bed itself to Naseem Akhtar, her chief of staff). President Musharraf even sent a warning through a top aide to Amna Buttar, a courageous Pakistani-American physician who was planning to accompany Mukhtar on a visit to New York: Mukhtar should watch her tongue in America, because the Pakistani government could hire local thugs to kill her and make it look like a mugging. Buttar passed the warning on to us.

Naseem told us: 'I want you to know that no matter how we are killed, even if it looks like an accident, it isn't. So if we die in a train accident, or a bus accident, or a fire – then tell the world that it was not actually an accident.'

Mukhtar's courage is having an impact, and she has shown that great social entrepreneurs don't come just from the ranks of the privileged. Rapes used to be widespread in rural Pakistan, because there was no disincentive. But Mukhtar changed the paradigm, and women and girls began to fight back and go to the police.

In 2007, a case similar to Mukhtar's unfolded in a village called Habib Labano. A young man eloped with his high-caste girlfriend, outraging the girl's family. So a high-caste council resolved to take revenge on a sixteen-year-old-girl, Saima, who was a cousin of the young man. Eleven men kidnapped the girl and paraded her naked through the village, and then, on council orders, two men raped her.

Inspired by Mukhtar, Saima didn't kill herself. Instead, her family sought prosecution. Saima went for a medical checkup that confirmed the rape, and aid groups moved to help her. After a protest that blocked a road, the higher authorities fired two police officers and arrested five of the lower-ranking suspects. It wasn't exactly justice, but it was progress. Raping poor girls is no longer always a penalty-free sport, and so rapes appear to have declined considerably in the southern Punjab. There is no data, but inhabitants in village after village say that rapes used to be common and are now rare.

Mukhtar has also galvanized other change-makers, creating echoes of herself. Farooq Leghari is a bull of a man, a tough cop who speaks English and has been seasoned by service in some of the toughest parts of Pakistan. In a long conversation at a police post that he commands, he spoke of ruling by fear, of beating up suspects to make them confess. Everything he knew was the law of the jungle, and then he was sent to Meerwala to be the top cop looking after Mukhtar. He was taken aback by Mukhtar and her commitment to the poor and helpless, and in spite of himself he came to admire her deeply.

'It is a spiritual feeling,' he recalled. 'I am very glad when I see Mukhtaran Bibi going abroad, when she opens schools or shelters.' As Farooq fell under Mukhtar's spell, he became increasingly uncomfortable with the orders from his superiors to spy on her and harass her. When his superiors scolded Farooq for protecting

Mukhtar, he told his bosses of her wonderful work. That's when he was abruptly transferred to a distant police post. Farooq continued to denounce the persecution of Mukhtar publicly, so we asked him why he risked his career to stand up for a woman he was supposed to have punished.

'I have been a bad cop,' he said. 'To bad people, yes, but I was bad. One day I was thinking, in my life, have I ever done anything good? Well, now I have a chance from God to do something good. She is helping people, and I must help Mukhtaran Bibi. I must do something good. That is why in spite of every danger to my life, to my career, I support Mukhtaran Bibi.'

Farooq said that his personnel reviews were now highly negative, and that his police career was effectively over. He feared that he could be murdered. But through watching Mukhtar, he had found a new purpose in life: protecting and speaking up for impoverished women in the villages.

After the Musharraf government collapsed in 2008, a cloud lifted from Mukhtar's operations. The intelligence agencies began to spy on terrorists instead of on Mukhtar. Pakistani spies no longer tailed us when Mukhtar showed us around the nearby villages. The government stopped harassing her, and the dangers eased just a little, allowing Mukhtar to step up her activities. In 2009, Mukhtar married a policeman who had long pleaded for her hand. She became his second wife, making Mukhtar an odd emblem of women's rights, but the marriage proceeded only after the first wife convinced Mukhtar that this was what she genuinely wanted. It was another unusual chapter in an unusual life. This uneducated woman from a tiny village had stood up to her country's president and army chief, and after years of enduring unremitting threats and harassment, she had outlasted him. She had taken a sordid tale of victimization and – through her extraordinary courage and vision – become an inspiration to us all.

CHAPTER FIVE

The Shame of 'Honor'

If a man takes a wife and, after lying with her, dislikes her
and slanders her and gives her a bad name, saying, 'I married
this woman, but when I approached her, I did not find proof
of her virginity,' then the girl's father and mother . . . shall
display the cloth [that the couple slept on] before the elders
of the town . . . If, however, the charge is true and no proof
of the girl's virginity can be found, she shall be brought to
the door of her father's house and there the men of her town
shall stone her to death.

— DEUTERONOMY 22:13–21

Of all the things that people do in the name of God, killing a
girl because she doesn't bleed on her wedding night is
among the most cruel. Yet the hymen — fragile, rarely seen, and
pretty pointless — remains an object of worship among many reli-
gions and societies around the world, the simulacrum of honor.
No matter how much gold may sell for, a hymen is infinitely more
valuable. It is frequently worth more than a human life.

The cult of virginity has been exceptionally widespread. Not
only does the Bible advocate stoning girls to death when they fail
to bleed on their wedding sheets, but Solon, the great lawgiver of
ancient Athens, prescribed that no Athenian could be sold into
slavery save a woman who lost her virginity before marriage. In
China, a neo-Confucian saying from the Song Dynasty declares:
'For a woman to starve to death is a small matter, but for her to
lose her chastity is a calamity.'

This harsh view has dissipated in most of the world, but survives in the Middle East, and this emphasis on sexual honor is today a major reason for violence against women. Sometimes it takes the form of rape, because – as with Mukhtar – often the simplest way to punish a rival family is to violate the daughter. Sometimes it takes the form of honor killing, in which a family kills one of its own girls because she has behaved immodestly or has fallen in love with a man (often there is no proof that they have had sex, and autopsies of victims of honor killings frequently reveal the hymen to be intact). The paradox of honor killings is that societies with the most rigid moral codes end up sanctioning behavior that is supremely immoral: murder.

Du'a Aswad was a beautiful Kurdish girl living in northern Iraq. She was seventeen years old when she fell in love with a Sunni Arab boy. One night she stayed out with him. Nobody knows if they actually slept together, but her family assumed that they had. When Du'a returned the next morning, she saw the rage in her family and ran to seek shelter in the home of a tribal elder, but religious leaders and her own family members insisted that she must die. So eight men stormed the elder's house and dragged her out into the street, as a large crowd gathered around her.

Honor killings are illegal in Iraqi Kurdistan, but security forces were present as Du'a was attacked, and they did not interfere. At least one thousand men joined in the assault. So many men in the crowd shot video clips with their cell phones that on the Web you can find a half-dozen versions of what happened next.

Du'a was thrown to the ground, and her black skirt was ripped off to humiliate her. Her long, thick hair cascaded around her shoulders. She tried to get up, but the men kicked her around as if she were a soccer ball. Frantic, she tried to fend off the blows, to get up, to cover herself, to find a sympathetic face in the crowd. Then the men gathered rocks and concrete blocks and dropped them on her. Most rolled off, but she began bleeding. Some of the rocks struck her head. It took thirty minutes for Du'a to die.

When she was dead and could no longer feel shame, some men in the crowd covered her legs and bottom again. This seemed to be meant as a sanctimonious gesture of righteousness, as if the obscenity were a teenage girl's bare flesh rather than her bleeding corpse.

The United Nations Population Fund has estimated that there are 5,000 honor killings a year, almost all in the Muslim world (Pakistan's government uncovered 1,261 honor killings in 2003 alone). But that estimate appears too low, because so many of the executions are disguised as accidents or suicides. Our estimate is that at least 6,000 and probably far more, honor killings take place annually around the world.

In any case, that figure doesn't begin to capture the scope of the problem, because it doesn't include what might be called honor rapes – those rapes intended to disgrace the victim or demean her clan. In recent genocides, rape has been used systematically to terrorize certain ethnic groups. Mass rape is as effective as slaughtering people, yet it doesn't leave corpses that lead to human rights prosecutions. And rape tends to undermine the victim groups' tribal structures, because leaders lose authority when they can't protect the women. In short, rape becomes a tool of war in conservative societies precisely because female sexuality is so sacred. Codes of sexual honor, in which women are valued based on their chastity, ostensibly protect women, but in fact they create an environment in which women are systematically dishonored.

In Darfur, it gradually became clear that the Sudanese-sponsored Janjaweed militias were seeking out and gang-raping women of three African tribes, then cutting off their ears or otherwise mutilating them to mark them forever as rape victims. To prevent the outside world from knowing, the Sudanese government punished women who reported rapes or sought medical treatment. When one student, Hawa, was gang-raped and beaten by the Janjaweed outside Kalma camp, her friends carried her to a clinic run by Doctors of the World, an aid group. Two French nurses immediately began caring for her injuries, but several truckloads of police stormed the clinic, pushed aside the French nurses who tried valiantly to resist, and burst in on Hawa. They dragged her out of the clinic and carried her off to prison, where she was chained to a cot by an arm and a leg.

The crime? Fornication, for by seeking treatment she was acknowledging that she had engaged in sex before marriage, and she did not provide the mandatory four adult male Muslim eye-witnesses to prove that it was rape. Sudan also blocked aid groups from bringing into Darfur postexposure prophylaxis kits, which can greatly reduce the risk that a rape victim will be infected with HIV.

Mass rapes have been reported at stunning levels in recent con-flicts. Half of the women in Sierra Leone endured sexual violence or the threat of it during the upheavals in that country, and a United Nations report claims that 90 percent of girls and women over the age of three were sexually abused in parts of Liberia during civil war there. Even in places like Pakistan, where there is no genocide or all-out war, honor rapes arise from an obsession with virginity and from the authorities' indifference to injustices suffered by the poor and uneducated. Shershah Syed, a prominent gynecologist in Karachi, says that he frequently treats young girls from the slums after rapes. And then, unless the girl kills herself, the family has to move away; otherwise, the perpetrators – who are usually rich and well connected – will terrorize the family and eliminate them as witnesses. And the police are worse than indif-ferent.

'When I treat rape victims, I tell the girls not to go to the police,' Dr. Syed added. 'Because if a girl goes to the police, the police will rape her.'

The world capital of rape is the eastern Congo. Militias consider it risky to engage in firefights with other gunmen, so instead they assault civilians. They discovered that the most cost-effective way to terrorize civilian populations is to conduct rapes of stunning brutality. Frequently the Congolese militias rape women with sticks or knives or bayonets, or else they fire their guns into the women's vaginas. In one instance, soldiers raped a three-year-old girl and then fired their guns into her. When surgeons saw her, there was no tissue left to repair. The little girl's grief-stricken father then committed suicide.

'All militias here rape women, to show their strength and to show your weakness,' said Julienne Chakupewa, a rape counselor in Goma, Congo. 'In other places, there is rape because the soldiers want a woman. Here, it's that but also a viciousness, a mentality of hatred, and it's women who pay the price.

'We say "women,"' Julienne added quickly, 'but these victims are not adults. They are girls of fourteen, even children of six.'

In 2008, the United Nations formally declared rape a 'weapon of war,' and Congo came up constantly in the discussions. Major General Patrick Cammaert, a former United Nations force commander, spoke of the spread of rape as a war tactic and said something haunting: 'It has probably become more dangerous to be a woman than a soldier in an armed conflict.'

One of those Congolese victims is Dina, a seventeen-year-old from the town of Kindu. She wore a blue shirt and bright multi-colored skirt as she told us her story, an orange head scarf fastened demurely over her head. Dina was shy, speaking softly through an interpreter, and she smiled often in nervousness.

One of six children, Dina grew up working on her parents' farm, growing bananas, cassava, and beans. Two of her brothers attended school for a bit, but none of the daughters did. 'It's more important to educate boys,' she explained, and she seemed to believe it.

All the local residents knew that there were soldiers from the Hutu Interahamwe militia in the area, so Dina was fearful whenever she went out to farm the crops. But the alternative was to starve. One day, because of the danger, Dina cut short her work in her bean field and headed back to town well before sunset. As she was walking home, five Hutu militia members surrounded her. They had guns and knives and forced her to the ground. One of them was carrying a stick.

'If you cry out, we will kill you,' one of them told Dina. So she kept quiet as, one by one, the five men raped her. Then they held her down as one of them shoved the stick inside her.

When Dina didn't come home, her father and friends bravely went out to the fields, and there they found her, half dead in the grass. They covered her and carried her back to her home. There was a health center in Kindu, but Dina's family couldn't afford to take her there to be treated, so she was cared for only at home. She lay paralyzed in her bed, unable to walk. The stick had broken into her bladder and rectum, causing a fistula, or hole, in the tissues. As a result, urine and feces trickled constantly through her vagina and down her legs. These injuries, rectovaginal and vesicovaginal fistulas, are common in Congo because of sexual violence.

'My people had no tribal conflict with them,' Dina said of the soldiers. 'Their only purpose was to rape me and leave me bleeding and leaking wastes.' This culture of brutality spread from militia to militia, from tribe to tribe. In just the Congolese province of South Kivu, the UN estimates that there were twenty-seven thousand sexual assaults in 2006. By another UN accounting, three quarters of the women in some areas had been raped. John Holmes, the UN undersecretary general for humanitarian affairs, says flatly: 'The sexual violence in Congo is the worst in the world.'

One of the warlords whose troops have been implicated in the rapes is Laurent Nkunda, a tall, genial man who served us dinner in his comfortable mountain lair. He passes himself off as a Pentecostal pastor and piously wore a REBELS FOR CHRIST button on his uniform, apparently because he thought it would win him American support. Before he offered us drinks and snacks, he said grace. Nkunda insisted that his troops never rape anybody, adding that the only time one of his soldiers did rape a woman, he executed the soldier. Yet everyone knows that rape is routine. When Nkunda presented some of the prisoners of war whom his soldiers had seized from rival armed militias, we asked them about rape.

'If we see girls, it's our right,' said one, Noel Rwabirinba, a sixteen-year-old who said he had carried a gun for two years. 'We can violate them.'

Noel Rwabirinba, a child soldier in Congo, said that it is the troops' right to rape women (Nicholas D. Kristof)

United Nations peacekeepers did little to stop the rapes. Former ambassador Stephen Lewis of Canada, one of the most eloquent advocates for the world's women, has suggested that UN Secretary-General Ban Ki-moon should make mass rape a priority and pledge to resign if member countries don't support him. 'We're talking about more than fifty percent of the world's population, amongst whom are the most uprooted, disinherited and impoverished of the earth,' Lewis said. 'If you can't stand up for the women of the world, then you shouldn't be Secretary-General.'

Women have suffered grievously in the genocides of Rwanda and Darfur. Men, too. In Rwanda, when the genocide was over, 70 percent of the country's population was female because so many more men were killed. In Darfur, after interviewing several women who told of having been raped when leaving their camps to get firewood, we asked the obvious question: 'If women are raped when they get firewood, then why don't they stay in the camp? Why don't the men collect firewood?'

'When men leave the camp, they're shot dead,' one of the women explained patiently. 'When the women leave, they're *only* raped.' In almost every conflict, mortality is disproportionately male. But whereas men are the normal victims of war, women have become a weapon of war – meant to be disfigured or tortured to terrorize the rest of the population. To travel in eastern Congo and talk to villagers is to uncover layers and layers of routinized rape. In a camp for displaced people, we asked to speak to a rape victim, and one was immediately brought over. To ensure her privacy, we took her under a tree away from other people, but after ten minutes a long line of women formed nearby.

'What are you all doing here?' we asked.

'We're all rape victims,' explained the woman in front. 'We're waiting to tell our stories, too.'

For Dina, lying incontinent and paralyzed in her home, life seemed to be over. Then neighbors began telling her family about a hospital where doctors could fix injuries like hers. The hospital is called HEAL Africa, and it is located in Goma, the biggest city in eastern Congo. The family contacted HEAL Africa's representative, and he arranged for a missionary plane to carry Dina to Goma for treatment. HEAL Africa covered the expense.

Dina was taken from the Goma airstrip by ambulance to the HEAL Africa hospital; it was the first time she had ever ridden in a car. Nurses gave her a plastic diaper and put her together with dozens of other women, all of whom were incontinent because of fistulas. This gave Dina the courage to try to stand and walk. The nurses gave her a crutch and helped her hobble about. They fed her and began a course of physical therapy, and added her name to a list of women waiting for fistula surgery. When Dina's day came, a doctor successfully sewed up her rectovaginal fistula. Then she underwent more physical therapy as she prepared for a second operation to repair the hole in her bladder. Meanwhile, Dina began to wonder what she would do postsurgery, and she decided to stay for the time being in Goma.

'If I return to Kindu,' she explained, 'I'll just be raped again.' Yet after the second surgery, which also succeeded, Dina decided to go back to Kindu after all. She missed her family, and in any case the war was also reaching into Goma. It seemed to Dina that she might be just as vulnerable if she stayed, so she chose to return to the maelstrom of Kindu.

'Study Abroad' – in the Congo

In the cauldron of violence and misogyny that is eastern Congo, the HEAL Africa hospital where Dina was treated is a sanctuary of dignity. It is a large compound of low white buildings where patients are respected. It's an example of an aid project that makes an extraordinary difference in people's lives. And one of those helping patients like Dina is a young American woman named Harper McConnell.

Harper has long, dirty-blond hair and very white skin that seems to redden more than tan under the tropical sun. She dresses casually, and with the exception of African necklaces dangling on her collar, she looks as if she could be on an American university campus. Yet here she is in war-torn Congo, speaking excellent Swahili and bantering with her new friends who grew up in the Congolese bush. She has taken a path that more young Americans should consider – traveling to the developing world to 'give back' to people who desperately need the assistance.

Young people often ask us how they can help address issues like sex trafficking or international poverty. Our first recommendation to them is to get out and see the world. If you can't do that, it's great to raise money or attention at home. But to tackle an issue effectively, you need to understand it – and it's impossible to understand an issue by simply reading about it. You need to see it firsthand, even live in its midst.

One of the great failings of the American education system, in our view, is that young people can graduate from university without any understanding of poverty at home or abroad. Study-abroad programs tend to consist of herds of students visiting Oxford or

Harper McConnell with a friend at the HEAL Africa hospital in Congo
(Nicholas D. Kristof)

Florence or Paris. We believe that universities should make it a
requirement that all graduates spend at least some time in the
developing world, either by taking a 'gap year' or by studying
abroad. If more Americans worked for a summer teaching English
at a school like Mukhtar's in Pakistan, or working at a hospital like
HEAL Africa in Congo, our entire society would have a richer
understanding of the world around us. And the rest of the world
might also hold a more positive view of Americans.

Young people, women especially, often worry about the safety
of volunteering abroad. There are, of course, legitimate concerns
about disease and violence, but mostly there is the exaggerated
fear of the unknown – the mirror image of the nervousness that
Africans or Indians feel when they travel to America for their studies. In reality, Americans and Europeans are usually treated
hospitably in the developing world, and are much less likely to be
robbed in an African village than in Paris or Rome. The most dangerous part of living in a poor country is often the driving, since
no one wears seat belts, and red lights – if they exist – tend to be
regarded as mere suggestions.

American women sometimes do get unwanted notice, particularly if they are blond, but it's rarely threatening. Once women

have settled in at their destination, they usually find it safer than they had imagined. Western women are often exempt from local indignities and harassment, partly because local men find them intimidating. Women volunteers often have more options than men do. For example, in conservative cultures, it may be inappropriate for an American man to teach female students or even talk to women, while an American woman may well be able to teach either boys or girls and to mix with local men and women alike.

There are countless opportunities to volunteer at the grassroots. Most of the aid programs we refer to in this book welcome volunteers, as long as they stay for a few months to make the visit worth the trouble. We've noted contact information for these organizations in the appendix. Time spent in Congo and Cambodia might not be as pleasant as in Paris, but it will be life-changing.

Harper, who grew up in Michigan and Kansas, was studying political science and English at the University of Minnesota, not sure what she would do afterward. She had studied poverty and development and was feeling restless and pressured with graduation looming. Then, in May of her senior year, she heard that her church was exploring a relationship with a hospital in Congo. The church, Upper Room, in Edina, Minnesota, understood something important: The congregation should not just be writing checks but also getting actively involved. So Harper talked to her pastor about the Congo arrangement, and by the end of the meeting Harper had agreed to go live in Goma to oversee the relationship with the HEAL Africa hospital.

'We want to educate our congregation about eastern Congo and give them the chance to come and see life here,' she says. 'I also provide the church with the reality on the ground to make sure that projects which are dreamed up in offices in the United States actually meet the needs in the field.'

Harper stays in a nice Western-style house in Goma, with the couple who founded the HEAL Africa hospital: a Congolese doctor, Jo Lusi, and his wife, Lyn, from England. Jo and Lyn take up one room in the house, which is always crowded with visitors and guests. And while it provides a sanctuary from the chaos of Congo, the generator still goes off at 10 p.m. – and don't count on a hot shower. Then there's the countryside, which often feels as if it's a century or two behind Goma. One day Harper was bubbling with news: 'One of our teams just went to a village that hadn't seen a car since the 1980s. They called it "a walking house."'

HEAL Africa is a major hospital. Officially it has 150 beds, but there are usually 250 patients, and it manages to accommodate them. There are 14 doctors and a total staff of 210, all of whom are Congolese except for Lyn, Harper, and one other person. The hospital manages to have clean sheets, but there are still just two gynecologists in an area with 5 million people. Getting electricity, water, and bandages for the hospital is a nightmare, and corruption is overwhelming. In 2002, a nearby volcano erupted, and when the lava reached the building the hospital burst into flames. Most of the hospital grounds were covered in eight feet of lava, but with support from American donors, the hospital was rebuilt as soon as the lava had cooled.

For a young, single person, living in a place like Goma can be tedious and confining. Harper broke up with her boyfriend of two years when she moved to Congo, and although she regularly gets marriage proposals from drivers, there isn't any dating scene. Once she contracted malaria and ended up in her own hospital. But she felt a measure of pride at finally enduring the standard African ailment. As she was lying feverishly in her hospital bed, nourished by an IV drip, she awoke thinking that she saw Ben Affleck looming over her hospital bed. She soon realized it was not a figment of her delirium: Affleck was visiting Congo and had come by to wish her well.

There are also compensations for the lack of shopping malls and Netflix movies. Harper has undertaken two major projects that make her excited to get out of bed each morning. First, she started a school at the hospital for children awaiting medical treatment. It can take several months before children with orthopedic problems receive care, and they often come from rural areas with no decent schools. So Harper found teachers and put together a class-room. The children now can go to school six days a week. At the age of twenty-three, Harper became the principal of her own school.

Second, Harper started a skills-training program for women awaiting surgery. Many of the patients, like Dina, spend months at the hospital, and they can now use the time to learn to sew, read, weave baskets, make soap, and bake bread. Typically a woman chooses one of the skills and then works with a trainer until she is confident that she can make a living at it. When the woman leaves, HEAL Africa gives her the raw materials she needs – even a pedal sewing machine, if she has learned tailoring – so that she can generate income for her family afterward. Those who have trouble absorbing vocational skills are at least given a big block of salt so that they can break it up and sell little bags of salt in the market to survive. The ability to earn a living transforms the women's lives.

'The women are so excited about Harper's program,' said Dada Byamungu, whom Harper hired to teach sewing. As we talked, a raucous group of women surrounded Harper, teasing her and thanking her in Swahili, all at the same time – and she was laugh-ing and retorting in rapid-fire Swahili. Dada translated what the women were saying: 'They say that they will lift Harper up and make her their queen!'

If you were to come to dinner at our home, you would see lovely woven reed placemats made by women at HEAL Africa. Harper has set up a little shop at the hospital to sell goods like these that the women are making, and she's trying to sell them on the Internet and in American department stores as well. If you're an American university student, there's something else that Harper did that may be more relevant: She is setting up a study-abroad program for Americans who want to spend a month at ULPGL, a university in Goma. The Americans will take courses with Congolese students, spend time in the classroom and the field, and write research papers together in small groups. Harper also tries to encourage donors in the United States. The hospital has an annual budget of $1.4 million, more than one third of which is contributed by individual Americans (more information is at www.healafrica.org). Only 2 percent of those donations go to overhead and administrative expenses; the rest is plowed into the hospital. The hospital even accepts gifts of airline miles, to fly staff back and forth, and it eagerly welcomes volunteers and visitors.

'I'd rather have someone come here and see what's going on than write a check for one or two thousand dollars, because that visit is going to change their life,' Harper says. 'I have the privilege of hearing from church members and other visitors about how their time at HEAL Africa has turned their worldview upside down and changed their lifestyle at home.'

As Harper jabbers away in Swahili with her African friends, it's clear that she is getting as well as giving. She agrees:

There are times when all I want is a fast Internet connection, a latte, and a highway to drive on. Yet the greetings I receive in the morning from my coworkers are enough to keep me here. I have the blessing of carrying a purse sewn by a woman waiting for fistula surgery at the hospital and watching how these new skills have changed her whole composure and confidence, of celebrating with my Congolese friend who was accepted for a job right after he graduated from university, of seeing children in school who previously never had the chance, of rejoicing with a family over their improved harvest, of dancing with my coworkers over a grant awarded for a program. The main factor that separates me from my friends here is the opportunities I was given as a first-world citizen, and I believe it is my responsibility to work so that these opportunities are available to all.

CHAPTER SIX

Maternal Mortality – One Woman a Minute

Preparation for death is that most Reasonable and Seasonable
thing, to which you must now apply yourself

– COTTON MATHER, IN A SERMON,
ADVISING PREGNANT WOMEN

No one reading this book, we hope, can fathom the sadistic cruelty of those soldiers who used a pointed stick to tear apart Dina's insides. But there is also a milder, more diffuse cruelty of indifference, and it is global indifference that leaves some 3 million women and girls incontinent just like Dina. Fistulas like hers are common in the developing world but, outside of Congo, are overwhelmingly caused not by rape but by obstructed labor and lack of medical care during childbirth. Most of the time, such women don't get any surgical help to repair their fistulas, because maternal health and childbirth injuries are rarely a priority.

For every Dina, there are hundreds like Mahabouba Muhammad, a tall woman who grew up in western Ethiopia. Mahabouba has light chocolate skin and frizzy hair that she ties back; today, she tells her story easily, for the most part, occasionally punctuated with self-mocking laughter, but there are moments when the old pain shines through in her eyes. Mahabouba was raised in a village near the town of Jimma, and her parents divorced when she was a child. As a result, she was handed over to her father's sister, who didn't educate her and generally treated her as a servant. So Mahabouba and her sister ran off together to town and worked as maids in exchange for room and board.

'Then a neighbor told me he could find better work for me,' Mahabouba recalled. 'He sold me for eighty birr [ten dollars]. He got the money, I didn't. I thought I was going to work for the man who bought me, in his house. But then he raped me and beat me. He said he had bought me for eighty birr and wouldn't let me go. I was about thirteen.'

The man, Jiad, was about sixty years old and had purchased Mahabouba to be his second wife. In rural Ethiopia, girls are still sometimes sold to do manual labor or to be second or third wives, although it is becoming less common. Mahabouba hoped for consolation from the first wife, but instead the woman whipped Mahabouba with savage relish. 'She used to beat me when he wasn't around, so I think she was jealous,' Mahabouba remembered angrily, and she paused for a moment as the old bitterness caught up with her.

The couple wouldn't let Mahabouba out of the house for fear she might run away. Indeed, she tried several times, but each time she was caught and thrashed with sticks and fists until she was black, blue, and bloody. Soon, Mahabouba was pregnant, and as she approached her due date Jiad relaxed his guard over her. When she was seven months pregnant, she finally succeeded in running away.

'I thought if I stayed, I might be beaten to death along with my child,' Mahabouba said. 'I fled to the town, but the people there said they would take me right back to Jiad. So then I ran away again, back to my native village. But my immediate family was no longer there, and nobody else wanted to help me because I was pregnant and somebody's wife. So I went to drown myself in the river, but an uncle found me and took me back. He told me to stay in a little hut by his house.'

Mahabouba couldn't afford a midwife, so she tried to have the baby by herself. Unfortunately, her pelvis hadn't yet grown large enough to accommodate the baby's head, a common occurrence with young teenagers. She ended up in obstructed labor, with the baby stuck inside her birth passage. After seven days, Mahabouba fell unconscious, and at that point someone summoned a birth attendant. By then the baby had been wedged there for so long that the tissues between the baby's head and Mahabouba's pelvis had lost circulation and rotted away. When Mahabouba recovered consciousness, she found that the baby was dead and that she had no control over her bladder or bowels. She also couldn't walk or even stand, a consequence of nerve damage that is a frequent by-product of fistula.

'People said it was a curse,' Mahabouba recalled. 'They said, "If you're cursed, you shouldn't stay here. You should leave."' Mahabouba's uncle wanted to help the girl, but his wife feared that helping someone cursed by God would be sacrilegious. She urged her husband to take Mahabouba outside the village and leave the girl to be eaten by wild animals. He was torn. He gave Mahabouba food and water, but he also allowed the villagers to move her to a hut at the edge of the village.

'Then they took the door off,' she added matter-of-factly, 'so that the hyenas would get me.' Sure enough, after darkness fell the hyenas came. Mahabouba couldn't move her legs, but she held a stick in her hand and waved it frantically at the hyenas, shouting at them. All night long, the hyenas circled her; all night long, Mahabouba fended them off.

She was fourteen years old.

When morning light came, Mahabouba realized that her only hope was to get out of the village to find help, and she was galvanized by a fierce determination to live. She had heard of a Western missionary in a nearby village, so she began to crawl in that direction, pulling her body with her arms. She was half dead when she arrived a day later at the doorstep of the missionary. Aghast, he rushed her inside, nursed her, and saved her life. On his next trip to Addis Ababa, he took Mahabouba with him to a compound of one-story white buildings on the edge of the city: the Addis Ababa Fistula Hospital.

There Mahabouba found scores of other girls and women also suffering from fistulas. On arrival, she was examined, bathed, given new clothes, and shown how to wash herself. Fistula patients often suffer wounds on their legs, from the acid in their urine eating away at the skin, but frequent washings can eliminate these sores. The girls in the hospital walk around in flip-flops, chattering with one another and steadily dripping urine – hospital staff joke that it is 'puddle city' – but the floors are mopped several times an hour, and the girls are too busy socializing with one another to be embarrassed.

The hospital is run by Catherine Hamlin, a gynecologist who is truly a saint. She has devoted most of her life to poor women in Ethiopia, undergoing danger and hardship while transforming the lives of countless young women like Mahabouba. Tall, lean, and white-haired, Catherine is athletic, welcoming, and wonderfully gentle – except when people suggest she is a saint.

'I love this work,' she said in exasperation the first time we met. 'I'm not here because I'm a saint or doing anything noble. I enjoy my life tremendously . . . I'm here because I feel God wants me to be here. I feel I'm doing some good and helping these women. It's very satisfying work.' Catherine and her late husband, Reg Hamlin, moved from their native Australia to Ethiopia in 1959 to work as ob-gyns. In Australia, they had never seen a single case of fistula; in Ethiopia, they encountered fistulas constantly. 'These are the women most to be pitied in the world,' Catherine says firmly. 'They're alone in the world, ashamed of their injuries. For lepers, or AIDS victims, there are organizations that help. But nobody knows about these women or helps them.'

Fistulas used to be common in the West, and there was once a fistula hospital in Manhattan, where the Waldorf-Astoria Hotel is today. But then improved medical care all but eliminated the problem; now almost no woman in the rich world spends four days in obstructed labor – long before then, doctors give her a C-section.

In 1975, Catherine and Reg founded the Addis Ababa Fistula Hospital, and it remains a lovely hillside compound of white buildings and verdant gardens. Catherine presides over the hospital, living in a cozy house in the center of the compound, and she plans to be buried in Addis Ababa alongside her husband. Catherine has presided over more than twenty-five thousand fistula surgeries and

Mahabouba on the grounds of the Addis Ababa Fistula Hospital in Ethiopia (Nicholas D. Kristof)

has trained countless doctors in the specialty. She is an exceptionally skilled surgeon, but because some patients don't have enough tissue left to repair they are given colostomies, so that feces leave the body through a hole made in the abdomen and are stored in a pouch that must be regularly disposed of. Patients with colostomies require ongoing care and live in a village near the hospital.

Mahabouba is one of those who couldn't be fully repaired. Physical therapy got her walking again, but she had to settle for a colostomy. Still, when she had recovered her mobility, Catherine put her to work in the hospital. At first Mahabouba simply changed linens or helped patients wash, but gradually the doctors realized that she was smart and eager to do more, and they gave her more responsibilities. She learned to read and write, and she blossomed. She found a purpose in life. Today, if you were to visit the hospital, you might well see Mahabouba walking around – in her nurse's uniform. She has been promoted to the position of senior nurse's aide.

It costs about $300 to repair a fistula, and about 90 percent of them are repairable. But the vast majority of women who suffer fistulas are impoverished peasants who are never taken to a doctor and never receive medical assistance. L. Lewis Wall, a professor of obstetrics at the Washington University School of Medicine who has campaigned tirelessly for a fistula hospital in West Africa, estimates that 30,000 to 130,000 new cases of fistula develop each year in Africa alone.*

Instead of receiving treatment, these young women – often just girls of fifteen or sixteen – typically find their lives effectively over. They are divorced from their husbands and, because they emit a terrible odor from their wastes, are often forced to live in a hut by themselves on the edge of the village, as Mahabouba was. Eventually, they starve to death or die of an infection that progresses along the birth canal.

'The fistula patient is the modern-day leper,' notes Ruth Kennedy, a British nurse-midwife who worked with Catherine at the fistula hospital. 'She's helpless, she's voiceless . . . The reason these women are pariahs is because they are women. If this happened to men, we would have foundations and supplies coming in from all over the world.'

Oprah Winfrey interviewed Catherine and was so taken with her that she later visited the fistula hospital and donated a new wing for it. Yet maternal health generally gets minimal attention because those who die or suffer injuries overwhelmingly start with three strikes against them: They are female, they are poor, and they are rural. 'Women are marginalized in the developing world,' says Catherine. 'They are an expendable commodity.'

Granted, health care is deficient in poor countries even for men. Eleven percent of the world's inhabitants live in sub-Saharan Africa, and they suffer 24 percent of the world's disease burden – which is addressed with less than 1 percent of the world's health

---

* It was Professor Wall's campaign that, in the 1990s, first introduced us to obstetric fistulas. Dr. Wall heads the Worldwide Fistula Fund (www.worldwidefistulafund.org) and is finally seeing his longtime dream of a fistula hospital in West Africa being realized. With support from Merrill Lynch and private American donors, the hospital is being built in Niger, although funding is still tight. Professor Wall has truly been a hero in the struggle to help these neglected women.

care spending. But maternal care is particularly neglected, never receiving adequate funding. For the 2009 fiscal year, President George W. Bush actually proposed an 18 percent cut in USAID spending for maternal and child care to just $370 million, or about $1.20 per American per year.

Conservatives battle forced abortions in China, and liberals fight passionately for abortion rights in foreign lands. But meeting the challenge of women dying in childbirth has never had much of a constituency. We in the news media can count inattention to the issue as another of our failures. The equivalent of five jumbo jets' worth of women die in labor each day, but the issue is almost never covered. The remedy? America should lead a global campaign to save mothers in childbirth. Right now the amount we Americans spend on maternal health is equivalent to less than one twentieth of 1 percent of the amount we spend on our military.

The World Health Organization estimates that 536,000 women perished in pregnancy or childbirth in 2005, a toll that has barely budged in thirty years. Child mortality has plunged, longevity has increased, but childbirth remains almost as deadly as ever, with one maternal death every minute.

Some 99 percent of those deaths occur in poor countries. The most common measure is the maternal mortality ratio (MMR). This refers to the number of maternal deaths for every 100,000 live births, although the data collection is usually so poor that the figures are only rough estimates. In Ireland, the safest place in the world to give birth, the MMR is just 1 per 100,000 live births. In the United States, where many more women fall through the cracks, the MMR is 11. In contrast, the average MMR in South Asia (including India and Pakistan) is 490. In sub-Saharan Africa, it is 900, and Sierra Leone has the highest MMR in the world, at 2,100.

While MMR measures the risk during a single pregnancy, women in poor countries undergo many pregnancies. So statisticians also calculate the lifetime risk of dying in childbirth. The highest lifetime risk in the world is in the West African country of Niger, where a girl or woman stands a 1-in-7 chance of dying in childbirth. Overall in sub-Saharan Africa, the lifetime risk of dying in childbirth is 1 in 22. India disgraces itself, because for all its shiny new high-rises, an Indian woman still has a 1-in-70 chance of dying in childbirth at some point in her life. In contrast, in the United States, the lifetime risk is 1 in 4,800; in Italy, it's 1 in 26,600; and in Ireland a woman has only 1 chance in 47,600 of dying in childbirth.

So lifetime risk of maternal death is one thousand times higher in a poor country than in the West. That should be an international scandal. The gap, moreover, is getting wider. WHO found that between 1990 and 2005, developed and middle-income countries reduced maternal mortality significantly, but Africa reduced it hardly at all. Indeed, because of growing populations, the number of African women who died in childbirth rose from 205,000 in 1990 to 261,000 in 2005.

Maternal morbidity (injuries in childbirth) occurs even more often than maternal mortality. For every woman who dies in childbirth, at least ten suffer significant injuries such as fistulas or serious tearinng. Unsafe abortions cause the deaths of seventy thousand women annually and cause serious injuries to another 5 million. The economic cost of caring for those 5 million women is estimated to be $750 million annually. And there is evidence that when a woman dies in childbirth, her surviving children are much more likely to die young as well, because they no longer have a mother caring for them.

Frankly, we hesitate to pile on the data, since even when numbers are persuasive, they are not galvanizing. A growing collection of psychological studies show that statistics have a dulling effect, while it is individual stories that move people to act. In one experiment, research subjects were divided into several groups, and each person was asked to donate $5 to alleviate hunger abroad. One group was told the money would go to Rokia, a seven-year-old girl in Mali. Another group was told that the money would go to address malnutrition among 21 million Africans. The third group was told that the donations would go to Rokia, as in the first group, but this time her own hunger was presented as part of a background tapestry of global hunger, with some statistics thrown in. People were much more willing to donate to Rokia than to 21 million hungry people, and even a mention of the larger problem made people less inclined to help her.

In another experiment, people were asked to donate to a $300,000 fund to fight cancer. One group was told that the money would be used to save the life of one child, while another group was told it would save the lives of eight children. People contributed almost twice as much to save one child as to save eight. Social psychologists argue that all this reflects the way our consciences and ethical systems are based on individual stories and are distinct from the parts of our brains concerned with logic and rationality. Indeed, when subjects in experiments are first asked to solve math problems, thus putting in play the parts of the brain that govern logic, afterward they are less generous to the needy.

So we would prefer to move beyond statistics and focus on an individual: Simeesh Segaye. If more people could meet this warm twenty-one-year-old peasant with a soft voice, we're sure 'maternal health' would suddenly become a priority for them. Simeesh was lying on her back in a bed at the end of the main ward in the Addis Ababa Fistula Hospital when we first saw her. Ruth Kennedy, the hospital's nurse-midwife, translated as Simeesh told us how she had enjoyed an eighth-grade education – very impressive for rural Ethiopia. She had married at nineteen and was thrilled when she became pregnant. Her girlfriends all congratulated her, and they all prayed that she would be blessed with a son.

When she went into labor, no baby emerged. After two full days of obstructed labor, Simeesh was barely conscious. Her neighbors carried her for hours to the nearest road and put her on a bus when one finally arrived. The bus took another two days to get to the nearest hospital, and by then the baby was dead.

When Simeesh began to recover back in the village, she found that she was crippled and leaking urine and feces. She was shattered and humiliated by the constant smell of her wastes. Her parents and husband saved $10 to pay a public bus to take her back to the hospital in the hope that her fistula could be repaired. When the bus came along, the other passengers took one whiff of her and

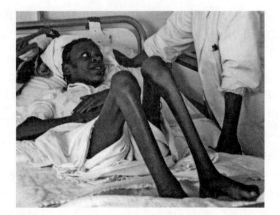

Simeesh Segaye, her legs stuck in this bent position, in the Addis Ababa
Fistula Hospital (Nicholas D. Kristof)

complained vociferously: *We shouldn't have to ride next to somebody who stinks like that! We paid for this ride – you can't make us put up with that stink! Put her off!*

The bus driver returned Simeesh's $10 and ordered her off the bus. Any prospect of a repair vanished. Simeesh's husband then abandoned her. Her parents stood by her, but they built a separate hut for her because even they couldn't abide her odor. Every day, they brought her food and water and tried to reassure her. Simeesh stayed in that hut – alone, ashamed, helpless. By one estimate, 90 percent of fistula patients have contemplated suicide, and Simeesh, too, decided she wanted to die. Depression swept over her, turning her numb and almost catatonic. People suffering from depression sometimes revert to the fetal position, and that's what Simeesh did – except that she almost never moved.

'I just curled up,' she says, 'for two years.' Once or twice a year, her parents took her out of the hut, but otherwise she just lay on the ground, hidden away, hoping that death would be her escape. She barely ate, because the more she ate or drank, the more wastes trickled down her legs. And so she began to starve to death.

Simeesh's parents loved their daughter, but they didn't know if doctors could help, and they had no money. She didn't ask for anything, barely spoke, just lay in her hut wishing she were dead.

113

After two excruciating years of watching their daughter suffer, her parents sold their livestock – all of their assets – to try to help Simeesh. It was clear that no bus would transport her, so they paid $250 for a private car to take them to a hospital in the city of Yirga Alem, a day's drive away. The doctors there found Simeesh's case too complex and referred her to the fistula hospital. The doctors there reassured Simeesh, telling her that they could solve her problems, and she began to emerge from her depression. At first she spoke only in furtive whispers, but slowly she began to reengage with people around her.

Before the doctors could try to repair the fistula, they had to address her other problems. After two years of constantly lying curled up in a fetal position, Simeesh's legs had withered and become permanently bent: She couldn't move them, let alone straighten them, and she was too emaciated and weak to operate on. Catherine and the other doctors tried to strengthen Simeesh by giving her good food, and nurses were helping her with physical therapy so that she could straighten her legs. Then doctors found that seven centimeters of her pubic joint had disappeared, apparently because of infection. The doctors performed a temporary colostomy, and after long and painful rounds of physical therapy – which Simeesh embraced as her depression faded – she was able to stand up again.

Then she developed stress fractures in her feet. So the doctors prescribed intensive physiotherapy, and several former patients massaged her and worked with her, always careful to stop when the pain grew too agonizing. Finally, after months and months of grueling work, Simeesh was able to stretch her legs and stand. Eventually she could even walk unassisted. Just as important, she had recovered her dignity and enthusiasm for life. Once she was strong again, the surgeons repaired her fistula, and she made a full recovery.

Women like Simeesh have been abandoned by almost everyone in the world. But for decades, one American doctor has led the fight to call attention to maternal health. Even as he lost ground to a lethal degenerative disease, he fought daily to lessen the toll of childbirth.

A Doctor Who Treats Countries, Not Patients

Allan Rosenfield grew up in the 1930s and 1940s in Brookline, Massachusetts, the son of a successful obstetrician in Boston. He went to medical school at Columbia and did a stint for the air force in South Korea. While in Korea, he volunteered on week-ends at a local hospital – and was shaken as he walked up and down the wards. Rural Korean women were suffering horrendous child-birth injuries unimaginable in the United States. Allan returned to America, but he was haunted by the memories of those stoic peas-ant women.

The Korean experience left Allan with a deep interest in the medical needs of poor countries. When he later heard about a position at a medical school in Lagos, Nigeria, he signed up. In 1966, he took his new bride, Clare, to Lagos, where they started a new life together. Allan was bowled over by what he saw in Nigeria, particularly by the need for family planning and for maternal care. He also was beset by doubts.

'I began to feel that the model of care we were giving wasn't appropriate for Nigeria,' he recalled. That practical encounter with the realities of Africa was the beginning of a lifelong interest in public health, preventing disease rather than just treating patients as they turned up. In the West, we tend to think of disease and mortality as the province of doctors, but by far the greatest strides in global health have been made by public health specialists. Models of the public health approach include smallpox vaccination programs, oral rehydration therapy to save babies with diarrhea, and campaigns to encourage seat belts and air bags in vehicles. Any serious effort to reduce maternal mortality likewise requires a

*Allan Rosenfield at Columbia University's Mailman School of Public
Health in New York City (Tanya Braganti)*

public health perspective – reducing unwanted pregnancies and
providing prenatal care so that last-minute medical crises are less
frequent.

Sometimes the most effective approaches aren't medical at all.
For example, one out-of-the-box way to reduce pregnancies is to
subsidize school uniforms for girls. That keeps them in school
longer, which means that they delay marriage and pregnancy until
they are better able to deliver babies. A South African study found
that giving girls a $6 uniform every eighteen months increased the
chance that they would stay in school and consequently significantly reduced the number of pregnancies they experienced. Allan
Rosenfield struggled to combine this public health perspective
with practical medicine – and he became a social entrepreneur in
the world of maternal health.

Allan had intended for his service in Nigeria to be an interlude,
his own version of the Peace Corps. But surrounded by such overwhelming needs, he began to feel a calling. He signed up for a job
with the Population Council in Thailand. The Rosenfields spent six
years there, starting a family, learning the Thai language, and utterly
falling in love with the country. Yet the beauty of Thai beaches were
a world apart from the horrors of the maternity wards. Moreover,

IUDs and the Pill were available only by prescription from a doctor, which meant that some of the most effective forms of contraception were unavailable to 99 percent of the population. So Allan worked with the ministry of health on a revolutionary scheme: allowing trained auxiliary midwives to prescribe the Pill. First, he developed a checklist of questions, so that a midwife could talk to a woman and either give her a prescription for the Pill or, if there were risk factors, refer her to a doctor. Soon the program was rolled out to three thousand sites around the country, and eventually the auxiliary midwives were authorized to insert IUDs as well. It's difficult to appreciate today how unusual this approach was, for physicians closely guarded their prerogatives, and it was heresy to entrust mere midwives with medical responsibilities.

'Because it was so different an approach, I would have trouble getting it approved today,' Allan said. 'But because I was on my own, I could do it.' The trajectory of his career was set: public health work to make it safe for women to have babies. In 1975, Allan moved to New York to head the Center for Population and Family Health at Columbia University. He developed a global network of allies in the field, and in 1985 published a landmark article along with Deborah Maine, a colleague, in *The Lancet*, the British journal that has been at the forefront of global health issues. It declared:

> It is difficult to understand why maternal mortality receives so little serious attention from health professionals, policy makers, and politicians. The world's obstetricians are particularly neglectful of their duty in this regard. Instead of drawing attention to the problem and lobbying for major programmes and changes in priorities, most obstetricians concentrate on subspecialties that put emphasis on high technology.

The article led to a global advocacy movement on behalf of maternal health, and it coincided with Allan's appointment as dean of Columbia's Mailman School of Public Health. Then, in 1999, with a $50 million grant from the Bill & Melinda Gates Foundation, he launched an organization called Averting Maternal Death and Disability (AMDD), which undertook a pioneering global effort to make childbirth safe.

Increasingly, Allan began approaching maternal death not just as a public health concern but also as a human rights issue. 'The technical solutions to reduce maternal mortality are not enough,' Allan wrote in one essay. 'As a basic human right, women should be able to have a child safely and with good quality of care. The human rights "system" – laws, policies, and conventions – must be used to hold states accountable for obligations undertaken pursuant to treaties.'

Allan was a trailblazer when he first headed abroad, but the field has caught up with him. 'In my day, we didn't even know what global health care was,' he recalled. 'What I did was off the wall. But today a lot of kids want to get into it.' In medical schools today, global public health is a hot topic, and doctors like Paul Farmer of Harvard Medical School, who spends more time running hospitals in Haiti and Rwanda than in his office in Boston, are viewed by students as icons.

Allan's own life took a tragic course in 2005. He was diagnosed with ALS and also myasthenia gravis, two diseases that affect motor nerves. He had always been athletic and outdoorsy, but now he found himself increasingly frail. He lost weight, had trouble walking and breathing, and then was consigned to a wheelchair. He worried about being a burden to his family. Yet he went to work every day and even attended international conferences. At the International Women's Health Coalition banquet in January 2008, he could barely move but was a center of attention, lionized by admirers from all over the world. In October 2008, he died.

AMDD is now saving lives in fifty poor countries. We saw its impact when we stopped by a clinic in Zinder, in eastern Niger, the country with the highest lifetime risk of maternal mortality in the world. Niger has only ten ob-gyns in the entire country, and rural areas are lucky to have a physician of any kind in the vicinity. The Zinder clinic staff were startled and excited to see a couple of Americans, and they happily gave us a tour – even pointing out one heavily pregnant woman, Ramatou Issoufou, who was lying on a stretcher, gasping and suffering convulsions. Between gasps, she complained that she was losing her vision.

The sole doctor in the clinic was a Nigerian, Obende Kayode, placed there as part of a Nigerian foreign aid program (if Nigeria can send doctors abroad as foreign aid, so can America!). Dr. Kayode explained that Ramatou probably had eclampsia, a pregnancy complication that kills about fifty thousand women a year in the developing world. So she needed a cesarean section; once the baby was out, the convulsions would end as well.

Ramatou was a mother of six, thirty-seven years old, and her life was ebbing away in the little hospital waiting room. 'We're just calling for her husband,' Dr. Kayode explained. 'When he provides the drugs and surgical materials, we can do the operation.'

The Zinder clinic, it turned out, was part of a pilot program in Niger arranged by the United Nations Population Fund (UNFPA)* and AMDD to fight maternal mortality. As a result, all the materials needed for a C-section were kept in sealed plastic bags and available if the family paid $42. That was a great improvement over the previous approach of having the families run all over town, spending far more to buy bandages here, gauze there, scalpels somewhere else. But what if Ramatou's family didn't have $42?

In that case, she would probably die. 'If the family says they have no money, then you have a problem,' Dr. Kayode acknowledged. 'Sometimes you help, with the expectation that you will be paid back. At the beginning, I helped a lot, but then afterward people didn't pay me back.' He shrugged, and added: 'It depends on the mood. If the staff feel they can't pay out again, then you just wait and watch. And sometimes she dies.'

Still, the hospital staff didn't want Ramatou to die with us watching. The nurses wheeled her into the operating room and

---

* The UN is so wretched at public relations that it can't even match its abbreviations with its organizations. This agency originally was called the UN Fund for Population Activities, and it remained UNFPA even after it changed its name to the UN Population Fund.

scrubbed her belly, and a nurse administered a spinal anesthetic. Ramatou lay on the gurney, breathing heavily and irregularly, otherwise motionless apparently unconscious. Dr. Kayode came in, quickly sliced through Ramatou's abdomen, and held up a large organ that looked a bit like a basketball. That was her uterus. He carefully cut it open and pulled out a baby boy, whom he handed to a nurse. The baby was quiet, and it wasn't immediately clear if he was alive. Likewise, Ramatou was suspiciously comatose as Dr. Kayode stitched up her uterus, put it back in her abdomen, and then sewed up the outer cut on her stomach. But twenty minutes later, Ramatou was regaining consciousness, wand and exhausted but no longer suffering convulsions or labored breathing.

'I'm okay,' she managed to say, and then the nurse brought her baby son to her – now squawking, wriggling, and very much alive. Ramatou's face lit up, and she reached out with her hands to hold her baby. It truly seemed a miracle, and it showed what is possible if we make maternal health a priority. One doctor and a few nurses in a poorly equipped operating theater in the middle of the desert had brought a woman back to life and saved her baby as well. And so Allan Rosenfield's public health legacy included two more lives saved.

CHAPTER SEVEN

Why Do Women Die in Childbirth?

Would the world stand by if it were men who were dying
just for completing their reproductive functions?

— ASHA-ROSE MIGIRO,
UN DEPUTY SECRETARY GENERAL, 2007

The first step to saving mothers' lives is to understand the reasons for maternal mortality. The immediate cause of death may be eclampsia, hemorrhage, malaria, abortion complications, obstructed labor or sepsis. But behind the medical explanations are the sociological and biological ones. Consider the factors that converged to kill Prudence Lemokouno.

We found Prudence lying on a bed in the little hospital of Yokadouma, in the wild southeastern corner of Cameroon, in roughly the area where (genetic evidence suggests) AIDS first jumped to humans in the 1920s. A twenty-four-year-old mother of three children, Prudence was wearing an old, red-checked dress that bulged out hugely at the belly; a sheet covered her lower parts. She was in tremendous pain, and she periodically grabbed the side of the bed, though she never cried out.

Prudence had been living with her family in a village seventy-five miles away, and she had received no prenatal care. She went into labor at full term, assisted by a traditional birth attendant who had had no training. But Prudence's cervix was blocked, and the baby couldn't come out. After three days of labor, the birth attendant sat on Prudence's stomach and jumped up and down. That ruptured Prudence's uterus. The family paid a man with a motorcycle to take

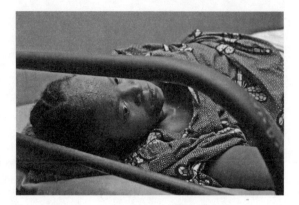

Prudence Lemokouno in her hospital bed in Cameroon,
untreated by the staff (Naka Nathaniel)

Prudence to the hospital. The hospital's doctor, Pascal Pipi, real-ized that she needed an emergency cesarean. But he wanted $100 for the surgery, and Prudence's husband and parents said that they could raise only $20. Dr. Pipi was sure that the family was lying and could pay more. Perhaps he was right, for one of Prudence's cousins had a cell phone. If she had been a man, the family proba-bly would have sold enough possessions to raise $100.

Dr. Pipi was short and solidly built, with spectacles, a serious and intelligent manner, superb French – and a resentful contempt for local peasants. He worked diligently, and he was very pleasant to us, but he excoriated the nearby villagers like Prudence who didn't take care of themselves and didn't seek medical attention early enough.

'Even the women who live in town, right next to the hospital, they have their babies at home,' he said. Overall, he estimated, only about 5 percent of local women deliver in the hospital. Supplies are almost nonexistent, he complained, and in the history of the hospital nobody had ever given a voluntary blood donation. Dr. Pipi came across as bitter – angry at the women, and also at himself for being stuck in a remote provincial backwater. He was utterly unsympathetic to their needs.

We had come upon the clinic by accident and dropped in to

inquire about maternal health in the area. Dr. Pipi gave an intelligent assessment of conditions in the region, and then we stumbled upon Prudence in an unused room in the hospital. She had been lying there untreated for three days, according to her family – only two days, Dr. Pipi indignantly told us later. The fetus had died shortly after she arrived at the hospital, and now it was decaying and slowly poisoning Prudence.

'If they had intervened right away, my baby would still be alive,' Alain Awona, Prudence's twenty-eight-year-old husband, said angrily as he hovered beside his wife. A teacher at a public school, he was educated enough to be indignant and assertive at the mistreatment of his wife. 'Save my wife!' he pleaded. 'My baby is dead. Save my wife!'

Dr. Pipi and his staff were furious at Alain's protests and embarrassed at having a woman die in front of visitors. They argued that the problem was a resource shortage compounded by uneducated villagers who refuse to pay for medical services.

'Most of the time in emergencies, the family doesn't pay,' scoffed Emilienne Mouassa, the senior nurse, who appeared to have veins full of antifreeze. 'They just run away.'

Dr. Pipi said that without intervention Prudence had only hours to live, and that he could operate on her if he had the remaining $80. So we agreed to pay it then and there. Then Dr. Pipi said that Prudence was probably anemic and would need a blood transfusion to get her through a C-section. A nurse consulted Prudence's records and reported back that her blood was type A, Rh positive.

Nick and Naka Nathaniel, the videographer, looked at each other. 'I'm A positive,' Nick whispered to Naka.

'And I'm O positive – a universal donor,' Naka whispered back. They turned to Dr. Pipi.

'What if we gave blood?' Nick asked. 'I'm A positive and he's O positive. Could you use that blood for the transfusion?'

Dr. Pipi shrugged agreement.

So Nick and Naka handed over some money to send a nurse to town to buy what supposedly were brand-new disposable needles. The lab technician then drew blood from each of them.

Prudence didn't seem fully aware of what was going on, but her mother had tears of joy streaming down her cheeks. The family had been sure that Prudence was going to die, and now it suddenly seemed that her life could be saved. Alain insisted that we stick around to see the surgery through. 'If you go,' he warned bluntly, 'Prudence will die.'

Emilienne and the other nurses had been arguing with the family again, shaking them down for more money, but we intervened and paid some more. Then the nurses hooked up the blood units on a drip, and blood from Nick and Naka began coursing into Prudence's bloodstream. She almost immediately perked up and, in a weak voice, she thanked us. The nurses said that everything was ready for Prudence's surgery, but the hours dragged by and nothing happened. At 10 p.m., we asked the duty nurse where Dr. Pipi was.

'Oh, the doctor? He went out the back door. He's gone home. He'll operate tomorrow. Probably.' It appeared that Dr. Pipi and the nurses had decided to teach Alain and Prudence's family a lesson for being uppity.

'But by tomorrow it will be too late!' Nick protested. 'Prudence will be dead. The doctor himself said that she might have only a few hours.'

The nurse shrugged. 'That is up to God, not us,' she said. 'If she dies, that would be God's will.' We came close to strangling her.

'Where does Dr. Pipi live?' Nick asked. 'We'll go to his house right now.' The nurse refused to say. Alain was watching, flabbergasted and dazed.

'Come on, you must know where the doctor lives. What if there's a crisis in the night?'

At that point, our Cameroonian interpreter tugged us aside. 'Look, I'm sure we could find out where Dr. Pipi lives if we ask around,' he said. 'But if we go to his house and try to drag him back here to do surgery, he'll be incredibly angry. Maybe he'll do the surgery, but you don't know what he'll do with the scalpel. It wouldn't be good for Prudence. The only hope is to wait for morning, and see if she's still alive.' So we gave up and headed back to our guesthouse.

'Thank you,' Alain said. 'You tried. You did your best. We thank you.' But he was crushed – partly because he knew the hospital staff was doing this to spite him. Prudence's mother was too angry to speak; her eyes glowed with tears of frustration.

The next morning, Dr. Pipi finally operated, but by then at least three days had elapsed since Prudence had arrived at the hospital, and her abdomen was severely infected. He had to remove twenty centimeters of her small intestine, and he had none of the powerful antibiotics that were necessary to fight the infection.

The hours passed. Prudence remained unconscious, and gradually everybody realized that it wasn't just the anesthesia; she was in a coma. Her stomach expanded steadily because of the infection, and the nurses paid her little heed. When the bag of urine from her catheter overflowed, no one changed it. She was vomiting lightly, and it was left to Prudence's mother to clean it up.

As the hours passed, the mood in the room became increasingly grim. Dr. Pipi's only comments were criticisms of Prudence's family, especially of Alain. Prudence's stomach ballooned grotesquely, and she was spitting up blood. She began fighting for her breath, in huge, terrifying rattles. Finally, the family members decided that they would take her home to the village to die. They hired a car to take them back to the village, and they drove back, somber and bitter. Three days after the surgery, Prudence died.

That's what happens, somewhere in the world, once every minute.

It wasn't only Prudence's ruptured uterus that was responsible for her death. There were four other major factors.

- *Biology.* One reason women die in childbirth has to do with anatomy, arising from two basic evolutionary trade-offs. The first is that once our ancient ancestors began to walk upright, too large a pelvis made upright walking and running inefficient and exhausting. A narrow pelvis permits fast running. That, however, makes childbirth exceedingly difficult. So the evolutionary adaptation is that women generally have medium-sized pelvises that permit moderately swift locomotion and allow them to survive childbirth – most of the time.

The other trade-off is head size. Beginning with our Cro-Magnon ancestors, human skull size expanded to accommodate more complex brains. Larger brains offer an evolutionary advantage once a child is born, but they increase the chance that a large-headed fetus will never emerge alive from the mother.

Humans are the only mammals that need assistance in birth, and some evolutionary psychologists and evolutionary biologists have argued that as a result perhaps the first 'profession' to emerge in prehistoric days was that of the midwife. The risk to the mother varies with anatomy, and human pelvises are categorized by shapes that reflect alternate evolutionary compromises: gynecoid, android, anthropoid, and platypelloid. There is some disagreement among specialists about how significant the pelvic distinctions are, and *The Journal of Reproductive Medicine* has suggested that they reflect childhood environmental factors as much as genetics.

In any case, the most common pelvis for women is gynecoid, which is most accommodating of the birth process (but is not found on great women runners) and is particularly common among Caucasian women. In contrast, the anthropoid pelvis is elongated, permits fast running, and is more likely to result in obstructed labor. Data on pelvis shapes is poor, but African women seem disproportionately likely to have anthropoid pelvises, and some experts on maternal health offer that as one reason maternal mortality rates are so high in Africa.

- *Lack of Schooling.* If villagers were better educated, Prudence would have had a better chance, for several reasons. Education is associated with lower desired family size, greater use of contraception, and increased use of hospitals. So with more education, Prudence would have been less likely to have become pregnant and, if she had become pregnant, would have been more likely to deliver in the hospital. And if the birth attendant had been better schooled, she would have referred a case of obstructed labor to the hospital – and she certainly would not have sat on Prudence's stomach.

Education and family planning also tend to leave families better able to earn a living and more likely to accumulate savings. The result is that they are better able to afford health care, and educated families are also more likely to choose to allocate savings to the mother's health. Prudence's family, if educated, would therefore have been better able to afford the $100 for her surgery, and more likely to consider it a wise expense. The World Bank has estimated that for every one thousand girls who get one additional year of education, two fewer women will die in childbirth. As we'll see, such studies sometimes overstate the power of education, but even if the magnitude is exaggerated, an effect is clear.

- *Lack of Rural Health Systems.* If Cameroon had had a better health care structure, the hospital would have operated on Prudence as soon as she arrived. It would have had powerful antibiotics available to treat her infection. It would have had trained rural birth attendants in the area, equipped with cell phones to summon an ambulance. Any one of these factors might have saved Prudence.

One of the impediments to constructing a health system is the shortage of doctors in rural Africa. Dr. Pipi was unsympathetic, but it's also true that he was a hard worker who was hugely overburdened – and Cameroon just didn't have enough physicians to post a second one at the hospital in Yokadouma. Doctors and nurses in rural Africa get ground down by the relentless hours, lack of supplies, and difficult conditions (including the dangers to their own health), so they try to move to the capital. Very often, they also emigrate to Europe or America, amounting to a kind of foreign aid from Africa to the West and leaving women like Prudence without anyone to operate on them.

One problem with our proposal for donor countries to invest heavily in maternal care in Africa is that those countries lack the doctors – at least those willing to serve in rural areas. It's far easier to build an operating theater in a rural area than to staff it. One sensible response is to start training programs in Africa that produce many more health care professionals, but in two- or three-year programs that don't grant MDs that allow the graduates to find jobs abroad. Africa would be better off grad- uating fewer doctors if the trade-off were that more health professionals would be forced to remain in their home coun- tries. The purpose of medical training isn't to fuel emigration but to address health needs at home.

Another common problem is that doctors and nurses often don't show up for work, particularly in rural clinics. In one careful study across six countries in Africa, Asia, and Latin America, on any one day 39 percent of doctors were absent from clinics when they were supposed to be on duty. Western donor governments and UN agencies should try supporting not just the building of clinics, but also a system of auditors to con- duct random inspections. The pay of medical staff who are unaccountably absent would then be docked, and that just might prove a cheap way to make existing clinics more efficient and effective.

- *Disregard for Women.* In much of the world, women die because they aren't thought to matter. There's a strong correlation between countries where women are marginalized and coun- tries with high maternal mortality. Indeed, in the United States, maternal mortality remained very high throughout the nine- teenth century and beginning of the twentieth century, even as incomes rose and access to doctors increased. During World War I, more American women died in childbirth than American men died in war. But from the 1920s to the 1940s in the United States, maternal mortality rates plunged – apparently because the same society that was giving women the right to vote also found the political will to direct resources to maternal health. When women could vote, suddenly their lives became more important, and enfranchising women ended up providing a huge and unanticipated boost to women's health.

Unfortunately, maternal health is persistently diminished as a 'women's issue.' Such concerns never gain a place on the mainstream international agenda, and never gain sufficient resources. 'Maternal deaths in developing countries are often the ultimate tragic outcome of the cumulative denial of women's human rights,' noted the journal *Clinical Obstetrics and Gynecology*. 'Women are not dying because of untreatable diseases. They are dying because societies have yet to make the decision that their lives are worth saving.'

It might also help if women didn't menstruate and childbirth involved storks. As *The Lancet* noted:

The neglect of women's issues . . . does reflect some level of unconscious bias against women at every level, from the community to high-level decisionmakers . . . While we may ignore it, maternal health does involve sex and sexuality; it is bloody and messy; and I think many men (not all, of course) have a visceral antipathy for dealing with it.

In most societies, mythological or theological explanations were devised to explain why women *should* suffer in childbirth, and they forestalled efforts to make the process safer. When anesthesia was developed, it was for many decades routinely withheld from women giving birth, since women were 'supposed' to suffer. One of the few societies to take a contrary view was the Huichol tribe in Mexico. The Huichol believed that the pain of childbirth should be shared, so the mother would hold on to a string tied to her husband's testicles. With each painful contraction, she would give the string a yank so that the man could share the burden. Surely if such a mechanism were more widespread, injuries in childbirth would garner more attention.

Poverty is obviously also a factor, but high rates of maternal mortality are not inevitable in poor countries. Exhibit A is Sri Lanka. Since 1935 it has managed to halve its maternal deaths every six to twelve years. Over the last half century, Sri Lanka has brought its maternal mortality ratio down from 550 maternal deaths for every 100,000 live births to just 58. A Sri Lankan woman now has just one chance in 850 of dying in pregnancy during her lifetime.

That is a stunning achievement, particularly since Sri Lanka has been torn apart by intermittent war in recent decades and ranks 117th in the world in per capita income. And it's not just a matter of throwing money at the problem, for Sri Lanka spends 3 percent of GNP on health care, compared to 5 percent in India next door – where a woman is eight times more likely to die in childbirth. Rather, it's about political will: Saving mothers has been a priority in Sri Lanka, and it hasn't been in India.

More broadly, Sri Lanka invests in health and education generally, and pays particular attention to gender equality. Some 89 percent of Sri Lankan women are literate, compared to just 43 percent across South Asia. Life expectancy in Sri Lanka is much higher than in surrounding countries. And an excellent civil registration system has recorded maternal deaths since 1900, so that Sri Lanka actually has data, in contrast to vague estimates in many other countries. Investments in educating girls resulted in women having more economic value and more influence in society, and that seems to be one reason that greater energy was devoted to reducing maternal mortality.

Beginning in the 1930s, Sri Lanka set up a nationwide public health infrastructure, ranging from rudimentary health posts at the bottom to rural hospitals one tier up, and then district hospitals with more sophisticated services, and finally provincial hospitals and specialist maternity centers. To make sure that women could get to the hospitals, Sri Lanka provided ambulances.

Sri Lanka also established a major network of trained midwives, spread across the country and each serving a population of three thousand to five thousand. The midwives, who have undergone eighteen months of training, provide prenatal care and refer risky cases to doctors. Today, 97 percent of births are attended by a skilled practitioner, and it is routine even for village women to give birth in a hospital. Over time, the government added obstetricians to its hospitals, and it used its data to see where women were slipping through the cracks – such as those living on the tea estates – and then to open clinics targeting those women. A campaign against malaria also reduced maternal deaths, since pregnant women are especially vulnerable to that disease.

Sri Lanka shows what it takes to reduce maternal mortality. Family planning and delayed marriage help, and so do mosquito nets. A functioning health care system in rural areas is also essential.

'Looking at maternal mortality is a great way to look at a health system as a whole, because it requires you to do a great many things,' says Dr. Paul Farmer, the Harvard public health specialist. 'You need family planning, you need a district hospital for C-sections, and so on.'

There are other possible innovations as well. One study found that giving Vitamin A supplements to pregnant women in Nepal reduced maternal mortality by 40 percent, apparently because that reduced infections in malnourished women. Anecdotal evidence in Bangladesh and other countries suggests that loosening controls over antibiotics and encouraging women to take them postpartum will reduce death from sepsis.

One of the most interesting experiments is under way in India, where a pilot program in some areas is paying $15 to poor women to deliver in health centers. In addition, rural health workers get a $5 bounty for each woman brought in for delivery. Vouchers are also provided so that pregnant women can get transportation to the clinic. The initial results have been very impressive. The proportion of women delivering in health centers rose from 15 percent to 60 percent, and mortality plunged. In addition, after the delivery the women were more likely to return to the health center for birth control and other services.

'We have what it takes,' said Allan Rosenfield. 'Those countries that have paid attention to the problem have made a real difference in maternal mortality.' The World Bank summed up the experience in a 2003 report: 'Maternal mortality can be halved in developing countries every 7–10 years . . . regardless of income level and growth rate.'

Because progress on maternal health is possible, people have often assumed it is virtually guaranteed. In 1987, partly as a result of Allan's landmark article in *The Lancet*, a UN conference convened in Nairobi to launch the Safe Motherhood Initiative; the goal was to 'reduce maternal mortality by 50 percent by the year 2000.' Then, in 2000, the UN formally adopted the Millennium Development Goal of reducing maternal mortality by 75 percent by 2015. The first target wasn't achieved, and the millennium goal will be missed by a wide margin.

In retrospect, advocates of maternal health made a few strategic errors. The dominant camp – which was backed by the World Health Organization and initially prevailed – insisted that the solution lay in improving primary care. The idea was to create programs like China's old 'barefoot doctors' or Sri Lanka's network of midwives, because this would be much more cost-effective than training doctors (who in any case would probably serve only city-dwellers). After a WHO conference in 1978 emphasized funding for rural birth attendants, some countries even dismantled obstetric programs at hospitals.

Those training programs for birth attendants probably helped save newborn babies – by teaching midwives to use sterile razor blades to cut the cord – but they didn't much help maternal survival. In Sri Lanka, training midwives worked because they were part of a complete health care package and could refer patients to hospitals, but in most of the world training birth attendants was only a cheap substitute for a comprehensive program.

A minority camp, led in part by Allan Rosenfield, had argued that the crucial step for saving pregnant women was to provide emergency obstetric services. Training birth attendants is useful, Allan argued, but cannot save all pregnant women. Worldwide, about 10 percent of women giving birth need C-sections, and the percentage is higher in the poorest countries where pregnant women are more likely to be malnourished or very young. Probably too many women get C-sections in the West, but too few do in Africa. Without C-sections, there is simply no way to save the lives of many women, and ordinary birth attendants

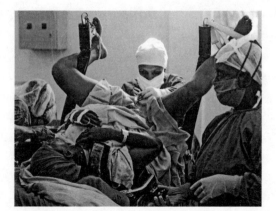

Mamitu Gashe, herself an obstetric fistula patient who never attended even elementary school, now regularly performs surgery – a reminder that nonphysicians can perform some jobs we think of as the domain only of doctors. Here Mamitu repairs a fistula at the Addis Ababa Fistula Hospital. (Nicholas D. Kristof)

cannot provide that service. It may not take an ob-gyn to perform a C-section, but it does take more than a birth attendant with a razor blade.

Further evidence of the centrality of emergency obstetrics came from a study of a fundamentalist Christian church in Indiana whose members were affluent, well-educated, and well-nourished Americans, yet who for spiritual reasons eschewed doctors and hospitals. The group's maternal mortality ratio was 872 per 100,000 live births. That's seventy times the rate in the United States as a whole, and it's almost twice as high as in India today. It's difficult to avoid the conclusion that the critical factor for saving mothers is access to doctors in an emergency. As the *International Journal of Gynecology & Obstetrics* put it in an editorial, emergency obstetric care is the 'keystone in the arch of safe motherhood.'

The practical challenge is how to provide emergency obstetric services. Such services are neither simple nor cheap. They require an operating theater, anesthesia, and a surgeon. And the reality is that rural parts of Africa often have none of these. In puzzling over that challenge, Allan Rosenfield kept thinking back to his experience as a young doctor in Thailand, when he trained midwives to offer services that normally were the preserve only of physicians. Especially considering how MDs often emigrate, why couldn't nonphysicians be trained to perform emergency C-sections?

The Addis Ababa Fistula Hospital often makes use of medical staff without formal degrees. As is common in poor countries, those administering anesthesia at the Fistula Hospital are nurses, not doctors. Indeed, one of them started out as a porter. Most striking, one of the top surgeons is Mamitu Gashe, who never went to elementary school, let alone medical school. Mamitu grew up illiterate in a remote village in Ethiopia and suffered a fistula as a young wife in her first pregnancy. She made her way to the Addis Ababa Fistula Hospital for surgery, and afterward began helping out by making beds and assisting Reg Hamlin during surgeries. She would stand beside him and hand him the scalpel, and she watched closely. After a couple of years, he let her do simple work, like suturing, and over time he entrusted her with more and more of the surgery.

Mamitu had nimble fingers and first-rate technical skills, and even if her biological knowledge was limited, she steadily accumulated experience repairing internal injuries. Eventually, Mamitu was doing fistula surgery by herself. The fistula hospital does more fistula repairs than any institution in the world, and Mamitu was at the center of the whirlwind. She also began to take charge of the training program, so when elite doctors went to Addis Ababa for a few months to learn fistula surgery, their teacher was often an illiterate woman who had never been to a day of school. Eventually Mamitu tired of being a master surgeon who couldn't read, so she went to night school. Last time we visited her, she had reached the third grade.

'You can train midwives or senior nurses to do C-sections, and they will save lives,' notes Ruth Kennedy. Indeed, there have been some experiments in Mozambique, Tanzania, and Malawi with training non-physicians to perform C-sections; this approach would be a major lifesaver. But doctors are reluctant to give up their exclusive control over these surgeries, and so there has been no broader rollout.

Another impediment is that maternal health just doesn't have an international constituency. In the 2008 U.S. presidential election, candidates tried to prove their foreign aid bona fides by calling for increased spending to fight AIDS and malaria. But maternal health wasn't on the political horizon, and the United States and most other countries contributed negligible sums to address it. Norway and Britain are rare exceptions, having announced a major foreign aid program in 2007 to target maternal mortality. The United States could do a world of good – and bolster its international image – if it joined the British and Norwegians in that effort.

In pushing for a global campaign to reduce maternal deaths, it's crucial to avoid exaggerated claims. In particular, advocates should be wary of repeating assertions that investing in maternal health is highly cost-effective. A senior World Bank official told a maternal health conference in London in 2007, with typical enthusiasm: 'Investing in better health for women and their children is just smart economics.' Now, that's certainly true of educating girls, but the sad reality is that investments in maternal health are unlikely to be as cost-effective as other kinds of health work. Saving women's lives is imperative, but it is not cheap.

One study suggested that the millennium development goal of curbing deaths by 75 percent could be achieved by spending escalating sums ranging from an additional $1 billion in 2006 up to an additional $6 billion in 2015. Another study suggested that it would cost an additional $9 billion a year to provide all effective interventions for maternal and newborn health to 95 percent of the world's population. (In contrast, total international development assistance from all countries for maternal and neonatal health was a paltry $530 million in 2004.)

Suppose that the estimate of $9 billion per year is correct. It pales beside the $40 billion that the world spends annually on pet food, but it's still a great deal of money. If that $9 billion managed to save three quarters of the mothers who are now dying, that would mean that 402,000 women would be saved annually, in addition to many newborns (and many maternal injuries would be averted as well). The cost of each woman's life saved would be more than $22,000. Even if we're wrong by a factor of five, it would still cost more than $4,000 for each life saved. In contrast, a $1 vaccine can save a child's life. As one leader in the development field said: 'Vaccines are cost-effective. Maternal health isn't.'

So let's not overstate the case. Maternal mortality is an injustice that is tolerated only because its victims are poor, rural women. The best argument to stop it, however, isn't economic but ethical. What was horrifying about Prudence's death was not that the hospital allocated its resources poorly, but that it neglected a human being in its care. As Allan Rosenfield has been arguing, this is first and foremost a human rights issue. And it's time for human rights organizations to seize upon it.

An example of the measures we've been talking about – including emergency obstetrics to save lives in difficult environments – can be found in a wondrous hospital in a remote country that doesn't even exist . . .

Edna's Hospital

Edna Adan first scandalized her country by learning to read, and she's been shocking her neighbors ever since. Now she is startling those few Westerners who venture to the Horn of Africa and find, gleaming in the chaos, a beautiful maternity hospital.

Westerners have become so cynical about corruption and incompetence in the third world that they sometimes believe it's not even worth trying to support good causes in Africa. Edna and her maternity hospital bear witness to the fact that such cynics are wrong. She and a handful of donors in the United States together have built a monument that neither could have accomplished alone.

Hargeisa, where Edna grew up, is a town in the harsh desert of what was then the British protectorate of Somaliland, later Somalia, and now the breakaway republic of Somaliland. The people there are poor, and the society deeply traditional. The innumerable local camels often had more freedom than the women.

'I was of a generation that had no schools for girls,' Edna recalled as she sat in her modern living room in Hargeisa. 'It was considered undesirable to teach a girl to read and write. There were no schools for girls, because if girls are educated then they grow up to talk about genitals.' A mischievous glint in her eye revealed that she was joking – a little bit.

Edna grew up in an exceptional family. Her father, Adan, was a doctor who became the father of medical care in the country. Adan met Edna's mother, the daughter of the postmaster-general, at the tennis court of the British governor of Somaliland. Even in such an elite family, Edna's newborn brother died when the midwife dropped him on his head. And when Edna was about eight years old, her mother inducted her into Somali tradition: Edna's genitals were cut in the process called female circumcision. The intention is to reduce girls' sexual desire, curb promiscuity, and ensure that daughters will be marriageable.

'I was not consulted,' Edna says. 'I was caught, held down, and it was done. My mother thought it was the right thing to do. My father was out of town. When he came back and heard, that was the only time I ever saw him with tears in his eyes. And that encouraged me, because if he thought it was wrong, then that meant a lot.'

The cutting of Edna, who was very close to her father, led to a fierce argument between her parents and a souring of their marriage. And it is one reason Edna herself has become a passionate opponent of genital cutting. But at home, Edna's enlightened upbringing continued. A tutor came to her home to teach the boys of the family, and her parents allowed her to hover in the background and absorb the lessons. Edna soon proved her aptitude, and so her parents sent her to attend a primary school for girls in the nearby French colony of Djibouti. There was no high school for girls, so she returned to Hargeisa to work as an interpreter for a British doctor. 'It improved my English, got me into health, and whetted my appetite even more for health work,' says Edna.

In 1953, an elementary school for girls opened in another town, and at the age of fifteen Edna went off to work as a student teacher there. In the mornings she taught the girls, and in the afternoon she was taught privately by the same teacher who taught high school boys (since it would have been improper for Edna to sit with the boys). Every year there were a few scholarships for Somalis to go to Britain to study, and it was assumed that these would be for boys. But Edna was allowed to sit for the exams – in a separate room from the boys – and soon became the first Somali girl to study in Britain. She spent seven years there, studying nursing, midwifery, and hospital management.

Edna became her country's first qualified nurse-midwife, the first Somali woman to drive, and then Somalia's first lady, period. She married Somaliland's prime minister, Ibrahim Egal, who became Somalia's prime minister in 1967 after the former British and Italian Somali territories merged. She and her husband visited President Lyndon Johnson at the White House. In a photo she showed us, Edna is gorgeous as well as vivacious, and LBJ beams as he towers over her (she's five foot two).

Edna later divorced and was recruited by the World Health Organization. She lived the good life of a UN official and was posted around the world. But she dreamed of starting a hospital in her homeland – *the hospital my dad would have wanted to work in* – and in the early 1980s she began building her own private hospital in Somalia's capital, Mogadishu. When war broke out, the project had to be abandoned.

In the UN, Edna rose to be the top WHO official in Djibouti, with a lovely office and a Mercedes-Benz. But she didn't want her legacy to be a Mercedes; she wanted it to be a hospital. The dream nagged at her, and she felt unfulfilled. She knew that Somaliland has one of the highest maternal mortality rates in the world, though precise figures do not exist because no one keeps track of deaths. So when Edna retired from the World Health Organization in 1997, she announced to the Somaliland government – which by then had won a civil war and had broken off from Somalia – that she was going to sell her Mercedes and take the proceeds, as well as her savings and pension, to build a hospital.

You tried that, said Somaliland's president, who happened to be her ex-husband.

I have to do this, she replied. *I have to do this now more than ever, because what few health facilities we had were destroyed during the civil war.*

We'll give you land for the hospital on the edge of town, he said.

No, Edna said firmly. *That's not good for women who have babies at two a.m.*

There was only one available tract inside the town of Hargeisa. It had been a military parade ground for the previous government, notorious as the spot where people were imprisoned, flogged, and executed. After the civil war ended, the site had been abandoned, and Somalilanders used it as a dump. Edna initially recoiled when she visited it but also saw an advantage: It was in the poor part of town, near the people who needed her most. So Edna planned her own maternity hospital, funding it with $300,000 – her entire life savings.

It was an audacious dream, perhaps a foolish one. An official at the small UN outpost in Hargeisa said that Edna's vision was noble but too ambitious for Somaliland, and he had a point. African countries are littered with incomplete and abandoned projects, so skepticism was in order for a project driven less by balance sheets than by dreams. Another challenge in planning the hospital was that potential supporters like the UN and private aid groups are not very active in a breakaway country like Somaliland that no one recognizes and thus officially doesn't exist.

When the hospital was mostly built but still lacked a roof, Edna's money ran out. The UN and other donors were sympathetic but refused to provide the rest of the money needed. That's when Ian Fisher wrote an article in *The New York Times* about Edna and her dream. Anne Gilhuly, a recently retired English teacher at Greenwich High School in a wealthy suburb in Connecticut, with no particular interest in Africa or maternal health, read that article. She was teaching classics to adults in continuing education classes and pursuing her interest in Shakespeare and theater. But the article moved her, and so did the accompanying photo of Edna beside her incomplete hospital. A friend of Anne's in Greenwich, Tara Holbrook, had also read the article, and they spoke about it on the phone.

'We were so disgusted with the plastic toys our grandchildren wanted for Christmas that we leaped at the chance to do something better for the children of the world: help some of their mothers survive,' Anne recalls. She quickly adds, self-mockingly, 'Sounds corny, I know.'

So Anne and Tara contacted Edna. They asked various experts if Edna's goal was sensible, if it was achievable. Former American ambassador Robert Oakley and others said it just might be, and so Anne plowed ahead. Soon she and Tara found out about a group of people in Minnesota who had also read Ian's article and wanted to help. The Minnesota group included a few Somalilanders, led by a computer executive named Mohamed Samatar and a dynamo travel agent named Sandy Peterson. Sandy's daughter had been

Edna in front of her hospital in Somaliland (Nicholas D. Kristof)

raped at age six by a neighbor and had subsequently undergone the gamut of psychiatric counselisng, mental hospitals, and suicide attempts. Sandy realized that many African girls underwent equally traumatic experiences yet received no help whatsoever. The Minnesotans had created a support organization, Friends of Edna's Hospital, and applied for tax-exempt status. The two groups joined forces. When the tax-exempt status was granted the following June, Anne launched her appeals.

'Tara and I sent out our first fund-raising letter – mostly to women of our generation we thought would be proud of Edna for her achievements in a patriarchal society,' Anne recalled. 'And they did respond.'

With help from Anne and her friends, Edna completed her hospital, after upsetting all the protocols of the construction industry in Somaliland. First, she barred workers from chewing khat, a leaf that has amphetamine-like qualities and is enjoyed by men throughout the region. The workers didn't believe she could be serious – until she fired some of them for disobeying orders. Then Edna insisted that the masons teach women how to make bricks. They resisted at first, but she was paying the bills, so Somaliland soon had its first female brickmakers. Local merchants in Hargeisa also supported the hospital, allowing Edna to use construction equipment free of charge and even donating 860 bags of cement.

The result is a white three-story hospital with an English sign that reads EDNA ADAN MATERNITY HOSPITAL in front of it. There is no hint of the squalid dump it replaced. Anybody accustomed to dilapidated African hospitals would be astonished, for it gleams in the afternoon sun and has the hygiene and efficiency of a Western hospital. It has sixty beds and seventy-six staff members, and Edna lives in an apartment inside the hospital so that she can always be on call. She accepts no salary and uses her WHO pension to make up the shortfall in the hospital's operating expenses.

'Things like this are very precious to us,' she said, holding a surgical mask, unobtainable commercially anywhere in Somaliland. The hospital imports all medical supplies and survives thanks to gifts and hand-me-downs. The generator is from the Danish Refugee Council. The ultrasound machine is from a German doctor who had once visited; he sent his old one. The blood refrigerator is from a Somali who owed Edna a favor. The United Nations Refugee Agency donated an ambulance. The Netherlands donated two incubators. USAID, the American aid agency, built an outpatient center. Britain equipped the operating theater. UNICEF gives vaccines. WHO provides reagents for blood transfusions.

Friends of Edna's Hospital initially gathered equipment and medical supplies in the United States and shipped them to Somaliland. Gradually the emphasis shifted to fund-raising only, to pay for equipment and supplies that Edna buys closer to the hospital. The group is also financing two of Edna's former nursing students in medical school so that she will have two of 'her own' practicing full-time as physicians at the hospital. And the Friends are simultaneously trying to build an endowment so that the hospital can survive Edna's passing.

Somehow, improbably, it all comes together. At three o'clock one morning, a man arrived, pushing his wife in a wheelbarrow. She was in labor. The team leaped into action and rushed the woman into the delivery room. Another time, a nomadic woman gave birth in the desert and developed a fistula. Her husband couldn't stand her smell and constant wetness, and stabbed her in the throat; the knife went through her tongue and stopped at her palate. The other

Edna delivering a breech birth in her hospital (Nicholas D. Kristof)

nomads stitched her throat together with needle and thread and carried her to Edna's hospital. A visiting fistula surgeon patched the woman together again, from her throat to her bladder.

As Edna roams the hospital, she's like the weather in October: alternately stormy and sunny. One of her hospital's major roles is training a constant stream of midwives, nurses, and anesthetists, and she is constantly grilling the trainees in English, because she wants them all to speak English fluently. In the hallway, she pauses to upbraid one nursing student about an error, ensuring that she'll never make that mistake again. A moment later, Edna is all empathy as she talks to a fistula patient who sobs as she describes how her husband forced her to leave their home.

'I'm a woman, too!' Edna tells the girl, holding her hand. 'I feel like crying myself.'

Once a man drove through the hospital's front gate with his wife in labor in the backseat. The baby emerged just as they arrived, and so the man tried to drive right out again.

'No! No!' Edna shouted at him. 'You'll kill your wife. The placenta still has to come out.'

'I won't pay you,' the man shouted back. 'I'm leaving.'

'Close the gate!' Edna shouted to the guard, blocking the car from leaving. Then Edna turned to the husband.

'Forget about the payment,' she said, and she pulled out the placenta right there in the backseat before opening the gate and allowing him to go.

Somali superstition holds that burning a baby on the chest will prevent tuberculosis, so Edna constantly has to guard against mothers sneaking their newborn babies out of the hospital to burn them. At least once, a mother burned her new baby in the hospital kitchen.

The American backers of the hospital have been venturing out to Somaliland to see what they have wrought. Sandy Peterson, the travel agent, was the first to travel to Hargeisa. Then others went as well, including Anne Gilhuly and her husband, Bob, who visited when Edna was doing double duty as Somaliland's foreign minister a few years ago. Anne e-mailed us:

> Swimming with her, with all our clothes on naturally (except for Bob, who could wear a bathing suit because he was a man), in the Gulf of Aden at Berbera, in that warm turquoise water with the pink mountains in the distance and her bodyguard marching up and down the otherwise absolutely deserted beach with his machine gun, is a lot more interesting than playing bridge at the local Y.

Anne also saw the tougher side of Edna. Once a senior nurse waited too long before calling in the doctor to perform a cesarean. Believing that the nurse had endangered a woman's life, Edna erupted in full fury and gave the nurse such a ferocious tongue-lashing that Anne and Bob were shaken. Afterward, they decided that Edna was right: If she was going to save patients and change attitudes, she had to be ferocious.

'Edna was determined that that would not happen again, that they had not been sufficiently sensitive to the woman's condition,' Anne recalled. 'In her hospital there must be total attention paid to each individual. I definitely felt chastened. The incident brought home the extent of the task Edna has set for herself and how hard it is for us to comprehend fully what she is up against.'

CHAPTER EIGHT

Family Planning and the 'God Gulf'

Whenever cannibals are on the brink of starvation, Heaven
in its infinite mercy, sends them a nice plump missionary.

– OSCAR WILDE

Rose Wanjera, a twenty-six-year-old woman in Kenya, showed
up at a maternity clinic one afternoon. She had a small child
in tow, and her stomach bulged with another on the way. Rose was
sick and penniless and had received no prenatal care. She was an
unusual visitor to a slum clinic because she had attended college
and spoke English. She sat in a corner of the squalid, dimly lit
clinic, patiently waiting for the doctor, and told us how wild dogs
had mauled her husband to death a few weeks earlier.

A nurse eventually called her, and she lay on a cot. The doctor
examined her, listened to her abdomen, and then announced that
she had an infection that threatened her life and that of her unborn
baby. He enrolled her in a safe motherhood program, so that she
would get prenatal care and help with the delivery.

The clinic that Rose visited represents an unusual outpost of a
consortium formed by aid organizations to provide reproductive
health care for refugee women, who tend to be among the most
forlorn and needy people on Earth. The consortium includes
CARE, the International Rescue Committee, and AMDD, Allan
Rosenfield's organization at Columbia University. This particular
clinic was run by another member of the consortium, Marie
Stopes International – but then George W. Bush cut off funds to
Marie Stopes and the entire consortium, all around the world,

because Marie Stopes was helping to provide abortions in China. One might have understood cutting funds to the China program, but slashing funds for the consortium in Africa was abhorrent.

The funding cut forced Marie Stopes to drop a planned outreach program to help Somali and Rwandan refugees. It had to close two clinics in Kenya and to lay off eighty doctors and nurses – precisely the staff who were looking after Rose. She became one of untold victims of American abortion politics that effectively eliminated her only source of health care. 'These were clinics focusing on the poorest, the marginalized, in the slums,' said Cyprian Awiti, the head of Marie Stopes in Kenya.

This incident reflects the 'God Gulf' in American foreign policy. Religion plays a particularly profound role in shaping policies on population and family planning, and secular liberals and conservative Christians regularly square off. Each side has the best of intentions, yet each is deeply suspicious of the other – and these suspicions make it difficult to forge a broad left-right coalition that would be far more effective in confronting trafficking and overcoming the worst kinds of poverty. The great battleground in these conflicts has been whether to fund organizations like Marie Stopes that have some links to abortions.

Driven in part by conservative Christians, Republican presidents, including both Bushes, instituted the 'gag rule,' barring funds to any foreign aid group that, even with other money, counseled women about abortion options or had any link to abortions. As a result, said a Ghanaian doctor, Eunice Brookman-Amissah, 'contrary to its stated intentions, the global gag rule results in more unwanted pregnancies, more unsafe abortions, and more deaths of women and girls.'

One of the prime conservative targets has been the UNFPA, which works to promote family planning, maternal health, and newborn survival. United Nations agencies tend to be inefficient and bureaucratic, far less nimble and cost-effective than private aid groups, and probably do more for the photocopier industry than for the world's neediest – *but they're still irreplaceable.* Just recall the operating theater in Zinder, Niger, where the doctor saved

Ramatou and her baby; that hospital was equipped by UNFPA. Conversely, Prudence may have died in part because a UNFPA maternal health program in Cameroon didn't have the resources to reach her hospital.

When UNFPA was created in 1969, the Nixon administration was a strong supporter, and the United States government the biggest donor. But in the 1980s American antiabortion activists began to target UNFPA. Although the organization does not perform abortions or fund them, critics noted that it advises China on population issues and that China has a coercive family planning program. UNFPA did make the disgraceful mistake in 1983 of awarding its Population Award gold medal to Qian Xinzhong, the head of the Chinese family planning program, who was then presiding over a brutal family planning crackdown involving forced abortions. The Chinese Communist Party leaders themselves were sufficiently embarrassed by Qian's zealotry that they fired him a year later.

The United States government had no mechanism to punish China for forced abortions, so instead it pummeled UNFPA. In 1985, President Ronald Reagan reduced funding for it. Then George H. W. Bush and George W. Bush both eliminated U.S. funding for the agency. Representative Chris Smith, a New Jersey Republican, led the fight against UNFPA. He's a good man who genuinely cared about Chinese women and was horrified by coerced abortions. He wasn't trying to score cheap political points in criticizing UNFPA, since most New Jersey voters had never heard of the agency. This was an issue that Smith genuinely cared about.

The reality, though, was that while the Chinese abuses were real, UNFPA was not a party to them. After giving the gold medal to Qian, the UN turned around and became an important brake on Chinese behavior. A State Department fact-finding mission sent to investigate by the George W. Bush administration reported back: 'We find no evidence that UNFPA has knowingly supported or participated in the management of a program of coercive abortion or involuntary sterilization in the People's Republic of China.'

In the thirty-two counties in China where UNFPA operates pilot programs, it has reduced abortion rates by 40 percent, to a rate lower than that in the United States.

Indeed, UNFPA achieved a major breakthrough for Chinese women that it has never received credit for. In the past, women in China had always used a steel-ring IUD that cost only four cents to make but often failed or caused severe discomfort. That steel ring led to millions of unintended pregnancies and then to abortions. Under UNFPA pressure, China grudgingly switched to a kind of IUD called the copper-T. This kind was more expensive to manufacture – twenty-two cents each – but far more comfortable and effective. That was a huge advance for the 60 million Chinese women with IUDs, and it averted about 500,000 abortions every year. In short, since then, UNFPA has prevented nearly 10 million abortions in China. That's a record far better than that of any pro-life organization.

That has been the pattern again and again: With the best of intentions, pro-life conservatives have taken some positions in reproductive health that actually hurt those whom they are trying to help – and that result in more abortions. Pro-choice and pro-life camps, despite their differences, should be able to find common ground and work together on many points, in particular on an agenda to reduce the number of abortions. Visit clinics in Estonia, where abortions were widely used as a form of birth control, where some women had ten or more abortions, and you see the resulting high levels of infertility and other complications. And in poor countries, abortions are sometimes as lethal to the mother as to the fetus. For every 150 unsafe abortions in sub-Saharan Africa, a woman dies; in the United States, the risk is less than 1 in 100,000. So liberals and conservatives should be able to agree on steps that prevent unwanted pregnancies and thus reduce the frequency of abortion.

Yet that doesn't happen. One of the scandals of the early twenty-first century is that 122 million women around the world want contraception and can't get it. Whatever one thinks of abortion, it's tragic that up to 40 percent of all pregnancies globally are unplanned or unwanted – and that almost half of those result in induced abortions. By some measures, more than one quarter of all maternal deaths could be avoided if there were no unplanned and unwanted pregnancies. It's an added disgrace that over the last dozen years there has been negligible progress in providing family planning, particularly in Africa. Only 14 percent of Ethiopian women use modern forms of contraception today.

'We've lost a decade,' Professor John Cleland, a British fertility expert, told a parliamentary study group in 2006. 'Contraceptive use in Africa has hardly increased in the last ten years in married women. It is a disaster.'

Curbing population growth isn't nearly as simple as Westerners assume. In the 1950s, one pioneering family planning project in Khanna, India, sponsored by the Rockefeller Foundation and Harvard University, gave intensive help with contraception to eight thousand villagers. After five years, the birth rate among those people was higher than that of a control group given no contraception. Far more commonly, contraception programs have a modest effect in reducing fertility, but still less than supporters expect.

One carefully conducted experiment in Matlab, Bangladesh, found that after three years family planning programs reduced the average number of births to 5.1 in the target area, compared to 6.7 in the control area. That's not a revolution, but it reflects a meaningful impact. Peter Donaldson of the Population Council asserts that family planning programs accounted for at least 23 percent of the fertility decline in poor countries between 1960 and 1990.

The key to curbing population is often less a technical matter of providing contraceptives and more a sociological challenge of encouraging smaller families. One way to do that is to reduce child mortality, so that parents can be sure that if they have fewer children, they will survive. Perhaps the most effective way to encourage smaller families is to promote education, particularly for girls. For example, England slowed its fertility rate seriously in the 1870s, probably because of the Education Act of 1870, which called for compulsory education. That reflects a very strong global correlation between rising education levels and declines in family size. It appears that the most effective contraceptive is education for girls, although birth control supplies are obviously needed as well.

There's some evidence that decisions about childbearing reflect deep-seated tensions between men and women about strategies to pass on their genes. Polling tends to confirm what evolutionary biologists have sometimes suggested, that at a genetic level men often act like Johnny Appleseed, betting that the best way to achieve a future crop is to plant as many seeds as possible, without doing much to nurture them afterward. Given biological differences, women prefer to have fewer children but to invest heavily in each of them. One way to curb fertility, therefore, may be to give women more say-so in the family.

Quite apart from laying a foundation for economic development, family planning programs are also crucial these days in fighting AIDS. HIV is a special problem for women, in part because of biology: Women are about twice as likely to be infected during heterosexual sex with an HIV-positive partner as men are. That's because semen has a higher viral load than vaginal secretions do, and because women have more mucous membranes exposed during sex than men.

One of the greatest moral and policy failures of the last thirty years is the indifference that allowed AIDS to spread around the globe. That indifference arose in part from the sanctimony of the moralizers. In 1983, Patrick Buchanan declared, 'The poor homosexuals – they have declared war against nature, and now nature is exacting an awful retribution.' In retrospect, the grossest immorality of the 1980s took place not in San Francisco bathhouses, but in the corridors of power where self-righteous leaders displayed callous indifference to the spread of the disease.

One of the challenges in curbing the virus is a suspicion of condoms held by many conservatives. Many of them fear that even discussing how to make sex safer also makes it more likely; there may be an element of truth to that, but condoms unquestionably also save lives. Today, condoms cost two cents each when purchased in bulk and are extraordinarily cost-effective in reducing diseases. A University of California study suggested that the cost of a year of life saved through a condom distribution program was $3.50, versus $1,033 in an AIDS treatment program (admittedly, that was when AIDS medications were more expensive). Another study found that each $1 million spent on condoms saved $466 million in AIDS-related costs.

Yet even though condoms are so cost-effective, they are rationed with extraordinary stinginess. In Burundi, which the World Bank counts as the poorest country in the world, donor countries provide fewer than three condoms per man per year. In Sudan, the average man receives one condom every five years. Someday people will look back and wonder: What were they thinking?

Some critics of condoms began spreading the junk science that condoms have pores ten microns in diameter, while the AIDS virus is less than one micron in diameter. That is untrue, and evidence from discordant couples (where one partner has HIV and the other doesn't) suggests that condoms are quite effective in preventing AIDS, albeit not as effective as abstinence. In El Salvador, the Catholic Church helped push through a law requiring condom packages to carry a warning label declaring that they do not protect against AIDS. Even before the law, fewer than 4 percent of Salvadoran women used condoms the first time they had sex.

George W. Bush never signed on entirely to the anticondom campaign being waged by many within his administration, and the United States continued to donate more condoms than any other country, with mild increases over the years. Ironically, it was the Clinton administration (and a stingy Republican Congress at the time) that gutted American donations of condoms: from 800 million condoms donated annually during the George H. W. Bush administration to a low of 190 million in 1999. The George W. Bush administration donated more than 400 million condoms a year during its second term.

The Bush administration focused its AIDS prevention campaign on abstinence-only programs. There is some evidence that abstinence education can be helpful, when paired with a discussion of condoms, contraception, and reproductive health. But the Bush program went beyond underwriting abstinence education; it insisted on 'abstinence only' for young people, meaning no discussion of condoms in schools (although the Bush AIDS program did distribute condoms readily to high-risk groups, such as prostitutes and truck drivers in Africa). Indeed, one third of AIDS prevention spending was funneled by law to abstinence-only education. One American-sponsored abstinence-only approach consists of handing out heart-shaped lollipops inscribed with the message: DON'T BE A SUCKER! SAVE SEX FOR MARRIAGE. Then the session leader invites girls to suck on the lollipops and explains:

> Your body is a wrapped lollipop. When you have sex with a man, he unwraps your lollipop and sucks on it. It may feel great at the time, but, unfortunately, when he's done with you, all you have left for your next partner is a poorly wrapped, saliva-fouled sucker.

Studies on the impact of abstinence-only programs aren't conclusive and seem to depend to some extent on the ideology of those conducting the study. But on balance, the evidence suggests that they slightly delay the debut of sexual activity; once it has been initiated, however, kids are less likely to use contraception. The studies suggest that the result is more pregnancies, more abortions, more sexually transmitted diseases, and more HIV. Advocacy groups like the International Women's Health Coalition fought heroically for evidence-based policies on sexual health, and Congresswoman Carolyn Maloney battled tenaciously for UNFPA programs, but the White House wasn't listening. Finally, President Barack Obama – shortly after taking office – announced that he would end the 'gag rule' and restore full funding to family planning groups and to UNFPA.

One of the premises of the abstinence-only campaign had been that Africa's AIDS problem was a consequence of promiscuity, but that may not have been true, particularly for African women. Emily Oster, an economist at the University of Chicago, notes that about 0.8 percent of American adults are infected with HIV, compared to 6 percent of adults in sub-Saharan Africa. When she examined the data, she couldn't find any indication that Africans are more promiscuous. In fact, Americans and Africans report a similar number of sexual partners (although some experts believe that in Africa they are more likely to be concurrent rather than consecutive). The biggest difference, Oster found, was that transmission rates are much higher in Africa than in America. For any given unprotected sexual relationship with an infected person, Africans are four or five times more likely to get HIV themselves.

That higher rate can be explained in part because Americans get treated for genital sores; Africans often don't. At any one time, 11 percent of Africans have untreated bacterial genital infections, and these sores allow for easy transmission of the virus. Public health experts widely acknowledge that one of the most cost-effective ways to treat HIV is to provide free checkups and treatment for such STDs. Oster notes that when AIDS prevention resources are devoted to treating STDs, the cost per year per life saved from AIDS is only about $3.50.

In any case, for women the lethal risk factor is often not promiscuity but marriage. Routinely in Africa and Asia, women stay safe until they marry, and then they contract AIDS from their husbands. In Cambodia, a twenty-seven-year-old former prostitute told us of her struggles with AIDS, and we assumed that she had caught the virus in the brothel.

'Oh, no,' she said. 'I got AIDS later, from my husband. In the brothel, I always used condoms. But when I was married, I didn't use a condom. A woman with a husband is in much more danger than a girl in a brothel.'

That's an exaggeration, but it underscores a central reality: AIDS is often a disease of gender inequality. Particularly in southern Africa, young women frequently don't have the power to say no to unprotected sex. Teenage girls, for example, often become the baubles of middle-aged men, and so HIV spreads relentlessly. As Stephen Lewis, the former UN ambassador for AIDS, puts it: 'Gender inequality is driving the pandemic.'

One test of a program should be how it handles the challenge of a fourteen-year-old girl like Thabang, who lives in the village of Kwa-Mhlanga in the northeastern part of South Africa. Tall, flirtatious, and liberal with makeup, Thabang is a rebellious adolescent who would be a challenge for any program. Thabang's father, an electrician, died after a protracted battle against AIDS that consumed the family savings. Thabang's mother, Gertrude Tobela, tested positive, apparently after getting the disease from her husband, and then infected her youngest child, Victor, during childbirth. Gertrude had been the first in her family to go to high school and college, and the family had enjoyed a middle-class standard of living. But soon Gertrude was too sick to work, and the family had to survive on $22.50-a-month government payments. The atmosphere in the shack in which they lived was despairing.

Thabang is smart and talented, and like any teenager she yearned for fun and warmth and love. She dreaded the misery of the shack, so she began to hang out in town. She had her hair done fashionably and wore sexy clothes, seeking the diversions of boys to escape the claustrophobia of her home. She also wanted more independence, yearned to be a grown-up, and resented her mother's efforts to rein her in. Thabang also has the misfortune of being strikingly attractive, so men flattered her with their attentions. In South Africa, successful middle-aged men often keep young teenage girls as mistresses, and many teenagers see such 'sugar daddies' as a ladder to a better life.

When Thabang began flirting with men, Gertrude screamed at her and beat her. Thabang was the only member of the family who didn't have AIDS, and Gertrude was aghast at the possibility that Thabang would contract the virus as well. But Gertrude's beatings infuriated Thabang, confirmed the girl's suspicion that her mother hated her, and prompted her to run away. Thabang also seemed to feel embarrassed by her AIDS-ridden mother, weak and frail and

*Thabang in front of the shack she dreads in South Africa, where her
mother is dying of AIDS (Nicholas D. Kristof)*

poor, and all their fighting left Gertrude even more exhausted and
depressed. Gertrude spoke in a composed way about her own
imminent death and Victor's, but she broke down completely
when she spoke of Thabang.

'My daughter left me because she wants liberty,' Gertrude said,
sobbing. 'She is so sexually active, and she stays in bars and rental
rooms.' Gertrude looked upon Thabang's fondness for makeup and
tight clothes with horror and couldn't bear the thought that the
cycle of AIDS would be repeated in the next generation. For her
part, Thabang insisted that while her friends slept with men for
cash or gifts, she herself did not.

'I'm a virgin, whatever my mother says,' Thabang said, and she
began to cry as well. 'She never believes me. She just yells at me.'

'Your mother loves you,' Nick told her. 'The only reason she
scolds you is that she loves you and cares what happens to you.'

'She doesn't love me!' Thabang replied fiercely, tears trickling
down her cheeks as she stood outside her home fifteen feet away
from her mother, who was also crying. 'If she did, she would talk
to me instead of beating me. She wouldn't say these things about
me. She would accept my friends.'

There's no question that the local schools should encourage

abstinence for girls like Thabang. But those programs shouldn't stop there. They should explain that condoms can dramatically reduce the risk of HIV transmission, and they should demonstrate how to use condoms properly. Governments should encourage male circumcision, which reduces HIV risk significantly, and should encourage free screening and treatment for sexually transmitted diseases. Testing for HIV should become routine, requiring people to opt out instead of to opt in. That way, nearly all adults would know their AIDS status, which is crucial, because it's impossible to contain an epidemic when people do not know whether or not they have been infected. That kind of comprehensive approach to prevention would be most effective in reducing the risks to a girl like Thabang. And these prevention methods are much cheaper than treating an AIDS patient for years.

Most of the studies on preventing AIDS aren't rigorous, but scholars at the Massachusetts Institute of Technology's Poverty Action Lab – which does some of the finest research on development anywhere – have examined four different strategies against AIDS in careful trials in Africa. Each strategy was tried in randomly chosen areas, and the results were compared to results in control areas. Success was measured by pregnancies averted (compared to the control areas), since they presumably reflected the amount of unprotected sex that could also transmit AIDS.

One strategy was to train elementary school teachers in AIDS education; that cost only $2 per student but had no impact on reducing pregnancies. A second approach was to encourage student debates and essays on condoms and AIDS; that cost only $1 per student but was not shown to reduce pregnancies. A third approach was to provide students with free uniforms to encourage them to stay in school longer; that cost about $12 per student and did reduce pregnancies. Using their comparisons with the control areas, the researchers calculated that the cost was $750 per pregnancy averted. The fourth and by far the most cost-effective approach was also the simplest: warning of the perils of sugar daddies. Schoolchildren were shown a brief video of the dangers of teenage girls going out with older men, and then were informed that older men have much higher HIV infection rates than boys. Few students had been aware of that crucial fact.

The warning didn't reduce girls' sexual activity, but they did end up sleeping with boyfriends their own age rather than with older men. The boys were more likely to use condoms – apparently because they were shaken by learning from the school presentation that teenage girls were much more likely than teenage boys to have HIV. This simple program was a huge success: It cost less than $1 per student, and a pregnancy could be averted for only $91. It's also a reminder of the need for relentless empiricism in developing policies. Conservatives, who have presumed that the key to preventing AIDS is abstinence-only education, and liberals, who have focused on distribution of condoms, should both note that the intervention that has tested most cost-effective in Africa is neither.

Religious conservatives have fought against condom distribution and battled funding for UNFPA, but they have also saved lives in vast numbers by underwriting and operating clinics in some of the neediest parts of Africa and Asia. When you travel in the poorest countries in Africa, you repeatedly find diplomats, UN staff, and aid organizations in the capitals or big cities. And then you go to the remote villages and towns where Western help is most needed, and aid workers are suddenly scarce. Doctors Without Borders works heroically in remote areas, and so do some other secular groups. But the people you almost inevitably encounter are the missionary doctors and church-sponsored aid workers.

Nick's plane once crashed while he was flying into central Congo, so he decided to drive out. In nearly a week of traversing a vast stretch of this war-torn country, the only foreign presence he encountered was two Catholic missions. The priest in one had just died of malaria, but the other mission was run by an Italian priest who distributed food and clothing and tried to keep a clinic going in the middle of a civil war.

Likewise, Catholic Relief Services fights poverty all over the world – not least by supporting Sunitha's shelter for former prostitutes in India. All told, some 25 percent of AIDS care worldwide is provided by church-related groups. 'In most of Africa, these are the cornerstone of the health system,' Dr. Helene Gayle, the head of CARE, said of the Catholic-run clinics. 'In some countries, they serve more people than the government health system.'

Moreover, the Catholic Church as a whole has always been much more sympathetic to condoms than the Vatican has been. Local priests and nuns often ignore Rome and quietly do what they can to save parishioners. In Sonsonate, in the poor southwestern part of El Salvador, the Catholic hospital advises women about IUDs and the Pill, and urges them to use condoms to protect themselves from AIDS. 'The bishop is in San Salvador and never comes here,' explained Dr. Martha Alica De Regalada. 'So we never get in trouble.' Nor was she worried that she would get into trouble for being quoted speaking so frankly.

Missionaries have been running indispensable health and education networks in some of the poorest countries for decades, and it would be enormously beneficial to bring their schools and clinics into a global movement to empower women and girls. Those missionaries have invaluable on-the-ground experience. Aid workers and diplomats come and go, but missionaries burrow into a society, learn the local language, send their children to local schools, sometimes stay for life. True, some missionaries are hypocritical or sanctimonious – just like any group of people – but many others are like Harper McConnell at the hospital in Congo, struggling to act on a gospel of social justice as well as individual morality.

If there is to be a successful movement on behalf of women in poor countries, it will have to bridge the God Gulf. Secular bleeding hearts and religious bleeding hearts will have to forge a common cause. That's what happened two centuries ago in the abolitionist movement, when liberal deists and conservative evangelicals joined forces to overthrow slavery. And it's the only way to muster the political will to get now-invisible women onto the international agenda.

It is particularly crucial to incorporate Pentecostalism into a movement for women's rights around the globe, because it is gaining ground more quickly than any other faith, especially in Africa, Asia, and Latin America. The church with the largest Sunday attendance in all of Europe is now a Pentecostal megachurch in Kiev, Ukraine, founded in 1994 by a charismatic Nigerian, Sunday Adelaja. One person in ten is now a Pentecostal, according to the highest estimates; those estimates may be exaggerated several-fold, but there's no doubt about Pentecostalism's spread throughout poor countries. One reason for that is the suggestion made by some of its churches that God will reward adherents with riches in this life. Some also teach variations of faith-healing or claim that Jesus will protect its followers from AIDS.

We thus regard the Pentecostal boom with some suspicion, but without doubt it also has a positive impact on the role of women. Pentecostal churches typically encourage all members of the congregation to speak up and preach during the service. So for the first time, many ordinary women find themselves exercising leadership and declaring their positions on moral and religious matters. On Sundays, women come together and exchange advice on how to apply community pressure to bring wayward husbands back into line. Just as important, Pentecostalism and other conservative evangelical denominations discourage drinking and adultery, and these are both practices that have caused tremendous hardship to African women in particular.

Until the late 1990s, conservative Christians were mostly a force for isolationism, worrying (as Jesse Helms put it) that foreign aid is 'money down a rat hole.' But, under the influence of Franklin Graham (Billy Graham's son, now head of the Samaritan's Purse aid organization) and Senator Sam Brownback and many others, evangelicals and other conservative Christians have come to focus on issues like AIDS, sex trafficking, and poverty. Now the National Association of Evangelicals is an important force for humanitarian causes and foreign aid. It's because of encouragement from evangelicals, including Michael Gerson, a former White House chief speech writer, that George W. Bush sponsored his presidential initiative to fight AIDS – the best single thing he ever did, arguably saving more than 9 million lives. Michael Horowitz, an agitator for humanitarian causes based at the Hudson Institute in Washington, has rallied religious conservatives to back an initiative to repair obstetric fistulas. These days bleeding-heart evangelicals are out in front alongside bleeding-heart liberals in fighting for aid money to tackle these problems, as well as malaria. That's a landmark change from a decade or two ago.

'Poverty and disease just weren't on my agenda,' Rick Warren, pastor of the Saddleback megachurch in California and author of *The Purpose Driven Life*, told us. 'I missed the AIDS thing. I had no idea what the big deal was.' Then, in 2003, Warren went to South Africa to train pastors and found a small congregation in a tent, caring for twenty-five AIDS orphans. 'I realized that they were doing more for the poor than my entire megachurch,' he said, with cheerful exaggeration. 'It was like a knife in the heart.'

Since then Warren has galvanized his church to fight poverty and injustice in sixty-eight countries around the world. More than 7,500 members of the church have paid their own way to volunteer in poor countries – and once they see the poverty up close, they want to do more.

Liberals could emulate the willingness of many evangelicals to tithe – to donate 10 percent of their incomes each year to charity. The *Index of Global Philanthropy* calculates that U.S. religious organizations give $5.4 billion annually to developing countries, more than twice as much as is given by U.S. foundations. Arthur Brooks, an economist, has found that the one third of Americans who attend worship services at least once a week are 'inarguably more charitable in every measurable way' than the two thirds who are less religious. Not only do they donate more, he says, but they also are more likely to volunteer their time for charities. Brooks does find, however, that while liberals are less generous with their own money, they are more likely to favor government funding of humanitarian causes.

Both groups might work harder to ensure that their charitable contributions truly go to the needy. Conservative Christians contribute very generously to humanitarian causes, but a significant share of that money goes to build magnificent churches. Likewise, liberal contributions often go to elite universities or symphonies. These may be good causes, but they are not humanitarian. It would be good to see liberals and conservatives alike expand their range of giving so that more goes to help the truly needy.

It would also be useful if there were better mechanisms for people to donate time. The Peace Corps is a valuable program, but it requires an intimidating commitment of twenty-seven months, and the schedule does not follow the academic year to accommodate those who are trying to delay graduate school. Teach For America has generated enormous interest among public service-minded young people, but it is a domestic program. We need funding for Teach the World, an international version of Teach For America, to send young people abroad for a year, a term that would then be renewable. That would offer an important new channel of foreign assistance to support girls' education in poor countries, and it would also offer young Americans a potentially life-changing encounter with the developing world.

Jane Roberts and Her 34 Million Friends

When George W Bush announced early in his first administration that the United States would withhold all $34
million that had been allocated for the UNFPA, many people
grumbled about it. But Jane Roberts, a retired French teacher in
Redlands, California, grumbled herself into starting a movement.
It began with a letter to the editor of her local paper, the *San
Bernardino Sun:*

> A week has passed since the Bush Administration decided to
> deny the $34 million voted by Congress for the United
> Nations Population Fund. Ho Hum, this is vacation time.
> Columnists have written about it and newspapers have
> printed editorials of lament. Ho Hum. More women die in
> childbirth in a few days than terrorism kills people in a year.
> Ho Hum. Some little girl is having her genitals cut with a
> cactus needle. Ho Hum, that's just a cultural thing.
>
> As an exercise in outraged democracy, would 34 million
> of my fellow citizens please join me in sending one dollar
> each to the US Committee for UNFPA? That would right a
> terrible wrong . . . and drown out the Ho Hums.

Jane is blue-eyed with short blond hair and carries a hint of the
sixties in her dress and manner: a taste for African necklaces and
simple clothing like black loafers. She was now on a mission. Jane
contacted groups like the Sierra Club and League of Women
Voters. After she saw a mention in the newspaper about the
National Council of Women's Organizations, she barraged the

Jane Roberts (courtesy of Jane Roberts)

council with pestering phone calls and e-mails. A week later its board endorsed her effort.

At the same time, a grandmother in New Mexico named Lois Abraham was thinking along the same lines as Jane. She had read a column Nick had written from Khartoum, Sudan, about a teenage girl with an obstetric fistula, noting that the administration was now crippling one of the few organizations helping such girls. Lois angrily drafted a chain letter about the UNFPA and the funding cutoff. It ended:

> If 34,000,000 American women send one dollar each to the UN Population Fund, we can help the Fund continue its 'invaluable work' and at the same time confirm that providing family planning and reproductive health services to women who would otherwise have none is a humanitarian issue, not a political one.
>
> PLEASE, NOW: Put a dollar, wrapped in a plain sheet of paper, in an envelope marked '34 Million Friends.' . . . Then mail it today. EVEN MORE IMPORTANT: Send this letter on to at least ten friends – more would be better! – who may join in this message.

Lois had cold-called the UNFPA and told an official she was sending out the e-mail. UNFPA didn't have much of a public image and rarely received contributions.

'Some in UNFPA were doubtful about such a grassroots effort,' recalled Stirling Scruggs, a former senior official in the agency. 'They thought it would last a few weeks and that the two women would tire and it would end quickly. That is, until bags of mail started piling up at UNFPA's mail room.'

The deluge of dollar bills triggered by Lois and Jane soon caused a problem. UNFPA had pledged that all the money would go to programs, but somebody had to handle all the mail. At first, staff members devoted their lunch hours to opening envelopes. Then supporters of the U.S. Committee for UNFPA volunteered their help. Finally, the UN Foundation gave grants to hire staff to handle the mail.

Most of the money consisted of $1 bills from women – and some men – all across the country. Some sent larger amounts. 'This $5 is in honor of the women in my life: my mother, my wife, my two daughters, and my granddaughter,' one man wrote. UNFPA informed Lois and Jane about each other, and they joined forces, formalizing their campaign as 34 Million Friends of UNFPA (www.34millionfriends.org). They began going on speaking tours, and the movement gained steam. People around the country were exasperated by the social conservatives' campaigns against reproductive health – the defunding of UNFPA, the denunciations of condoms and comprehensive sex education, the attempts to cut off support for family planning by aid groups like Marie Stopes International – and they were eager to do something concrete to help. Sending in a dollar bill wasn't a panacea, but it was very easy to do.

'No one can say I can't give a dollar,' Jane noted. 'We're even getting donations from college students and high school students. You can take a stand for the women of the world for just the price of a soda.'

Both Ellen Goodman and Molly Ivins wrote columns praising Jane and Lois and their work, and donations reached two thousand a day. Jane traveled with UNFPA to Mali and Senegal – her first visit to Africa – and began speaking and campaigning nonstop.

'From that time on, I have given my life to this,' she told Sheryl. 'I'm going to follow this to the ends of the earth to further this cause . . . Forty women every minute seek unsafe abortions – to me this is just a crime against humanity.'

After President Obama announced in January 2009 that he would restore funding for UNFPA, the question arose: Is 34 Million Friends still necessary? Should it fade away? But by then the group started by two indignant women had raised a total of $4 million, and they saw vast needs remaining – so they decided to continue their work as a supplement to American government funding of UNFPA. 'There is a huge unmet demand for family planning in the world today,' Jane said. 'There is huge need for fistula prevention and treatment. With population pressures and environmental pressures, and economic pressures in much of the world, women will bear the brunt of gender-based violence even more than now. So for me 34 Million Friends is my work. It is my passion. I don't think any cause is greater for the long term for people, the planet, and peace. So for me, on we go!'

CHAPTER NINE

Is Islam Misogynistic?

A majority of the dwellers of hell will be women, who curse
too much and are ungrateful to their spouses.

– MUHAMMAD IMRAN, *Ideal Woman in Islam*

On Nick's first trip to Afghanistan, he employed an interpreter who had studied English in university. He was a very brave man and seemed very modern until one particular discussion.

'My mother has never been to a doctor,' the interpreter said, 'and she never will go.'

'Why not?' Nick asked.

'There are no female doctors here now, and I cannot allow her to go to a male doctor. That would be against Islam. And since my father died, I'm in charge of her. She cannot leave the house without my permission.'

'But what if your mother were dying, and the only way to save her would be to take her to a doctor?'

'That would be a terrible thing,' the interpreter said gravely. 'I would mourn my mother.'

A politically incorrect point must be noted here. Of the countries where women are held back and subjected to systematic abuses such as honor killings and genital cutting, a very large proportion are predominantly Muslim. Most Muslims worldwide don't believe in such practices, and some Christians do – but the fact remains that the countries where girls are cut, killed for honor, or kept out of school or the workplace typically have large Muslim populations.

To look at one broad gauge of well-being, of 130 countries rated in 2008 by the World Economic Forum according to the status of women, 8 of the bottom 10 were majority Muslim. Yemen was in last place, with Chad. Saudi Arabia, and Pakistan right behind it. No Muslim country ranks in the top 40. Kazakhstan ranks highest, at number 45, followed by Uzbekistan, at 55.

We tend to think of Latin America, with its legacy of machismo, as a man's world. But Mexico and other Latin countries actually do pretty well at educating girls and keeping them alive. Most Latin nations have populations that are majority female. Maternity hospitals even in poor neighborhoods of South American cities such as Bogota and Quito provide free prenatal care and delivery, because saving women's lives is considered by society to be a priority.

In contrast, opinion polls underscore that Muslims in some countries just don't believe in equality. Only 25 percent of Egyptians believe that a woman should have the right to become president. More than 34 percent of Moroccans approve of polygamy. Some 54 percent of Afghan women say that women should wear the burka outside the house. Conservative Muslims often side with the top religious authority in Saudi Arabia, Grand Mufti Sheikh Abdulaziz, who declared in 2004: 'Allowing women to mix with men is the root of every evil and catastrophe.'

Muslims sometimes note that such conservative attitudes have little to do with the Koran and arise from culture more than religion. That's true: In these places, even religious minorities and irreligious people are often deeply repressive toward women. In Pakistan, we met a young woman from the Christian minority who insisted on choosing her own husband; infuriated at this breach of family honor, her brothers bickered over whether they should kill her or just sell her to a brothel. While they argued, she escaped. After the Taliban was ousted in Afghanistan, banditry spread and Amnesty International quoted an aid worker as saying: 'During the Taliban era, if a woman went to market and showed an inch of flesh, she would have been flogged; now, she's raped.' In short, often we blame a region's religion when the oppresion instead may be rooted in its culture. Yet, that acknowledged, it's also true that

A fully covered woman in Kabul, Afghanistan, with her daughter
(Nicholas D. Kristof)

one reason religion is blamed is that it is often cited by the oppressors. In the Muslim world, for example, misogynists routinely quote Muhammad to justify themselves.

So let's face the question squarely: Is Islam misogynistic?

One answer is historical, and it is no. When Muhammad introduced Islam in the seventh century, it was a step forward for women. Islamic law banned the previously common practice of female infanticide, and it limited polygamy to four wives who were supposed to be treated equally. Muslim women routinely owned property, with rights protected by the law, while women in European countries often did not have the equivalent property rights. All in all, Muhammad comes across in the Koran and the traditions associated with him as much more respectful of women than early Christian leaders. After all, the apostle Paul wanted women to keep silent in church, and the early Christian leader Tertullian denounced women as 'the gateway of the devil.'

Yet over the centuries Christianity has mostly moved beyond that. In contrast, conservative Islam has barely budged. It is still frozen in the world view of seventh-century Arabia, amid attitudes that were progressive for the time but are a millennium out of date. When a girls' junior high school caught fire in Saudi Arabia in 2002, the religious police allegedly forced teenage girls back into the burning building rather than allow them to escape without head coverings and long black cloaks. Fourteen girls were reportedly burned to death.

The Koran explicitly endorses some gender discrimination: A woman's testimony counts only half as much as a man's, and a daughter inherits only half as much as a son. When these kinds of passages arise in the Bible, Christians and Jews mostly shrug them off. It has been much harder for pious Muslims to ignore unpleasant and antiquated passages in the Koran, because it is believed to be not just divinely inspired but literally the word of God.

Still, many modern-minded Muslims are pushing for greater gender equality. Amina Wadud, an Islamic scholar in the United States, has written a systematic reinterpretation of chauvinist provisions in the Koran. For example, verse 4:34 refers to wives and is usually translated roughly like this: 'As for those from whom ye fear rebellion, admonish them and banish them to beds apart, and beat them.' Feminist scholars like Wadud cite a barrage of reasons to argue that this is a mistranslation. For example, the word translated above as 'beat' can have many other meanings, including to have sex with someone. Thus one new translation presents that same passage this way: 'As for women you feel are averse, talk to them persuasively; then leave them alone in bed (without molesting them), and go to bed with them (when they are willing).'

The Islamic feminists, as these scholars are known, argue that it is absurd for Saudi Arabia to bar women from driving, because Muhammad allowed his wives to drive camels. They say that the stipulation that two female witnesses equal one male witness applied only to financial cases, because women at the time were less familiar with finance. That situation is now obsolete, they say, and so is that provision. The feminist exegesis argues if the Koran originally was progressive, then it should not be allowed to become an apologia for backwardness.

A useful analogy is slavery. Islam improved the position of slaves compared to their status in pre-Islamic societies, and the Koran encourages the freeing of slaves as a meritorious act. At the same time, Muhammad himself had many slaves, and Islamic law unmistakably accepts slavery. Indeed, Saudi Arabia abolished slavery only in 1962, and Mauritania in 1981. In the end, despite these deep cultural ties, the Islamic world has entirely renounced slavery. If the Koran can be read differently today because of changing attitudes toward slaves, then why not emancipate women as well?

Muhammad himself was progressive on gender issues, but some early successors, such as the Caliph Omar, were unmitigated chauvinists. One reason for their hostility to strong women may have been personality clashes with the Prophet's youngest wife, Aisha, the Islamic world's first feminist.

Aisha was the only one of Muhammad's wives who was a virgin when he married her, and she grew to be a strong-willed woman with whom he spent a great deal of time. Aisha knew firsthand the perils of a society that treated a woman as a fragile chalice of honor, for she herself was once accused of adultery. While traveling across the desert in a caravan, she lost a necklace and went to look for it – and then was left behind by the caravan. A man named Safwan found Aisha and rescued her, but since they had been together without a chaperone, they were accused of having an affair. Muhammad sided with her – that's when he had the revelation about needing four witnesses to attest to adultery before punishment could be applied – and ordered that the accusers be flogged with forty lashes.

After Muhammad died in Aisha's arms (according to Sunni doctrine, which is disputed by Shiites), she took on an active and public role, in a way that annoyed many men. Aisha vigorously contested views of Islam that were hostile to women, and she recorded 2,210 hadith, or recollections of Muhammad used in Islam to supplement and clarify Koranic teachings. Ultimately Aisha even led an armed rebellion against a longtime adversary, Ali, after he became caliph. That insurrection is called the Battle of the Camel, because Aisha commanded her troops by riding among them on a camel. Ali crushed the rebellion, and then for centuries Islamic scholars discounted Aisha's importance and rejected her feminist interpretations. All but 174 of her hadith were discarded.

Yet in recent decades some Islamic feminists, such as Fatema Mernissi, a Moroccan, have dusted off Aisha's work to provide a powerful voice for Muslim women. There is, for example, a well-known statement attributed to Muhammad stipulating that a man's prayers are ineffective if a woman, dog, or donkey passes in front of the believer. As Mernissi notes, Aisha ridiculed that as nonsense: 'You compare us now to donkeys and dogs. In the name of God, I have seen the Prophet saying his prayers while I was there.' Likewise, Aisha denied various suggestions that her husband considered menstruating women to be unclean.

Another dispute about the Koran concerns the idyllic black-eyed virgins who supposedly will attend to men in the Islamic afterlife. These are the houri, and some Islamic theologians have been quite specific in describing them. A ninth-century scholar, Al-Tirmidhi, recounted that houri are gorgeous young women with white skin, who never menstruate, urinate, or defecate. He added that they have 'large breasts' that are 'not inclined to dangle.' Suicide bombers have often written about their expectations of being rewarded by the houri, and Muhammad Atta reassured his fellow hijackers on the eve of 9/11: 'The houri are calling you.'

The bombers may be in for a surprise. The Arabic language was born as a written language only with the Koran, and so many of its words are puzzling. Scholars are beginning to examine early copies of the Koran with academic rigor, and some argue that a number of these puzzling words may actually have been Syriac or Aramaic. A scholar who uses the pseudonym Christoph Luxenberg for his own protection argues that 'houri' is probably a reference to the Aramaic word for 'white grapes.' That would be plausible, because the Koran compares the houri to pearls and crystal, and because accounts of Heaven from the time of the Koran often included bounteous fruit, especially grapes to refresh the weary.

Would there be as many suicide bombers if the presumption was that martyrs would arrive at the Pearly Gates and be handed a dish of white grapes?

*

Westerners sometimes feel sorry for Muslim women in a way that leaves them uncomfortable, even angry. When Nick quizzed a group of female Saudi doctors and nurses in Riyadh about women's rights, they bristled. 'Why do foreigners always ask about clothing?' one woman doctor asked. 'Why does it matter so much what we wear? Of all the issues in the world, is that really so important?' Another said: 'You think we're victims, because we cover our hair and wear modest clothing. But we think that it's Western women who are repressed, because they have to show their bodies – even go through surgery to change their bodies – to please men.' A third doctor saw that Nick was taken aback at the scolding, and she tried to explain the indignation.

'Look, when we're among ourselves, of course we complain about the rules,' she said. 'It's ridiculous that we can't drive. But these are our problems, not yours. We don't want anybody fighting for us – and we certainly don't want anybody feeling sorry for us.'

Americans not only come across as patronizing but also often miss the complexity of gender roles in the Islamic world. 'I'm a Nobel Peace Prize-winner and a university professor, but if I testify in a court, it won't take my testimony because I'm a woman,' notes Shirin Ebadi, an Iranian lawyer. 'Any uneducated man would be taken more seriously . . . Iran is a bundle of contradictions. Women can't testify fully in court, and yet women can be judges presiding over the court. We do have women judges. Any woman who wants to travel abroad needs the consent of her husband. But our vice president is a woman. So when our vice president travels abroad, she needs the consent of her husband. Meanwhile, sixty-five percent of Iranian university students are women, because they do better on entrance exams than men do.'

Across the Middle East, attitudes are changing. Partly because of the leadership of prominent women such as Queen Rania of Jordan and Sheikha Mozah, the first lady of Qatar, acceptance of women's rights is spreading. A UN survey in Egypt, Jordan, Lebanon, and Morocco found that more than 98 percent of people in each country believed that 'girls have the same right to education as boys.'

Jordan, Qatar, and Morocco have been among the leaders in giving women greater roles. In Morocco, King Muhammad VI married a computer engineer who does not veil herself and who has become a role model for many Moroccan women. King Muhammad also reformed family law, giving women more rights in divorce and marriage, and he supported the pathbreaking appointment of fifty women imams, or preachers.

One of the promising efforts to stimulate change in the Arab world is led by Soraya Salti, a thirty-seven-year-old Jordanian woman who is promoting entrepreneurship in middle schools and high schools. Soraya's program, Injaz, teaches kids how to devise a business plan and then start and operate a small business. Many of them end up actually starting businesses, and the skills are especially useful for girls because of the discrimination that women face in the formal job market. By giving women an alternative way to pursue careers and earn incomes, as entrepreneurs, Injaz also facilitates the expansion of the labor force and economic development as a whole. Queen Rania has strongly backed Soraya, and the program has earned rave reviews. Injaz has now spread to twelve Arab countries and teaches 100,000 students a year how to launch businesses. 'If you can capture the youth and change the way they think, then you can change the future,' Soraya says.

A window into the squandered human resources in conservative Muslim societies is the Women's Detention Center in Kabul, Afghanistan. The jail is a single-story compound behind a high wall in the heart of the city, without guard towers or coils of barbed wire. Its inmates include teenage girls and young women who were suspected of having a boyfriend and then subjected to a 'virginity test' – a hymen inspection. Those whose hymens were not intact were then prosecuted and typically jailed for a few years.*

Rana, the middle-aged woman who serves as director of the detention center, is in some ways a pioneer for working women,

* Examination of the hymen obviously is an unreliable gauge of virginity. But it is perceived as reliable enough in poor countries with low levels of education, and woe to the girl who has lost hers.

having risen through the police ranks to direct the jail. But she believes that girls who lack a hymen should be prosecuted, if only to protect them from their families. Every year, Afghanistan's president pardons some inmates during the Eid al-Fitr festival that ends Ramadan. When women are freed, some of them are shot by relatives or, worse, 'accidentally' scalded to death with boiling water. Jail is sometimes the safest place for a bold Afghan woman.

One inmate, Ellaha, a nineteen-year-old with short black hair and a round self-confident face, startled us by greeting us in English and approaching us. She sat down in the dingy little jail room and unselfconsciously spoke of graduating from high school and attending one year of university while her family lived as refugees in Iran. Ellaha is charming, disciplined, and ambitious; in another culture, she would be an entrepreneur. Her problems began when the family returned to Afghanistan from Iran. Ellaha chafed at the more rigid Afghan customs, from the burka to the expectation that a woman will stay home all her life.

'My family wanted to force me to marry my cousin,' she said. 'I didn't agree to marry him, because he is not educated and I don't like his job – he is a butcher! Plus, he's three years younger than me. I wanted to study and continue my education, but my father and uncle wouldn't let me.'

Ellaha found work with an American construction company and quickly impressed the managers with her intelligence and diligence. Her family was torn between horror at their daughter working with infidels and delight at the money she brought home. Then one of her bosses, an American named Steve, arranged for Ellaha to study at a university in Canada on a full scholarship. Ellaha saw this as an opportunity that could transform her life, and she leaped at it – even though her parents worried that it would be un-Islamic for a woman to travel so far away and study with men. The family also still wanted Ellaha to marry her cousin, partly because he was the son of her father's oldest brother, the family patriarch. Ellaha's sister, two years younger, was meant to marry the cousin's younger brother, but the sister followed Ellaha's example and resisted. So the family struck back.

'When it was almost time for me to go to Canada and I was asking about flights, they tied me up and locked me in a room,' Ellaha said. 'It was in my uncle's house. My father said, "Okay, beat her." I'd never been beaten like that in all my life. My uncle and cousins were all beating me. They broke my head, and I was bleeding.' Ellaha's sister endured the same treatment. After a week of daily beatings as they lay with their wrists and ankles chained, Ellaha and her sister agreed to marry the cousins.

'My mother guaranteed that we would not escape, and our family took us back to our home after we promised we would be obedient,' Ellaha said. The family allowed Ellaha to resume her job, but her boss rescinded his offer of foreign study when he realized her family adamantly opposed the plan. Ellaha was heartbroken but continued to work hard. To help her do her work, she was given a mobile phone. Her family was aghast that she now could communicate unsupervised with men. The family demanded that she give up her phone.

'Then our father decided that we must marry . . . My mother came and said, "I have no power to help." So we escaped.' Ellaha and her sister fled to a cheap guesthouse, planning to go to Iran and stay with relatives while attending university there. But someone spotted Ellaha at the guesthouse and told her parents, so the police came to arrest her and her sister as runaways. The police subjected them to virginity checks, but their hymens were intact.

They were jailed 'because their lives were in danger,' explained Rana. 'To protect her from the anger of her father, she's here.' Ellaha acknowledged that that was a legitimate concern. 'They were very angry,' she said of her father and uncle. 'I was scared that they might kill me.' Ellaha's father, a carpenter named Said Jamil, was indignant when we tracked him down in Kabul. He didn't want us inside his house, so we spoke on the street. We asked him to promise not to harm Ellaha, and he did so, but he also vowed that he would no longer allow her 'to be so free.'

We don't blame Ellaha's difficulties on the Prophet Muhammad or on Islam as such. Islam itself is not misogynistic. But as many Muslims have themselves pointed out, as long as smart, bold women like Ellaha disproportionately end up in prison, or in coffins, in some Muslim nations, then those countries are undermining their own hopes for development.

There are many reasons for the boom in Muslim terrorists in recent decades, including frustration at backwardness in the Islamic world, as well as resentment of corrupt rulers. But another reason may be the youth bulge in Islam – partly because of lagging efforts on family planning – and the broader marginalization of women.

A society that has more men than women – particularly young men, is often associated with crime or violence. The historian David Courtwright has argued that one reason America is relatively violent, compared to Europe, is the legacy of a male surplus. Until World War II, the United States was disproportionately male, and the frontier was overwhelmingly so. The result, he suggests, was a tradition of aggressiveness, short tempers, and violence that still echoes in America's relatively high homicide rates. The same analysis, while controversial, may also help explain why male-dominated Muslim societies have similar threads emphasizing self-reliance, honor, courage, and a quick resort to violence.

All this is compounded when the men are young. In Western countries, the cohort aged fifteen through twenty-four makes up an average of 15 percent of the adult population. In contrast, in many Muslim countries, this share has been more than 30 percent. 'For each percentage-point increase of youth in the adult population,' says Norwegian researcher Henrik Urdal, 'the risk of conflict increases by more than 4 percent.'

Youth bulges may well be particularly destabilizing in conservative Muslim countries, because women are largely passive and silent – amplifying the impact of young men. Moreover, in other parts of the world, young men aged fifteen through twenty-four spend many of their waking moments chasing young women. In contrast, in conservative Muslim countries, some young men make war, not love.

In strict Muslim countries such as Afghanistan, many young

men have little hope of ever finding a partner. Typically in such nations, there are at least 3 percent more males than females, partly because females don't receive the same medical care as males. Also, polygamy means that the wealthiest men take two or three wives, leaving even fewer women available for the poor. The inability of a young man to settle down in a family may increase the likelihood of his drifting toward violence.

Young men in such countries grow up in an all-male environment, in a testosterone-saturated world that has the ethos of a high school boys' locker room. Organizations made up disproportionately of young men – whether they be gangs or boys' schools or prisons or military units – are often particularly violent. We suspect that the same can be true of entire countries.

Countries that repress women also tend to be backward economically, adding to the frustrations that nurture terrorism. Farsighted Muslim leaders worry that gender inequality blocks them from tapping their nations' greatest unexploited economic resource – the half of the population that is female. In Yemen, women make up only 6 percent of the nonagricultural labor force; the figure is 9 percent in Pakistan. Contrast that with between 40 percent and 50 percent in countries such as China and the United States. As a UN Arab Human Development Report put it: 'The rise of women is in fact a prerequisite for an Arab renaissance.'

Bill Gates recalls once being invited to speak in Saudi Arabia and finding himself facing a segregated audience. Four fifths of the listeners were men, on the left. The remaining one fifth were women, all covered in black cloaks and veils, on the right. A partition separated the two groups. Toward the end, during the question-and-answer session, a member of the audience noted that Saudi Arabia aimed to be one of the top ten countries in the world in technology by 2010 and asked if that was realistic. 'Well, if you're not fully utilizing half the talent in the country,' said Gates, 'you're not going to get too close to the top ten.' The small group on the right erupted in wild cheering, while the larger audience on the left applauded tepidly.

Some evidence suggests that where families repress women,

governments end up repressing all citizens. 'The status of women, more than other factors that predominate in Western thinking about religious systems and politics, links Islam and the democracy deficit,' writes the scholar M. Steven Fish. That may be because an authoritarian and patriarchal home environment is mirrored in an authoritarian and patriarchal political system.

The consequences of repressing women may run even deeper. David Landes, the eminent Harvard historian, in his magisterial book, *The Wealth and Poverty of Nations*, explores why it was Europe that nurtured an industrial revolution, and not Asia or the Middle East. He argues that one of the key forces working in Europe's favor was openness to new ideas, and that one of the best gauges of that openness was how a country treated its women:

> The economic implications of gender discrimination are most serious. To deny women is to deprive a country of labor and talent, but – even worse – *to undermine the drive to achievement of boys and men*. One cannot rear young people in such ways that half of them think themselves superior by biology, without dulling ambition and devaluing accomplishment. One cannot call male children 'Pasha,' or, as in Iran, tell them that they have a golden penis,* without reducing their need to learn and do . . .
>
> In general, the best clue to a nation's growth and development potential is the status and role of women. This is the greatest handicap of Muslim Middle Eastern societies today, the flaw that most bars them from modernity.

---

* Landes is correct that Iranians often call baby boys *doudoul tala*, or 'golden penis.' But this is not necessarily evidence of gender bias, since Iranians call baby girls an equivalent: *nanaz tala*, or 'golden pubic area.'

The Afghan Insurgent

The best-known aid effort in Afghanistan and Pakistan is the school-building project of Greg Mortenson, a mountain climber who came down half dead from a failed attempt to climb the second-highest peak in the world, K2. Himalayan villagers revived Greg and shared what little they had with him. When he recovered, he found that the village had seventy-eight boys and four girls studying schoolbooks out in the open – with no school and no teacher – and he promised to return and build them a school. Greg sent out 580 letters appealing for funds and got one check, from Tom Brokaw. Eventually he found other donors and sold his car, his books, and even his beloved climbing gear to raise the money. Ever since, Greg has been building schools throughout the region, following the lead of local people in each instance.

Greg became famous as the school-builder of Pakistan and then Afghanistan, always working in remote areas and always focusing on girls' schools. 'You educate a boy, and you're educating an individual,' Greg says, quoting an African proverb. 'You educate a girl, and you're educating an entire village.' More recently, Greg has been training graduates in maternal health care and adding a medical component to his programs. Greg wrote about his work in his powerful book, *Three Cups of Tea*, and it's the kind of grassroots, rural program with local buy-in that has often been most successful in the developing world.

Alas, it's also atypical, and Western aid efforts have been particularly ineffective in Muslim countries like Afghanistan and Pakistan. After the American-backed victory over the Taliban in Afghanistan at the end of 2001, well-meaning aid groups

Sakena Yacoobi visiting one of her clinics, in Herat, Afghanistan
(Afghan Institute of Learning)

dispatched hardy young Americans to Kabul. They rented homes and offices – sending Kabul real estate prices through the roof – and bought fleets of white SUVs. Kabul nightlife boomed, restaurants and DVD shops sprouted, and Kellogg's corn flakes appeared in grocery stores. On a weekend evening in Kabul, you could drop by a restaurant catering to aid workers and see $1 million worth of SUVs parked out front.

The flood of aid programs targeted Afghan women, and they did some good. But typically they didn't reach far into the countryside, where they were most needed. Moreover, many Afghans felt threatened by Christians or Jews entering their country, walking around naked (by Afghan standards), and urging women: *Learn to read! Get a job! Empower yourself! Throw off your burka!* One aid group, innocently trying to gather names of local people for a database, asked for the names not only of men in each household, but also of women and girls. That was perceived as scandalously intrusive.

Another Western aid group, trying to improve the hygiene and health of Afghan women, issued them bars of soap – nearly causing a riot. In Afghanistan, washing with soap is often associated with post-coital activity, so the group was thought to be implying that the women were promiscuous.

At the other extreme of effectiveness is Sakena Yacoobi, a force of nature who runs an aid organization called the Afghan Institute of Learning. Short and stout, her hair bundled in a scarf, waving greetings to one person while bantering in rapid-fire English with another, Sakena is perpetually in motion. Perhaps the reason fundamentalists haven't silenced her yet is that she herself is an Afghan Muslim, less threatening than an outsider. American organizations would have accomplished much more if they had financed and supported Sakena, rather than dispatching their own representatives to Kabul. That's generally true: The best role for Americans who want to help Muslim women isn't holding the microphone at the front of the rally but writing the checks and carrying the bags in the back.

Sakena grew up in Herat in northwestern Afghanistan, and although she was accepted by Kabul University, she couldn't attend because of the violence at the time. So she traveled halfway around the world to Stockton, California, attending the University of the Pacific on a scholarship as a premed student. Afterward, she studied public health at Loma Linda University (while bringing thirteen members of her family to safety in the United States). But Sakena wanted to help her people, and so she moved to Pakistan to work in the Afghan refugee camps, where she tried to provide health care and education. She began by opening a girls' school in Peshawar with three hundred pupils; a year later, she had fifteen thousand students. The Taliban barred girls from getting an education in Afghanistan, but Sakena nonetheless opened a string of secret schools for girls there.

'It wasn't easy, and it was very risky,' she recalls. 'I negotiated that if people supplied houses and protected the schools and the students, then we would pay the teachers and provide supplies. So we had thirty-eight hundred students in underground schools. We had rules that the students would arrive at intervals, no men were allowed inside, and people would work as lookouts.'

The operation was immensely successful, protecting eighty secret schools and suffering only one Taliban raid. 'That was my fault,' Sakena admits. 'I allowed an Englishwoman to visit, and the children talked and the Taliban raided the next day. But we had advance warning, and so the teacher dispersed the children and turned the classroom into a regular room of the house. It was okay in the end.'

Sakena's operation for Afghan refugees in Pakistan was even larger and included a university for women as well as literacy classes for adults. Once the Taliban fell, Sakena moved her Afghan Institute of Learning back to Kabul, and she now provides education and other services for 350,000 women and children in Afghanistan. The institute has 480 staff members, 80 percent of them women, and it operates in seven provinces. Many of the women students at Kabul University are graduates of her programs.

The institute runs a teacher-training program, as well as workshops that focus on teaching women their legal rights both in civil law and Islamic law. That's a sensitive issue, of course, but it is more palatable to the clerics when it comes from a Muslim woman in a head scarf than from American infidels.

'Education is the key issue for overcoming poverty, for overcoming war,' Sakena says. 'If people are educated, then women will not be abused or tortured. They will also stand up and say, "My child should not be married so young."'

The institute teaches religion as well, but in a way that might horrify fundamentalists. Moderate passages from the Koran are taught, so that women can direct their husbands to passages that call for respect for women. Often it is the first time that either women or men have realized that there are such verses in the Koran.

Sakena runs an archipelago of fixed and mobile health clinics, which offer Afghans family planning services and free condoms. Another fundamental part of her work involves economic empowerment measures. 'When people have empty stomachs, they can't learn,' she says. So the institute offers classes in a range of skills that enable women to earn an income. These include sewing, embroidery, hairstyling, and computer science. Young women who can master computer skills can get jobs as soon as they graduate for $250 per month, several times what most young men earn.

Sakena has now been widely recognized for her work, and UNFPA and other groups channel assistance through her. Bill Drayton's team selected Sakena to be the first Ashoka Fellow from Afghanistan. She is indeed one of the great social entrepreneurs of Afghanistan (a perfect model for Ellaha, the young Afghan woman in jail, if she isn't murdered by her father), and constantly in danger. She shrugs it off.

'Every day there is a death threat.' She laughs. 'I'm always changing cars, changing bodyguards.' It pains her, as a pious Muslim, that some fundamentalists want to kill her in the name of Islam. She leans forward and becomes even more animated. 'From my heart, I tell you: If they were educated, they would not behave like that. The Koran has quotation after quotation that says you must treat women well. Those people who do bad things, they are not educated. I am a Muslim. My father was a good Muslim, and he prayed every day, but he did not try to marry me off. There were many offers for me when I was in the sixth grade, and he said no.

'That is why these people are afraid of educating women – they are afraid that then the women will ask questions, will speak up . . . That's why I believe in education. It is such a powerful tool to overcome poverty and rebuild the country. If we took the foreign aid that goes to guns and weapons and just took one quarter of that and put it into education, that would completely transform this country.'

Sakena shakes her head in exasperation, and adds: 'The international community should focus on education. On behalf of the women and children of Afghanistan, I beg you! If we are to overcome terrorism and violence, we need education. That is the only way we can win.'

CHAPTER TEN

Investing in Education

If you think education is expensive, try ignorance.

– DEREK BOK

As a newly married couple living in China almost twenty years ago, we came to know a scrawny thirteen-year-old girl in the hard-scrabble Dabie Mountains of central China. The girl, Dai Manju, lived with her mother, father, two brothers, and a great-aunt in a dilapidated wooden shack on a hillside, a two-hour hike from the nearest road. The family members had no electricity, no running water, no bicycle, no wristwatch, no clock, no radio – virtually no possessions of any kind – and they shared their home with a large pig. The family could afford to eat meat just once annually, to celebrate the Chinese New Year. There was almost no furniture in the dim shack except for a coffin that the father had made for the great-aunt. 'I'm healthy now,' the great-aunt explained cheerfully, 'but it's best to be prepared.'

Dai Manju's parents were elementary school dropouts and barely literate. They didn't see much point in girls getting an education. Why would a woman need to read or write when she was going to spend her days hoeing fields and darning socks? The school fee – $13 a year for elementary school – seemed a waste of the family's tattered banknotes when the money could be used for something useful, like buying rice. So when Dai Manju was entering the sixth grade, they told her to drop out of school.

A short, thin girl with stringy black hair and a timid air, Dai Manju was a head shorter than an average American thirteen-year-

Dai Manju, an unwilling sixth-grade dropout,
in front of her school in China, with her principal
(Nicholas D. Kristof)

old would be. She couldn't afford textbooks or even pencils and paper, but she was the star pupil in her grade, and she yearned to continue her education.

'My parents were ill, and they said they couldn't afford sending me to school,' she said shyly, looking at her feet and speaking so quietly she was barely audible. 'Since I am the oldest child, my parents asked me to drop out and help with the housework.' She was hanging around the school, hoping to learn something even if her parents wouldn't pay the fees, and she still dreamed of becoming the first person in her family to graduate from elementary school. The teachers doted on Dai Manju, giving her old bits of pencils and scraps of paper, hoping to support her studies, and they introduced us to her when we first visited the school. On our next visit, Dai Manju led us on a four-mile hike up a foot trail to her shack to visit her parents.

We wrote an article about her in 1990, and a sympathetic reader in New York wired us $10,000 to pay for her tuition, through his bank, the Morgan Guaranty Trust Company. We conveyed the donation to the school, which was exultant. 'Now we can educate all the children here,' the principal declared. 'We can even build a new school!' The money was indeed used to construct a much-improved elementary school and to provide scholarships for girls in the area. When a fair amount of the money had already been spent, we called the donor to give him a report.

'You were very, very generous,' we said, genuinely enthused. 'You wouldn't believe how much difference ten thousand dollars will make in a Chinese village.'

There was a startled pause. 'But I didn't give ten thousand dollars,' he said. 'I gave a hundred.'

After some investigation, it turned out that Morgan Guaranty had erred. We called up a senior Morgan Guaranty executive and asked him on the record if he intended to dispatch bankers to force children to drop out of school to make up for the bank's mistake.

'Under the circumstances,' he said, 'we're happy to make a donation of the difference.'

The villagers were mightily impressed by American generosity – and carelessness. Since Dai Manju was the one who had inspired the gift, the authorities provided her with tuition-free schooling as long as she was able to pass exams. She finished elementary school, junior high school, high school, and then the equivalent of accounting school. She found work in Guangdong Province, as an accountant for local factories. After she had worked there for a couple of years, she found jobs for friends and family members. She sent growing sums of money home to her family, so that her parents became among the richest in the village. When we made a return visit a few years ago, Dai Manju's parents were rattling around a six-room concrete house (the great-aunt had died). There was still a pig, but it lived in the old shack, which was now a barn. The family had electricity, a stove, a television, and a fan.

Dai Manju married a skilled worker – an expert in molding – in 2006 and had a baby girl the following year, when she was thirty years old. She was working as an executive in a Taiwanese electronic company in the town of Dongguan, but she was thinking of starting her own company. Her boss agreed to support her, and it seemed to offer her an opportunity to become a *dakuan*, or tycoon.

Because of all the scholarships funded by Morgan Guaranty, many other girls on the hillside had also enjoyed an unusual spurt in education and gone off to find jobs in the factories of Guangdong. They sent money back home and helped pay to educate their younger siblings, who eventually also found good jobs in coastal China. All this brought the hillside more prosperity and influence, and so a road was built to the village, going right by the new Dai home. Someday, there may be a statue there of the donor, or of Dai Manju – or of a muddled bank clerk.

That is the power of education. One study after another has shown that educating girls is one of the most effective ways to fight poverty. Schooling is also often a precondition for girls and women to stand up against injustice, and for women to be integrated into the economy. Until women are numerate and literate, it is difficult for them to start businesses or contribute meaningfully to their national economies.

Unfortunately, the impact of girls' education is quite difficult to examine statistically. Few areas of development have been more studied, but those conducting and financing the research have mostly been so convinced of the virtues of educating girls that the work hasn't been very rigorous. The methodology of such studies is typically weak, and it doesn't adequately account for cause and effect. 'The evidence, in most cases, suffers from obvious biases: educated girls come from richer families and marry richer, more educated, more progressive husbands,' notes Esther Duflo of MIT, one of the most careful scholars of gender and development. 'As such, it is, in general, difficult to account for all these factors, and few of the studies have tried to do so.' Correlation, in short, is not causation.*

Advocates also undermine the trustworthiness of their cause by

---

* Larry Summers offers an example to emphasize the distinction between correlation and causation. He notes that there is an almost perfect correlation between literacy and ownership of dictionaries. But handing out more dictionaries will not raise literacy.

cherry-picking evidence. While we argue that schooling girls does stimulate economic growth and foster stability, for example, it is also true that one of the most educated parts of rural India is the state of Kerala, which has stagnated economically. Likewise, two of the places in the Arab world that have given girls the most education were Lebanon and Saudi Arabia, yet the former has been a vortex of conflict and the latter a breeding ground for violent fundamentalists. Our own view is that these are exceptions: Kerala was held back by its anti-market economic policies, Lebanon by competing religious sects and bullying neighbors, and Saudi Arabia by a deeply conservative culture and government. But the world is complicated, and whenever we see a silver bullet we try to conduct an assay test. Education isn't always a panacea.

All those caveats noted, the case for investing in girls' education is still very, very strong. Anecdotally, we know of many women who, with education, were able to obtain jobs or start businesses and transform their lives and the lives of those around them. More broadly, it's generally accepted that one of the reasons East Asia has prospered in recent decades is that it educates females and incorporates them into the labor force, in a way that has not been true of India or Africa.

A few studies with unimpeachable methodology examined the consequences when there was a huge expansion in schooling for girls, even those from poor or conservative homes. Between 1973 and 1978, for example, Indonesia vastly increased school attendance. One study, by Lucia Breierova and Professor Duflo of MIT, suggests that this led women to marry later and have fewer children. Educating girls had more of an impact than educating boys in reducing fertility.

Similarly, Una Osili of Indiana University and Bridget Long of Harvard examined a vast expansion of primary education that began in 1976 in Nigeria. They concluded that each additional year of primary education leads a girl to have .26 fewer children – a considerable reduction. It's often said that a high school education is what's most crucial, but this study found that even elementary education has a vast impact on fertility.

The challenges are manifest: Of the 115 million children who have dropped out of elementary school, 57 percent are girls. In South and West Asia, two thirds of the children who are out of school are girls.

Americans often assume that the way to increase education is to build schools, and in some areas that is necessary. We ourselves have recently built a school in Cambodia, like those students in Seattle under Frank Grijalva, but there are drawbacks. School construction is expensive, and there is no way to verify that teachers will do their jobs. One study in India found that 12 percent of all schools were closed at any time because teachers had not gone to work that day.

One of the most cost-effective ways to increase school attendance is to deworm students. Intestinal worms affect children's physical and intellectual growth. Indeed, ordinary worms kill 130,000 people a year, typically through anemia or intestinal obstruction, and the anemia particularly affects menstruating girls. When deworming was introduced in the American South in the early twentieth century, schoolteachers were stunned at the impact: The children were suddenly far more alert and studious. Likewise, a landmark study in Kenya found that deworming could decrease school absenteeism by a quarter.

'The average American spends fifty dollars a year to deworm a dog; in Africa, you can deworm a child for fifty cents,' says Peter Hotez of the Global Network for Neglected Tropical Disease Control, a leader in the battle against worms. Increasing school attendance by building schools ends up costing about $100 per year for every additional student enrolled. Boosting attendance by deworming children costs only $4 per year per additional student enrolled.

Another cost-effective way of getting more girls to attend high school may be to help them manage menstruation. African girls typically use (and reuse) old rags during their periods, and they often have only a single torn pair of underwear. For fear of embarrassing leaks and stains, girls sometimes stay home during that time. Aid workers are experimenting with giving African teenage girls sanitary pads, along with access to a toilet where they can change them. Initial findings are that this simple approach is effective in increasing female attendance at high schools.

FemCare, the arm of Procter & Gamble that makes Tampax tampons and Always pads, started its own project to distribute free pads in Africa, but it ran into unexpected challenges. First, the girls needed a place to change their pads and clean up, but many schools lacked toilets. So FemCare began building toilets – with running water – at the schools, and that added hugely to the costs. Then the project encountered cultural taboos about blood, such as resistance to disposing of used pads in the garbage. FemCare had to make special provision for the disposal of pads, in some places even distributing incinerators. The project was an education on both sides, and the outcome was a familiar one: Because corporations want their brand to be associated only with the best, they often support gold-plated projects that are very impressive but not particularly cost-effective.

Another tantalizingly simple way to boost girls' education is to iodize salt. Some 31 percent of households in the developing world do not get sufficient iodine from water or food. The result is occasional goiters and, much more frequently, brain damage when children are still in the womb. Fetuses need iodine in the first trimester to develop proper brains, and both human and animal studies show this is particularly true of female fetuses. A study in Ecuador suggests that iodine deficiency typically shaves ten to fifteen points off a child's IQ. Worldwide, iodine deficiency alone reduces humanity's collective IQ by more than 1 billion points. According to one estimate, just $19 million would pay for salt iodization in poor countries that need it. This would yield economic benefits that another study found were nine times the cost. The result is that while salt iodization is one of the least glamorous forms of assistance possible, development geeks rave about it.

Alternatively, a capsule of iodized oil can be given every two years to all women who may become pregnant – at a cost of only fifty cents per capsule. Research by Erica Field of Harvard focused on Tanzania, where these capsules were given to women in some areas beginning in 1986. Professor Field found that daughters of those women given capsules performed markedly better in school and were significantly less likely to be held back a grade.

Still another smart strategy to expand girls' education is bribery. (Nobody uses that word, but that's what it amounts to.) One of the pioneers is Mexico, where in 1995 the deputy finance minister, Santiago Levy, was alarmed that the crash of the peso and resulting recession would be devastating to the poor. The existing antipoverty program, built around food subsidies, was inefficient and served the needs mostly of food companies. So Levy quietly organized an experimental antipoverty program far away from the capital, in Campeche, where it wouldn't arouse interest or opposition. The essence of Levy's idea was to pay poor families to keep their children in school and take them in for regular medical checkups. Records were carefully kept, tabulating the results in villages where the program was introduced and in a control sample of comparable villages. Afterward, Levy showed President Ernesto Zedillo how successful the experiment had been, and Zedillo bravely agreed to phase out food subsidies and launch the new program nationwide. The program is now called Oportunidades.

About one quarter of Mexican families are served in some way by Oportunidades, and it is one of the most admired antipoverty programs in the world. The poor get cash grants in exchange for keeping children in school, getting them immunized, taking them to clinics for checkups, and attending health education lectures. Grants range from $10 per month for a child in the third grade to $66 for a girl in high school (grants are highest for high school girls because their dropout rates are highest). The payments are made directly by the central government, to reduce local corruption, and to mothers rather than fathers. That's because research has shown that mothers are more likely to use cash for the children's benefit, and because the payments elevate the status of the mothers within the household.

Oportunidades provided for rigorous evaluation – something that is lacking in too many aid programs. In this case, outside experts get contracts to perform the evaluations, making comparisons with control villages (villages are assigned randomly either to the experiment or to the control group), so that it is possible to measure how well the program worked. The outside evaluators, the International Food Policy Research Institute, rave about the program: 'After only three years, poor Mexican children living in the rural areas where Oportunidades operates have increased their school enrollment, have more balanced diets, are receiving more medical attention, and are learning that the future can be very different from the past.' The World Bank says that the program raised high school attendance by 10 percent for boys and 20 percent for girls. Children in the program grow one centimeter taller per year than those in the control group. In essence, Oportunidades encourages poor families to invest in their children, the way rich families already do, thus breaking the typical transmission path of poverty from generation to generation. Oportunidades is particularly beneficial for girls, and some early studies suggest it will pay for itself by creating more human capital to power Mexico's economy. The program is now widely copied in other developing countries, and even New York City is experimenting with paying bribes to improve school attendance.

Bribery comes into play as well in the UN's school feeding program, run by the World Food Programme (WFP) and UNICEF and long championed by former senator George McGovern. Typically, the WFP distributes food to a rural school, and local parents provide the labor to prepare daily meals with it. All the children at that school get a free meal – usually an early lunch, on the assumption that they've had no breakfast – as well as regular deworming. In addition, girls with good attendance often get a take-home ration as an inducement to parents to keep educating them.

'This helps keep girls in school,' said Abdu Muhammad, principal of the elementary school in Sebiraso, in a remote grassy plain of Eritrea in the Horn of Africa. He watched the students lining up as parents ladled stew onto their plates, and added: 'Now students can concentrate; they can follow the lesson. And we

A school feeding in Rutshuru, Congo, encourages children to stay in school.
(Nicholas D. Kristof)

haven't had any girls drop out since the feeding program started, except for those who got married. Girls used to drop out in fifth grade.'

School feeding programs cost just ten cents per child per day, and researchers have found that they considerably improve nutrition, reduce stunting, and increase school attendance, especially for girls. But money is short, so the WFP says there are some 50 million children who could benefit from the program but don't.

The approaches we've discussed have proven effective at increasing school attendance, but there's also the question of how to increase learning once the children are in school. One especially cost-effective way to do that is to offer small scholarships to girls who do well. A study in Kenya by Michael Kremer, a Harvard economist, examined six different approaches to improving educational performance, from providing free textbooks to child sponsorship programs. The approach that raised student test scores the most was to offer the top 15 percent of girls taking sixth-grade tests a $19 scholarship for seventh and eighth grade (and the glory of recognition at an assembly). The scholarships were offered in randomly chosen schools, and girls did significantly better in those schools than in the control schools — and that was true even of less able girls who realistically had little chance of winning a scholarship. Boys also performed better, apparently because they were pushed by the girls or didn't want to endure the embarrassment of being left behind.

Aid to these kinds of programs is of proven benefit, but not all aid programs are created equal. So in the last few years, there has been a backlash against calls for more foreign aid. Skeptics such as William Easterly, a New York University professor who has long experience at the World Bank, argue that aid is often wasted and sometimes does more harm than good. Easterly has unleashed withering sarcasm at the writings of Jeffrey Sachs, the Columbia University economist who has evangelized indefatigably for more aid to fight malaria and AIDS and to help countries fight their way out of poverty. Other economists have noted that it's difficult to find any correlation between amounts of aid going to a country and development in that country. As Raghuram Rajan and Arvind Subramanian put it in a 2008 article in *The Review of Economics and Statistics*:

> We find little robust evidence of a positive (or negative) relationship between aid inflows into a country and its economic growth. We also find no evidence that aid works better in better policy or geographical environments, or that certain forms of aid work better than others. Our findings suggest that for aid to be effective in the future, the aid apparatus will have to be rethought.

We're great admirers of Bono, who has been indefatigable in support of aid for Africa and who knows the subtleties of development; he talks poverty policy as well as he sings. Yet when Bono spoke at an international conference in Tanzania in 2007, he was heckled by some Africans who insisted that aid isn't what Africa needs and that he should back off. Andrew Mwenda, a Ugandan, complained about the calamitous consequences of 'the international cocktail of good intentions.' James Shikwati of Kenya has pleaded with Western donors: 'For God's sake, please just stop.'

The skeptics make some valid points. Anybody traveling in Africa can see that aid is much harder to get right than people usually realize. In 2000, a world health conference in Nigeria set a target: By 2005, 60 percent of African children would use bed nets to protect them from malaria. In reality, only 3 percent were using bed nets in 2005. There is also a legitimate concern that aid drives up the local exchange rate of African countries, undermining business competitiveness.

Even simple interventions, such as stopping mother-to-child transmission of HIV in childbirth, are more difficult to get right than anyone sitting in an armchair in America might imagine. A $4 dose of a drug called nevirapine will normally protect a baby from infection during childbirth, so this intervention has been dubbed the low-hanging fruit of public health. But even if a pregnant woman gets an AIDS test, and even if she goes to a hospital to deliver, and even if the hospital has nevirapine and the efficiency to administer it, and even if the woman is taught not to breast-feed the baby for fear of passing the virus in her milk, and even if the hospital gives the mother a free supply of infant formula and teaches her how to sterilize the bottles – even then, the system often fails. Many women simply discard the formula in the bushes outside the hospital as they walk home. Why? Because the women feel that they simply cannot feed a baby from a bottle in an African village. Every other villager would immediately realize that they were HIV-positive and would ostracize them.

While empowering women is critical to overcoming poverty, it represents a field of aid work that is particularly challenging in that it involves tinkering with the culture, religion, and family relations of a society that we often don't fully understand. A friend of ours was involved in a UN project in Nigeria that was meant to empower women, and his experience is a useful cautionary tale. The women in this area of Nigeria raise cassava (a widely eaten root, vaguely like a potato) and use it mostly for household food, while selling the surplus in the markets. When the women sold the extra cassava, they controlled the money, so the aid workers had a bright idea: *If we give them better varieties of cassava, they'll harvest more and sell more. Then they'll make more money, and then spend it on their families.* Our friend described what came next:

> The local women's variety of cassava produced 800 kilos per hectare, and so we introduced a variety that got three tons per hectare. The result was a terrific harvest. But then we ran into a problem. Cassava was women's work, so the men wouldn't help them harvest it. The women didn't have time to harvest such huge yields, and there wasn't a capacity to process that much cassava.
>
> So we introduced processing equipment. Unfortunately, this variety of cassava that we had introduced had great yields, but it also was more bitter and toxic. Cassava always produces a little bit of a cyanide-related compound, but this variety produced larger amounts than normal. So the runoff after processing had more cyanide, and we had to introduce systems to avoid contaminating ground water with cyanide – that would have been a catastrophe.
>
> So we dealt with that, and finally the project looked very successful. The women were making a lot of money on their cassava. We were delighted. But because the women were making so much, the men came in and kicked the women out of the cassava fields. The tradition was that women raise staple crops, and men raise cash crops. And the men reasoned that if cassava was so profitable, it must now be a man's crop. And so the men took over cassava, and they used the profits for beer. The women had even less income than when we started.

So let's freely acknowledge that Murphy's Law plays a role in the aid world. Foreign assistance is difficult to get right, and it sometimes is squandered. Yet it is equally clear that some kinds of aid do work; those that have been most effective have involved health and education. In 1960, 20 million children died before the age of five. By 2006, that figure had dropped below 10 million, thanks to campaigns for vaccination, sanitation, and oral rehydration to treat diarrhea. Think about that: *An extra 10 million children survive each year now, an extra 100 million per decade.* That's quite a success to weigh alongside the many failures of aid. Likewise, through his philanthropic efforts, Jimmy Carter has almost succeeded in wiping out guinea worm, an ancient parasite that has afflicted humans throughout recorded history.

Or consider the $32 million that the United States invested over ten years in the global battle to eradicate smallpox. Some 1.5 million people once died annually from smallpox; since it was eradicated in 1977, about 45 million lives have been saved. That's an astonishing total. And the United States recoups its $32 million investment in smallpox every two months, simply because Americans no longer need to pay to be vaccinated against it. Because of the money saved by eradication, that investment has yielded a 46 percent annual return in the three decades since smallpox was eradicated – a better investment than any stock in that period.

Ann and Angeline

Angeline Mugwendere's parents were impoverished farmers in Zimbabwe, and she was mocked by classmates when she went to school barefoot and in a torn dress with nothing underneath. Teachers would sternly send her home to collect school fees that were overdue, even though everyone knew there was no way her family could pay them. Yet Angeline suffered the humiliations and teasing and pleaded to be allowed to remain in school. Unable to buy school supplies, she cadged what she could.

'At break time, I would go to a teacher's house and say, "Can I wash your dishes?"' she remembers. 'And in return, they would sometimes give me a pen.'

At the end of primary school, she took the nationwide sixth-grade graduation examinations and had the best score not only in her school, but in the entire district – in fact, one of the highest marks in the nation. Yet she could not afford to go to secondary school. She was inconsolable. Angeline was destined to be another farmer or village peddler, another squandered African asset. Local people have a saying for it: *Those who harvest the most pumpkins are the ones who lack the pots to cook them.* In other words, the brightest children are often born into families that lack the means to educate them.

At that moment, though, Angeline's career intersected with that of Ann Cotton, a Welsh woman – 'very Welsh!' she says – trying to help girls in Zimbabwe. Ann has a finely tuned social conscience, nurtured as she grew up in Cardiff surrounded by family stories of mining and political struggle. She absorbed a passion for education and set up a center for schoolgirls with behavior problems. But her life found a deeper focus only after tragedy struck.

After a smooth pregnancy, Ann gave birth to her second child, a daughter named Catherine. The baby seemed healthy, and they returned home from the hospital. When Catherine was ten days old, a midwife came for a routine visit to check on the baby. She told Ann to rush the child to the hospital, that her life was in danger. At the hospital, a team standing by with a mobile oxygen tent took Catherine and placed her inside.

Catherine, it turned out, had a congenital lung defect. The alveoli, which transmit oxygen from the lungs into the blood, were not supplying her bloodstream with adequate amounts of oxygen. So the little girl's heart and lungs were failing. For the next six weeks, Catherine lived in an oxygen tent. Ann, her husband, and her son more or less lived in the hospital, becoming close with many other young parents whose children were in danger.

'Such agony!' Ann recalls. 'I have never felt so helpless. As a mother I was powerless to help my daughter. It was the greatest pain I have ever experienced.' The doctors and nurses worked heroically to save Catherine's life, but they couldn't.

'All we knew when she died was that we would honor her life and all she had taught us,' Ann says. But how to honor her wasn't clear. Ann's life was soon hectic with another boy and girl, for a total of three surviving children. Then Ann's husband took a job in the high-tech industry in Boston, and since Ann couldn't get a work permit under American visa rules, she enrolled in Boston University to study international relations. That revived her academic interests, and Ann later began a master's program in human rights and education at the University of London's Institute of Education.

As part of her program, Ann set off on a three-week visit to a particularly poor part of Zimbabwe, to research the low school attendance rates there among girls. The conventional wisdom was that for cultural reasons, many African families resisted sending daughters to school, and Ann brought along stacks of questionnaires and notepaper to probe that resistance. She focused on a school in a village called Mola, talking to children, parents, and

Ann Cotton reading to children in one of her schools in Zambia (Camfed)

school officials. She quickly realized that the big challenge wasn't culture, but poverty. Families didn't have the money to buy books and pay school fees for all their children, so they gave preference to their sons because it was more likely that boys could use the education to get good jobs afterward.

Ann was stirred by the determination of Zimbabwean girls to get schooling. She met two teenage sisters, Cecilia and Makarita, who had hiked sixty miles to Mola because it was cheaper than the school near their home. They invited Ann into the makeshift hut they had built, and they confessed that they didn't know where the money would come from to attend school the next term. It all reminded Ann of her grandmother's stories of Wales in harsher times, and it made her feel a kinship with these girls in the Tonga tribe in a remote nook of Zimbabwe. She imagined her own children enduring such deprivation.

'I was confronted by a level of poverty I had never before seen,' Ann says. She promised the local people that she would find a way to support girls' education. Village chiefs and school officials were enthusiastic, and they held a community meeting in which they pledged grassroots support for an initiative to educate girls – if Ann could help defray the costs.

Upon her return to her home in Cambridge, England, Ann was obsessed by the memories of those girls she had met. She and her husband started their own fund and asked friends and relatives for donations to pay the school fees for girls in Mola, but that wasn't enough. Ann is not an enthusiastic cook and had never done anything commercial, but she started making sandwiches and cakes at her kitchen table and peddling them in a stall at Cambridge Market, to raise funds for the girls. It was not a brilliant financial success: One freezing February day, Ann and two friends stood all day in the cold and brought back just £30.

Ann managed to raise enough money that first year to send thirty-two girls to high school, and their parents followed through on their pledges to support their daughters and make sure they attended school faithfully. Two years later, Ann turned her efforts into a formal organization, the Campaign for Female Education, or Camfed. One of the first girls whom Ann supported was Angeline; she went on to high school and, to nobody's surprise, performed brilliantly.

Camfed has expanded from Zimbabwe into Zambia, Tanzania, and Ghana, and it has won honors for its successes, enabling it to raise more money and expand further. Camfed's budget is still tiny compared to the big agencies – $10 million annually – but it now helps more than 400,000 children attend school each year. Right from the start, Camfed had only local staff in each country. There's a strong emphasis on ensuring that the community buys into the program, and it is a committee from the local community that chooses the girls who will get scholarships. Camfed staff review the decisions to make sure that there is no corruption. Moreover, Camfed has avoided the cult of personality that afflicts some aid groups. Camfed's Web site is about the schoolgirls, not about Ann, and there isn't a word about her baby Catherine, who inspired it all. We had to pry that out of Ann.

These kinds of grassroots efforts usually achieve more than the grand UN conferences that receive far more attention. We highlight Camfed partly because we believe an international women's movement needs to focus less on holding conventions or lobbying for new laws, and more time in places like rural Zimbabwe, listening to communities and helping them get their girls into schools.

For Camfed, support for a child typically begins when she is in elementary school, as part of a broad program to support needy students. Then, when the girls graduate from primary school, Camfed offers a full support package for high school, including shoes and a uniform if necessary. If a student lives too far from a high school, Camfed helps arrange for her to live in a dormitory and covers the costs. Camfed also supplies sanitary pads and underwear to all the girls, so that they do not miss school during their menstrual periods.

Ann and others have had to face the additional problem of sexual abuse by teachers. Particularly in southern Africa, some teachers trade good grades for sex: Half of Tanzanian women, and nearly half of Ugandan women, say they were abused by male teachers, and one third of reported rapes of South African girls under the age of fifteen are by teachers. 'If a girl feels that if she goes and talks to the teacher in private, she'll be fondled, then she's not going to do well,' Ann says. She also notes that Westerners sometimes create problems by sponsoring scholarships to be awarded by teachers or the principal. The scholarship winners are sometimes the prettiest girls, who in return are expected to sleep with the principal. Camfed avoids this problem by having the girls selected by a committee, without giving a central role to the principal.

Camfed supports its girls after they graduate from high school in starting a business or learning a skill such as nursing or teaching. Or, if they achieve sufficiently high grades, they are supported through college. Camfed has also started microfinance operations, and some of the girls are starting dairy farms or other businesses. Camfed alumni have also formed a social network, trading ideas and engaging in public advocacy on behalf of women's rights.

In Zimbabwe, for example, the graduates have banded together to call for tougher action against sexual abuse of girls. The graduates have also pushed to discourage routine virginity testing of teenage girls (a traditional practice to promote chastity), as well as campaigned against arranged marriages. In Ghana, a Camfed graduate named Afishetu was the only woman running in the district assembly elections in 2006 – and she won. Now she has her eye on a seat in the national parliament.

Perhaps the greatest surprise is that Camfed alumni have themselves become philanthropists. Even though their incomes are tiny by Western standards, they still support other schoolgirls. Ann says that Camfed's high school graduates are each helping an average of five other girls at any one time, not counting their own family members, whom they also support.

'They are becoming real role models in their communities,' Ann says. 'It may be that the neighbor's child can't go to school because she doesn't have a skirt, so she'll provide that. Or maybe she'll pay another girl's school fees. This was something that we didn't expect at all. It shows the power of education.'

Speaking of role models and the power of education, Camfed Zimbabwe has a new and dynamic executive director. She's a young woman who knows something about overcoming long odds and the impact a few dollars in tuition assistance can make in a girl's life.

It's Angeline.

CHAPTER ELEVEN

Microcredit: The Financial Revolution

It is impossible to realize our goals while discriminating against half the human race. As study after study has taught us, there is no tool for development more effective than the empowerment of women.

– KOFI ANNAN,
THEN UN SECRETARY-GENERAL, 2006

Saima Muhammad would dissolve into tears every evening. She was desperately poor, and her deadbeat husband was unemployed and not particularly employable. He was frustrated and angry, and he coped by beating Saima each afternoon. Their house, in the outskirts of Lahore, Pakistan, was falling apart, but they had no money for repairs. Saima had to send her young daughter to live with an aunt, because there wasn't enough food to go around.

'My sister-in-law made fun of me, saying, "You can't even feed your child,"' Saima recalled. 'My husband beat me up. My brother-in-law beat me up. I had an awful life.'

Sometimes Saima would take the bus to the market in Lahore, an hour away, to try to sell things for money to buy food, but that only led her neighbors to scorn her as a loose woman who would travel by herself. Saima's husband accumulated a debt of more than $3,000, and it seemed that this debt would hang over the family for generations. Then, when Saima's second child was born and turned out to be a girl as well, her mother-in-law, a crone named Sharifa Bibi, exacerbated the tensions.

Saima in front of her remodeled home near Lahore, Pakistan
(Nicholas D. Kristof)

'She's not going to have a son,' Sharifa told Saima's husband, in front of her. 'So you should marry again. Take a second wife.' Saima was shattered and ran off sobbing. Another wife might well devastate the family finances and leave even less money to feed and educate the children. And Saima herself would be marginalized in the household, cast off like an old sock. For days Saima walked around in a daze, her eyes red, and the slightest incident would send her collapsing into hysterical tears. She felt her whole life slipping away.

It was at that point that Saima joined a women's solidarity group affiliated with a Pakistani microfinance organization called Kashf Foundation. Saima took out a $65 loan and used the money to buy beads and cloth, which she transformed into beautiful embroidery to sell in the markets of Lahore. She used the profit to buy more beads and cloth, and soon she had an embroidery business and was earning a solid income – the only one in her household to do so. Saima brought her eldest daughter back from the aunt and began paying off her husband's debt.

When merchants wanted more embroidery than Saima could produce, she paid neighbors to work for her. Eventually thirty families were working for Saima, and she put her husband to work as well – 'under my direction,' she explained with a twinkle in her eye. Saima became the tycoon of the neighborhood, and she was able to pay off her husband's entire debt, keep her daughters in school, renovate the house, connect running water to the house, and buy a television.

'Now everyone comes to me to borrow money, the same ones who used to criticize me,' Saima said, beaming in satisfaction. 'And the children of those who used to criticize me now come to my house to watch TV.'

A round-faced woman with thick black hair that just barely peeks out from under her red-and-white-checked scarf, Saima is now a bit plump and displays a gold nose ring as well as several other rings and bracelets on each wrist. She dresses well and exudes self-confidence as she offers a grand tour of her home and work area, ostentatiously showing off the television and the new plumbing. She doesn't even pretend to be subordinate to her husband. He spends his days mostly loafing around, occasionally helping with the work but always having to take orders from his wife. He is now more impressed with females in general: Saima had a third child, also a girl, but that's not a problem. 'Girls are just as good as boys,' he explained.

'We have a good relationship now,' said Saima. 'We don't fight, and he treats me well.' And what about finding another wife who might bear him a son? Saima chuckled at the question: 'Now nobody says anything about that.' Sharifa Bibi, the mother-in-law, looked shocked when we asked whether she wanted her son to take a second wife to bear a son. 'No, no,' she said. 'Saima is bringing so much to this house . . . She's an exemplary daughter-in-law. She puts a roof over our heads and food on the table.'

Sharifa even allows that Saima is now largely exempt from beatings by her husband. 'A woman should know her limits, and if not then it's her husband's right to beat her,' Sharifa said. 'But if a woman earns more than her husband, it's difficult for him to discipline her.'

Saima's new prosperity has also transformed the family's educational prospects. She is planning to send all three of her daughters through high school, and maybe to college as well. She brings in tutors to improve their schoolwork, and her eldest child, Javaria, is ranked first in her class. We asked Javaria what she wanted to become, thinking she might aspire to be a doctor or lawyer.

Javaria cocked her head. 'I'd like to do embroidery,' she said.

Saima is an unusually successful participant in the microcredit revolution sweeping the developing world. In place after place, markets and microlending are proving a powerful system to help people help themselves. Microfinance has done more to bolster the status of women, and to protect them from abuse, than any laws could accomplish. Capitalism, it turns out, can achieve what charity and good intentions sometimes cannot.

Kashf is typical of microfinance institutions in that it lends almost exclusively to women, in groups of twenty-five, who guarantee one another's debts and meet every two weeks to make their payments and discuss a social issue. Topics include family planning, schooling for girls, or *hudood* laws used to punish rape victims. The meetings are held in the women's homes, in rotation, and they create a 'women's space' where they freely discuss their concerns. Many Pakistani women are not supposed to leave the house without their husbands' permission, but husbands tolerate the insubordination because it is profitable. The women return with cash and investment ideas, and over time they earn incomes that make a significant difference in household living standards. Typically, the women start small, but after they have repaid the first loan in full they can borrow again, a larger amount. This keeps them going to the meetings and exchanging ideas, and it builds the habit of dealing with money and paying debts promptly.

'Now women earn money and so their husbands respect them more,' said Zohra Bibi, a neighbor of Saima who used Kashf loans to buy young calves that she raises and sells when they are grown. 'If my husband starts to hit me, I tell him to lay off or next year I won't get a new loan. And then he sits down and is quiet.'

*

Kashf is the brainchild of Roshaneh Zafar, a Pakistani woman who sounds more like a banker than an aid worker. Roshaneh grew up in a wealthy, emancipated family of intellectuals who allowed her to study at the Wharton School at the University of Pennsylvania and later earn her MA in development economics at Yale. Many of Roshaneh's friends in Pakistan and at Wharton wanted to get rich, but she wanted to save the world, and so she joined the World Bank.

'I didn't want to create wealth for people who were already wealthy,' Roshaneh said. 'I thought I would go to the World Bank and make a difference. But it was like screaming against the wind. Everywhere we went, we would tell people to use better hygiene. And they would say: "You think we're stupid? If we had money, we would." I wondered what we were doing wrong. We had megamillion-dollar projects, but the money never got down to the villages.'

Then Roshaneh happened to find herself seated at a dinner next to Muhammad Yunus, the ebullient Bangladeshi professor who much later won the 2006 Nobel Peace Prize for pioneering microfinance. Yunus wasn't famous then, but he was attracting interest in development circles for starting Grameen Bank, which championed loans for poor women. Roshaneh had heard stories of Yunus's success and quizzed him over dinner. He talked animatedly about Grameen's work, and it was exactly the kind of pragmatic grassroots effort that she yearned to join. So Roshaneh took a leap of faith: She quit her job at the World Bank and wrote a letter to Yunus telling him that she wanted to become a microfinancier. He promptly sent her an air ticket to Bangladesh. Roshaneh spent ten weeks there, studying the work of Grameen. Then she returned to Lahore and set up the Kashf Foundation that helped Saima.

Kashf means 'miracle,' and at first it seemed a miracle would be needed to make it work. Pakistanis told Roshaneh that microfinance was impossible in a conservative Muslim country like Pakistan, that women would never be allowed to borrow. In the summer of 1996, she started combing poor neighborhoods, looking for clients. Roshaneh discovered, to her horror, that women were reluctant to take money. 'We went from door to door,

Roshaneh Zafar, the founder of Kashf, with clients in a village
(Nicholas D. Kristof)

attempting to convince women to start a credit relationship with us,' she recalled. Finally, Roshaneh found fifteen women willing to borrow and handed out 4,000 rupees ($65) to each of them.

Roshaneh brought in another dynamic Pakistani woman, Sadaffe Abid, who had studied economics at Mount Holyoke College. Roshaneh and Sadaffe made a striking pair: Well educated, well connected, well dressed, and beautiful, they prowled through poor villages looking to ordinary Pakistanis more like movie stars than anyone's idea of bankers. And for all their brilliance, Roshaneh and Sadaffe ran into difficulties because they had no intimate knowledge of the poverty they were trying to defeat.

'We only had one hundred clients, and thirty of them were delinquent,' Sadaffe remembers. Relentlessly empirical, focused on refining their business model, Roshaneh dispatched Sadaffe to be branch manager in a poor village. But even that proved difficult. 'Nobody would rent to us, because we were an NGO [a nongovernmental organization] and an NGO full of women,' Sadaffe said. Many Pakistanis also believed that no unmarried woman of honor would leave her parents' home and live on her own, so the Kashf women staff attracted leers and frowns. In later years, Roshaneh had to bend to reality and hire some male branch heads, because it is so difficult to find women willing to relocate to poor villages.

Roshaneh and Sadaffe spent their first few years tweaking the business model. Because delinquent loans were a problem, they began tracking loan payments daily rather than weekly. A loan officer began doing basic checking on a client's creditworthiness: Does she buy from the local grocery store on credit? Does she pay utility bills? But mostly the model depended on lending to a group of twenty-five women who would all be responsible if any one of them defaulted. That meant that those women did their own screening, for fear of admitting a weak link.

Finally, Kashf had a system in which virtually 100 percent of loans were repaid in full – if not by the borrower, then by other members of the group. Kashf then began expanding rapidly, more than doubling each year since 2000.

Kashf also began offering life insurance and health insurance, as well as home improvement loans. Roshaneh wanted to require that legal title to the home be transferred to the wife before the home improvement loan could be extended, but transfer of title in Pakistan turned out to require 855 steps and five years. So instead, Kashf requires the husband to sign a document pledging that he will never evict his wife, even if he divorces her.

Roshaneh was selected to be one of the early Ashoka Fellows, working with Bill Drayton. That put her in touch with other social entrepreneurs around the globe, building connections and exchanging ideas. By 2009, Kashf had 1,000 employees and 300,000 clients and was aiming for 1 million clients by 2010. Roshaneh cultivated a cadre of skilled female managers, with management training programs and sessions drilling staff in the 'seven habits of highly effective people.'

Kashf also started a bank, so that it could accept deposits as well as make loans. People usually think of microfinance in terms of loans, but savings are perhaps even more important. Not all poor people need loans, but all should have access to savings accounts. And if the family savings are in the woman's name, and thus in her control, that gives her more heft in family decision-making.

An in-house evaluation concluded that by the time the borrowers have taken their third loan, 34 percent have moved above the poverty line in Pakistan. A poll found that 54 percent said their husbands respected them more, and 40 percent said they had fewer fights with their husbands over money. As for the sustainability of the underlying business model, Roshaneh says crisply: 'Our return on equity is seven and a half percent.'

While microfinance has been exceptionally successful in parts of Asia, it remains an imperfect solution. Women's microbusinesses grow more slowly than men's, according to some studies, presumably because women are supposed to work from home and look after children at the same time – and these constraints also make it difficult for women-run businesses to graduate to a larger scale.

Moreover, microfinance hasn't worked nearly so well in Africa as it has in Asia. That may be because it is newer there and the models haven't been adjusted, or because populations are more rural and dispersed, or because the underlying economies are growing more slowly and so investment opportunities are fewer. Poor health and unexpected deaths from AIDS, malaria, and childbirth also create loan delinquencies that undermine the model. And the 'micro' refers to the amount of the loan, not to the interest rate: It's expensive to make small loans, and so borrowers often must pay annual interest rates of 20 or 30 percent – a bargain compared to commercial money-lenders, but a level that is horrifying to Americans or Europeans. The interest rate is fine when the money is pumped into a profitable new business, but if the money isn't invested soundly, then the borrowers become trapped in mounting debts. Then they are worse off than before – and we've heard of that happening to women in Kashf's programs.

'Microfinance is not a panacea,' Roshaneh says. 'You need health. You need education. If I were prime minister for a day, I would put all our resources in education.'

Not everybody can walk away from an international financial career like Roshaneh and Sadaffe and start an institution like Kashf. But absolutely anybody can join them in arranging microloans to needy women like Saima – by going to a Web site, www.kiva.org. Kiva is the brainchild of a young tech-savvy American couple, Matt and Jessica Flannery, who visited Uganda and saw the power of microfinance there. They knew that Americans would like to lend if only they knew the recipient, so Matt and Jessica thought: Why can't a Web site make the connection directly? That's when they started Kiva. If you go to the Kiva Web site, you see people all over the world who want to borrow to finance small businesses. Those would-be borrowers are vetted by a local on-the-ground microfinance organization.

A donor funds a Kiva account with a credit card, and then browses among the possible borrowers on the site to figure out to whom to lend money; the minimum loan is $25. Our own Kiva portfolio at the moment consists of loans to a pancake saleswoman in Samoa, an Ecuadorian single mother who has turned part of her home into a restaurant, and a woman furniture maker in Paraguay.

One reason microloans are almost always made to women, rather than to men, is that females tend to suffer the most from poverty. Mortality data show that in famines and droughts, it is mostly girls who die, not boys. A remarkable study by an American development economist, Edward Miguel, found that in Tanzania, extreme rainfall patterns – either droughts or flooding – are accompanied by a doubling in the numbers of unproductive old women killed for witchcraft, compared to normal years (other murders do not increase, only those of 'witches'). The weather causes crop failures, leading to worsening poverty – and that's when relatives kill elderly 'witches' whom they otherwise would have to feed.

Another reason for making women and girls the focus of antipoverty programs has to do with an impolitic secret of global poverty: Some of the most wretched suffering is caused not just by low incomes, but also by unwise spending – by men. It is not uncommon to stumble across a mother mourning a child who has just died of malaria for want of a $5 mosquito bed net and then find the child's father at a bar, where he spends $5 each week. Several studies suggest that when women gain control over spending, less family money is devoted to instant gratification and more for education and starting small businesses.

Because men now typically control the purse strings, it appears that the poorest families in the world typically spend approximately ten times as much (20 percent of their income on average) on a combination of alcohol, prostitutes, candy, sugary drinks, and lavish feasts as they do on educating their children. The economists Abhijit Banerjee and Esther Duflo examined spending among the very poor (those who earn less than $1 a day in some countries, less than $2 a day in others) in thirteen nations. They found that these impoverished families spent 4.1 percent of their money on alcohol and tobacco in Papua New Guinea; 5 percent in Udaipur, India; 6 percent in Indonesia; and 8.1 percent in Mexico. In addition, in Udaipur, the median household allocated 10 percent of its annual budget to weddings, funerals, or religious festivals, often involving conspicuous consumption. Ninety percent of South Africans spent money on festivals, as did a majority of people in Pakistan, Ivory Coast, and Indonesia. Roughly 7 percent of the total spending of the poorest people in India's Maharashtra State went to sugar. Go to little village shops in Africa or Asia, and you'll see plenty of candy for sale, but rarely vitamins or mosquito nets. There's no precise data, but in much of the world even some of the poorest young men, both single and married, spend considerable sums on prostitutes.

Among the poor in Udaipur, people seem by any measure to be malnourished. Sixty-five percent of men have a body mass index that makes them underweight by World Health Organization standards. Only 57 percent of adults said they had enough to eat throughout the year, and 55 percent are anemic. Yet, at least in Udaipur, the malnutrition could in most cases be eliminated if families bought less sugar and tobacco.

In contrast to the profligate spending on sugar and alcohol, the most impoverished families on the globe appear to spend about 2 percent of their incomes educating their children, even though that is the most reliable escalator out of poverty. If poor families spent only as much on educating their children as they do on beer and prostitutes, there would be a breakthrough in the prospects of poor countries. Girls, since they are the ones kept home from school now, would be the biggest beneficiaries.

Perhaps it seems culturally insensitive to scold the poor for indulging in festivals, cigarettes, alcohol, or sweets that make life more fun. Yet when resources are scarce, priorities are essential. Many African and Indian men now consider beer indispensable and their daughters' education a luxury. The service of a prostitute is deemed essential; a condom is a frill. If we're trying to figure out how to get more girls in school, or how to save more women from dying in childbirth, the simplest solution is to reallocate spending.

One way to do that is to put more money in the hands of women. One early pair of studies found that when women hold assets or gain incomes, family money is more likely to be spent on nutrition, medicine, and housing, and consequently children are healthier.

In Ivory Coast, one study focused on the different crops that men and women grow for their private kitties: men grow coffee, cocoa, and pineapple, and women grow plantains, bananas, coconuts, and vegetables. Some years the 'men's crops' have good harvests and the men are flush with cash; in other years it is the women who prosper. Money is to some extent shared. But even so, Professor Duflo found that when the men's crops flourish, the household spends more money on alcohol and tobacco. When the women have good crops, the households spend more money on food, particularly beef. Several other studies also suggest that women are more likely than men to invest scarce cash in education and small businesses.

In South Africa, one study examined the impact on child nutrition when the state pension system was extended to blacks after the collapse of apartheid. Suddenly many grandparents received a significant cash infusion (topping out at $3 per day, or twice the local median income). When the pensions went to grandfathers who cared for children, the extra cash had no impact on the children's height or weight. But when the pension went to a grandmother, there was a major impact. In particular, the granddaughters grew significantly in both height and weight, and such girls became taller and heavier than girls raised by grandfathers. That suggests that if one purpose of cash transfers is to improve the health of children, it's better to direct the transfers to women than to men.

Half a world away, in Indonesia, a woman continues to control economic assets that she brought into a marriage. A study found that if the wife has brought more resources into the marriage – and thus has more spending money afterward – then her children are healthier than those of families of equal wealth where the assets belong to the man. What matters to the children's well-being isn't so much the level of the family's wealth as whether it is controlled by the mother or by the father. As Duflo says:

> When women command greater power, child health and nutrition improves. This suggests that policies seeking to increase women's welfare in case of divorce or to increase women's access to the labor market may impact outcomes within the household, in particular child health . . . Increasing women's control over resources, even in the short run, will improve their say within the household, which will increase . . . child nutrition and health.

One implication is that donor countries should nudge poor countries to adjust their laws to give more economic power to women. For example, it should be routine for a widow to inherit her husband's property, rather than for it to go to his brothers. It should be easy for women to hold property and bank accounts, and countries should make it much easier for microfinance institutions to start banks. Women now own just 1 percent of the world's titled land, according to the UN. That has to change.

To its credit, the U.S. government has pushed for these kinds of legal changes. One of the best American foreign aid programs is the Millennium Challenge effort, and it has nudged recipients to amend legal codes to protect women. For example, Lesotho wanted Millennium Challenge money but did not allow women to buy land or borrow money without a husband's permission. So the

United States pushed Lesotho to change the law, and in its eagerness to get the funding it did so.

It may be politically incorrect to note these kinds of gender differences, but they are obvious to aid workers and national leaders alike. Botswana has been one of the fastest-growing countries in the world for decades, and its former president, Festus Mogae, was widely regarded as one of Africa's most able leaders. He laughed when we suggested delicately that women in Africa typically work harder and handled money more wisely than men, and he responded:

> You couldn't be more right. Women do work better. Banks were the first to see that and hired more women, and now everybody does. In homes, too, women manage affairs better than men. In the Botswanan civil service, women are taking over. Half of the government sector is now women. The governor of the central bank, the attorney general, the chief of protocol, the director of public prosecution — they are all women . . . Women perform better in Africa, much better. We see that in Botswana. And their profiles are different. Deferred consumption is higher among girls, and they buy durables and have higher savings rates. Men are more consumption oriented.

Some development experts hope to see more women enter politics and government, with the idea that they can do for their countries what they do for a household. Eighty-one countries have set aside certain positions for women, typically a share of seats in parliament, to boost their political participation. Eleven countries now have women as top leaders, and women hold 16 percent of national legislative seats around the world, up from 9 percent in 1987.

A former member of the U.S. Congress, Marjorie Margolies-Mezvinsky, has led a promising effort to get more women into governments around the world. In 1993, Margolies-Mezvinsky was a newly elected Democrat in the House of Representatives when the Clinton budget – complete with tax increases to balance the accounts – came before the chamber. In retrospect, that budget is often seen as a landmark that put America on a solid fiscal footing for the 1990s, but it was ferociously controversial at the time. As a newly elected member, Margolies-Mezvinsky was vulnerable, and Republicans vowed to defeat her if she voted for the tax increases. Yet in the end she cast the deciding vote for the Clinton budget. A year later, she was indeed defeated, by a slim margin. Her career as a politician was over.

Now Margolies-Mezvinsky runs Women's Campaign International, which coaches women grassroots activists on how to get attention for their causes, run for office, and put together coalitions to achieve their goals. In Ethiopia, where Women's Campaign International trained women to run effective campaigns, the proportion of women in parliament rose from 8 percent to 21 percent.

One rationale for seeking more female politicians is that women supposedly excel in empathy and forging consensus and thus may make, on average, more peaceful and conciliatory leaders than men. Yet we don't see much sign that women presidents or prime ministers have performed better, or more peacefully, than men in modern times. Indeed, women leaders haven't even been particularly attentive to issues like maternal mortality, girls' education, or sex trafficking. One reason may be that when women rise to the top of poor countries – think of Indira Gandhi, Benazir Bhutto, Corazón Aquino, Gloria Macapagal-Arroyo – they are almost always from elite families and have never directly encountered the abuses that poor women suffer.

On the other hand, the conventional wisdom in development circles is that women officeholders do make a difference at the local level, as mayors or school board members, where they often seem more attentive to the needs of women and children. One fascinating experiment took place in India after 1993, when the Indian constitution was amended to stipulate that one third of the positions of village chief were to be reserved for women. These were allocated randomly, so it became possible to compare whether villages run by women were governed differently from those ruled by men. Indeed, spending priorities were different. In villages run by women, more water pumps or taps were installed, and these were also better maintained. This may be because fetching water is women's work in India, but other public services were also judged to be at least as good as in men-run villages. The researchers could find no sign that other kinds of infrastructure were being neglected. Local people reported that they were significantly less likely to have to pay a bribe in the villages run by women.

Nevertheless, both male and female villagers declared themselves less satisfied with women leaders. The scholars conducting the study were puzzled by this: Services appeared to be superior, yet dissatisfaction was greater. It wasn't just male chauvinists who were upset; women villagers were also more dissatisfied. It seemed that ordinary citizens were discomfited by women leaders forced upon them, or resented the fact that the women leaders were less educated and experienced on average than male leaders. This does suggest that women politicians, at least in India, face a hurdle: Even if they do better than men at providing services, they initially are judged more harshly.

Follow-up research did find that after a village had once had a female leader, this bias against women chiefs disappeared. Women leaders were then judged by gender-neutral standards. Such research suggests that quotas for local female leaders may be worthwhile, because they overcome the initial hurdle that blocks women candidates. An Indian-style quota of women officeholders seems to break down gender barriers so that afterward the political system becomes more democratic and open.

Whatever the impact of women as leaders, we have some direct evidence from America's own history of the broad consequences of female political participation. As we noted earlier, maternal mortality in the United States declined significantly only once women gained the right to vote: When women had a political voice, their lives also became a higher priority. In addition, there is strong evidence that when women gained the vote, the political system responded by allocating more funds to public health programs, particularly for child health, because this was an issue that women voters were perceived as caring about strongly. Grant Miller, a scholar at Stanford University, has conducted a brilliant study of the health response when, state by state, women obtained the right to vote. He found that when women gained the vote, the politicians in that state scrambled to win favor from women voters by allocating more funds to child health care; this did not happen in states where women remained unable to vote. 'Within a year of suffrage law enactment, patterns of legislative roll call voting shifted, and local public health spending rose by roughly 35 percent,' Professor Miller wrote. 'Child mortality declined by 8–15 percent with the enactment of suffrage laws . . . Nationwide, these reductions translate into roughly 20,000 averted child deaths each year.'

The same thing happened at a national level. A year after the Nineteenth Amendment gave women all across the country the right to vote in 1920, Congress passed the Sheppard-Towner Act, a landmark program for public health. The 'principal force moving Congress was fear of being punished at the polls' by the new women voters, one historian wrote. The improvement in America's health during this period was stunning: The mortality rate for children aged one to four plummeted 72 percent between 1900 and 1930, although there are many other reasons for this decline as well, of course. As Professor Miller notes, opponents of women's political participation have often made the argument that if women get involved in outside activities, then children will suffer. In fact, the evidence from our own history is that women's political participation has proved to be of vast, life-saving benefit to America's children.

A CARE Package for Goretti

The lush landscape of northern Burundi constitutes one of the loveliest spots in Africa, with jutting hills looming over dark green fields and coffee trees swaying in the breezes. The climate is more pleasant here than in the lowlands, and the mud-walled huts are sparse. Yet this picturesque land is home to some of the most impoverished people on the planet, and one of the most forlorn of these was Goretti Nyabenda.

Goretti was largely a prisoner in her hut, which was made of red adobe clay. Women here are supposed to get their husband's permission each time they leave the property, and her husband, a grouchy man named Bernard, didn't like to give it. Goretti was thirty-five years old and a mother of six, but she wasn't even allowed to go to the market by herself.

Bernard and Goretti grew bananas, cassava, potatoes, and beans on a depleted half-acre plot, but they barely earned enough to survive. They were too poor to afford mosquito nets for all the children, even though malaria kills many people in the area. Bernard typically goes three times a week to a bar to drink homemade banana beer, spending $2 a session. His trips to the bar cost the family 30 percent of its disposable income.

Goretti, who had never been to school, was not permitted to buy anything, or to deal with cash at all. In her entire life, she had never touched even a one-hundred-franc note, worth less than ten American cents. She and Bernard would walk together to the market to shop, he would hand over the money to the seller, and then she would carry the goods home. Goretti's interactions with Bernard consisted mostly of being beaten, interspersed with having sex.

When we talked, she sat on a grass mat behind her hut. It was a sunny day, but the air was pleasantly cool and refreshing, and a chorus of insects serenaded her. Goretti was wearing a brown knit shirt – some American had donated it to charity and it had migrated to central Africa – over a colorful yellow wraparound skirt. She keeps her hair close-cropped, almost in a crew cut, because it is easier to manage that way, and she frowned as she described her mood: 'I was wretched. Because I always stayed in the house, I didn't know other people and I was all on my own. My husband said a wife's job is to cook, stay in the house, or work in the fields. I lived that way, so I was frustrated and angry.'

Then Goretti's mother-in-law told her about a program started in the village by CARE, the venerable American aid organization that has focused increasingly on the needs of women and girls. Eagerly, Goretti asked Bernard if she could go to one of the CARE meetings in the village. 'No,' Bernard said. Goretti sulkily stayed home. Then her grandmother began telling her how wonderful CARE was, reviving her longing to participate. Goretti pleaded with Bernard, and he continued to refuse. Then, one day, Goretti went without his permission. Bernard was initially furious, but Goretti had been careful to prepare dinner early and to attend to his every need.

CARE's program operates with 'associations' of about twenty women each. So with her grandmother and other women anxious to get involved, Goretti formed a new CARE association. The members promptly elected Goretti as their president. Often the members work together, cultivating one family's field one day and another's the next time. So the twenty women all came to Goretti's fields and tilled her entire parcel of land in one day.

'When my husband saw this, he was very happy,' Goretti said slyly. 'He said, "This group is really good." So he let me continue.'

Each woman brings the equivalent of a dime to each meeting. The money is pooled and loaned to one of the members, who must invest it in a money-making effort and then repay the sum with interest. In effect, the women create their own bank. Goretti borrowed $2, which she used to buy fertilizer for her garden. That was the first time she handled money. The fertilizer produced an excellent crop of potatoes that Goretti was able to sell over several days in the market for $7.50. So after just three months Goretti paid off her loan ($2.30, including interest), and the capital was then loaned to another woman.

Flush with cash from her potatoes, Goretti used $4.20 of the remaining profit to buy bananas to make banana beer, which sold very well in the market. That led her to launch a small business making and selling banana beer. When it was her turn to borrow again, Goretti took out another $2 loan to expand her beer business, and then she used the profits to buy a pregnant goat. The goat had its kid a month later, so Goretti now has two goats as well as her beer business. (At night, she brings the goats into the hut so that no one can steal them.)

Bernard looks longingly at Goretti's jars of banana beer, but she insists that he must not touch it – it is for sale, not consumption. Since Goretti is making money for the household, he grudgingly restrains himself. Her status rose when Bernard caught malaria and needed to be hospitalized. Goretti used the money she earned from selling beer, along with a loan from her CARE association, to pay the bill.

'Now Bernard doesn't bother me,' Goretti says. 'He sees that I can do things, so he asks my opinions. He sees that I can contribute.' The association members also use their meetings to trade tips on how to manipulate husbands, as well as to learn how to raise animals, to resolve family conflicts, and to start businesses. Visiting nurses provide health education, teaching the women when to take children for vaccinations, how to detect STDs, and how to avoid HIV. The women were also given the chance to take HIV tests, and Goretti tested negative.

'Before, some of the women here were sick with STDs, but they didn't know it,' Goretti says. 'Now they have been cured. I got injections for family planning, and if I'd known about this earlier, I wouldn't have had six kids. Maybe just three. But if I hadn't been in the group at all, I would have wanted ten kids.'

The CARE meetings are also teaching women to go to a hospital to give birth, and then to register the babies so that they have legal IDs. A vast challenge for girls in many countries is that they never get birth certificates or other legal documents, and so in official eyes they don't exist and aren't eligible for government assistance. There is a growing recognition in the aid community that a system of national ID cards, difficult to counterfeit, would help protect girls from being trafficked and would make it easier for them to get health services.

More fundamentally, women in the CARE program learn that appropriate behavior for a female doesn't consist of hanging back, that they can contribute at meetings and take firm positions. 'This was a culture where women couldn't speak,' Goretti said. 'There was an expression: "A hen cannot speak in front of a rooster." But now we can speak up. We're part of the community.' Many of the women, including Goretti, are also attending special literacy classes through CARE; she painstakingly wrote her name for us to show that she could.

The men here in northern Burundi tend to focus their efforts on the big local cash crop, coffee – either growing it themselves or working as paid-laborers on the plantations. At the end of the harvest, flush with cash, many men traditionally use the money to take what is called a second wife – a mistress, often just a teenager, who stays until the money runs out. The second wives are paid in clothing and jewelry, and they are a big drain on household income as well as an avenue for the spread of AIDS. Now, however, the women in the CARE program are trying to eradicate this tradition. If the husband of any woman in the association tries to take on a second wife, the other wives band together in a vigilante group and drive the mistress away. Sometimes they then go to the husband and announce that they are fining him $10; if they sound authoritative enough, he sometimes pays up, and the money goes into the association's coffers.

In a sign of how much times have changed, Bernard now goes to Goretti to ask for cash. 'I don't always give it to him, because we need to save,' she said. 'But sometimes I give him some. He allowed me to join the group and that gave me joy, so I want him

Goretti with her goats in front of her home in Burundi
(Nicholas D. Kristof)

to have the chance to have fun as well.' And Goretti has stopped asking permission every time she leaves the house. 'I do tell him when I'm going out,' she explained. 'But I inform him; I don't ask.'

Goretti is planning further expansion of her business. She wants to breed goats for sale, while continuing to peddle her beer. Plenty can still go wrong: Bernard may get jealous and take it out on her; wild animals could kill her goats; a drought could destroy her crops and leave her with debts; continued instability in Burundi could lead armed groups to pillage her crops. And all the beer she is making may simply turn more local men into drunkards. This rural microfinance model can help families, but there are limits.

Yet so far, so good – and the program is a bargain. CARE pays out less than $100 per woman over the three-year life of the project (after that, Goretti graduates, and the project begins in a new area). That means it costs a donor sixty-five cents a week to help Goretti. It improves life for her, but it also means that Burundi now has another person contributing to GNP. Likewise, Goretti's children now have money for pens and notebooks to further their education, as well as a model of what a woman can become.

'She has changed,' said Pascasie, Goretti's eldest child, a sixth-grade girl. 'Now if Dad isn't home, she can go to the market and buy us something that we need.'

As for Bernard, he was a bit reluctant to be interviewed, perhaps realizing that he was being cast for the least flattering role in the family drama. But after a bit of casual chatter about banana prices, he acknowledged that he was happier with a partner than he had been with a servant. 'I see my wife making money now, and bringing cash into the house,' he said. 'I have more respect for her now.'

It's possible that Bernard was just telling us what we wanted to hear. But Goretti is gaining a reputation as a husband-tamer, so she is in increasing demand. 'Now if there's a conflict in the neighborhood, I'm asked to help,' Goretti said proudly. She added that she wanted to become even more active in community projects and attend more village meetings. Bernard was listening and looked horrified, but Goretti wasn't fazed.

'Before, I underestimated myself,' Goretti said. 'I wouldn't say anything to anybody. Now I know I have good ideas, and I tell people what I think.'

CHAPTER TWELVE

The Axis of Equality

A woman has so many parts to her body, life is very hard
indeed.

– LUXUN, 'ANXIOUS THOUGHTS ON
"NATURAL BREASTS"' (1927)

We've been chronicling the world of impoverished women,
but let's break for a billionaire.

Zhang Yin is a petite, ebullient Chinese woman who started
her career as a garment worker, earning $6 a month to help sup-
port her seven siblings. Then, in the early 1980s, she moved to
the special economic zone of Shenzhen and found a job at a paper
trading company partly owned by foreigners. Zhang Yin learned
the intricacies of the paper business, and she could have stayed
and risen in the firm. But she is a restless, ambitious woman,
buzzing with entrepreneurial energy, so she struck out for Hong
Kong in 1985 to work for a trading company there. The company
went bankrupt within a year. Zhang Yin then started her own
company in Hong Kong, buying scrap paper there and shipping
it to firms throughout China. She soon realized that the grand
arbitrage opportunity was between waste paper in the United
States and in China. Since China has few forests, much of its
paper is made from straw or bamboo and is of execrable quality.
That made recyclable American scrap paper, derived from wood
pulp and worth very little locally, a valuable commodity in
China – particularly as industrialization led to soaring demand for
paper.

Working with her husband, a Taiwanese, Zhang Yin at first bought American scrap paper through intermediaries, but in 1990 she moved to Los Angeles and began to work out of her home. She drove around California in a used Dodge minivan, visiting garbage dumps and making arrangements to obtain their scrap paper. The dumps were happy to make deals with her.

'I had to learn from scratch,' Zhang Yin said. 'The business was just my husband and me, and I didn't speak a word of English.' She was able to ship scrap paper back to China cheaply, because ships were bringing toys and clothing from China to California ports but returning mostly empty. As Chinese demand for paper soared, Zhang Yin built up her company, and in 1995 she returned to China to open a paper-making plant in the southern boomtown of Dongguan. Her plants make containerboard, which is used to make corrugated cardboard boxes for Chinese exports.

Zhang Yin's recycling company in California, called America Chung Nam, is now the biggest American exporter to China by volume. Her Chinese paper manufacturer, Nine Dragons Paper, has more than five thousand employees, and she has grand ambitions for it. 'My goal is to make Nine Dragons, in three to five years, the leader in container-boards,' she told our *New York Times* friend David Barboza. 'My desire has always been to be the leader in an industry.'

By 2006, Zhang Yin had a net worth of $4.6 billion and topped some lists of China's richest people. She was arguably the world's richest self-made woman, although market turmoil later sent her net worth plunging and threatened her operations. In any case, there is something larger going on here: By the reckoning of the Huron Report, which tries to track China's wealth, six of the ten richest self-made women in the world are now Chinese.

All this reflects the way China has established a more equal playing field for women. In a larger sense, China has emerged as a model on gender issues for developing countries: It evolved from repressing women to emancipating them, underscoring that cultural barriers can be overcome relatively swiftly where there is the political will to do so. A broad range of countries around the world – Rwanda, Botswana, Tunisia, Morocco, Sri Lanka – have likewise made rapid progress in empowering women. Challenges remain, but these countries remind us that gender barriers can be dismantled, to the benefit of men and women alike.

We sometimes hear people voice doubts about opposition to sex trafficking, genital cutting, or honor killings because of their supposed inevitability. What can our good intentions achieve against thousands of years of tradition?

One response is China. A century ago, China was arguably the worst place in the world to be born female. Foot-binding, child marriage, concubinage, and female infanticide were embedded in traditional Chinese culture. Rural Chinese girls in the early twentieth century sometimes didn't even get real names, just the equivalent of 'No. 2 sister' or 'No. 4 sister.' Or, perhaps even less dignified, girls might be named Laidi or Yindi or Zhaodi, all variations of 'Bring a younger brother.' Girls were rarely educated, often sold, and vast numbers ended up in the brothels of Shanghai.

So was it cultural imperialism for Westerners to criticize foot-binding and female infanticide? Perhaps. But it was also the right thing to do. If we believe firmly in certain values, such as the equality of all human beings regardless of color or gender, then we should not be afraid to stand up for them; it would be feckless to defer to slavery, torture, foot-binding, honor killings, or genital cutting just because we believe in respecting other faiths or cultures. One lesson of China is that we need not accept that discrimination is an intractable element of any society. If culture were immutable, China would still be impoverished and Sheryl would be stumbling along on three-inch feet.

The battle for women's rights in China was as bitter as it is today in the Middle East, and there were setbacks. Chinese social conservatives were furious when young women began to cut their hair, saying that this made women look like men. In the late 1920s, street thugs would sometimes seize a woman with short hair and pull out all of her hair or even cut off her breasts. *If you want to look like a man,* they said, *this will do it.*

Communism after the 1949 revolution was brutal in China, leading to tens of millions of deaths by famine or repression, but its single most positive legacy was the emancipation of women. After taking power, Mao brought women into the workforce and the Central Committee of the Communist Party, and he used his political capital to abolish child marriage, prostitution, and concubinage. It was Mao who proclaimed: 'Women hold up half the sky.'

There were some setbacks for women with the death of ideology and the rise of a market economy in the 1980s, and Chinese women still face challenges. Even college-educated women experience discrimination in finding jobs, and sexual harassment is widespread. A Chinese cabinet minister once mistook Sheryl for a local secretary and tried to force himself on her; she got her revenge when she wrote about the incident in our book *China Wakes*. Concubinage has returned with *er nai*, or No. 2 wives, and China has millions of prostitutes again (although, in contrast to India, they mostly enter the business by choice). The combination of the one-child birth control policy and convenient access to ultrasound testing means that parents routinely check the sex of a fetus and get an abortion if it is female. The sex ratio of newborns is 116 boys for every 100 girls, meaning that many poor men will never be able to marry; this will be a source of future instability. Sadly, neither economic development nor the rise of education and a middle class seems to have affected the predilection for aborting female fetuses.

All that said, no country has made as much progress in improving the status of women as China has. Over the past one hundred years, it has become – at least in the cities – one of the best places to grow up female. Urban Chinese men typically involve themselves more in household tasks like cooking and child care than most American men do. Indeed, Chinese women often dominate household decision-making, leading to the expression '*qi guan yan*,' or 'the wife rules strictly.' And while job discrimination against women is real, it has less to do with sexism than with employers being wary of China's generous maternity benefits.

We could see the progress in Sheryl's ancestral village in southern China. When Sheryl's maternal grandmother was five years old, her mother tried to make her beautiful by wrapping cloth bandages around her feet from her toes to her heels, starting a process that would crush the tiny bones so that she could display dainty three-inch feet called golden lotuses. These were considered sensual: Nineteenth-century Chinese had far more erotic words for women's feet than for their breasts. Sheryl's grandmother stripped off the bandages after she moved with her husband to Toronto, but it was too late. She became the matriarch of seven strong-willed children but hobbled until the end of her life in tiny shoes, walking like a slim penguin on short stilts.

By the time we began visiting China, foot-binding had disappeared, but village women still mostly accepted second-class citizenship, pleading with the Goddess of Mercy for a son and sometimes drowning their own daughters after birth. Yet the spread of education and job opportunities for young women led to a rapid recalibration of perceptions concerning gender. Educating and empowering girls is certainly the right thing to do, but, most important in the eyes of many families, it is profitable! China has enjoyed a virtuous circle in which, once girls had economic value, parents invested more in them and gave them greater autonomy.

Chinese women are also making inroads in fields that were once overwhelmingly male. The majority of math and chemistry students in China are still male, but the edge is slimmer than in the United States. Chess is one of the most male-dominated pursuits all around the world, and that is also true in China – but women there are catching up more than elsewhere. In 1991, Xie Jun became the first women's world chess champion from China, and since then two other Chinese women – Zhu Chen and Xu Yuhua – have succeeded her. Moreover, a girl named Hou Yifan may be the greatest talent ever in women's chess. At the age of fourteen in 2008, she narrowly lost in the finals for the women's world championship, and she is still improving rapidly. If any female now playing is to wrest the title of world chess champion from men, it is likely to be her.

China is an important model because it was precisely its emancipation of girls that preceded and enabled its economic takeoff. The same is true of other rapidly growing Asian economies. As Homi Kharas, an economist who has worked on these issues for the World Bank and the Brookings Institution, advised us:

> Engineering an economic takeoff is really about using a nation's resources most efficiently. Many East Asian economies enjoyed a sustained boom by moving young peasant women from farms to factories, after giving them a basic education for free. In Malaysia, Thailand, and China, export-oriented industries like garments and semi-conductors predominantly employed young women who had previously been working in less productive family farms or doing household work. The economies got multiple benefits from this transition. By improving the labor productivity of the young women, growth was raised. By employing them in export industries, the countries got foreign exchange which could be used to buy needed capital equipment. The young women saved much of their money or sent it back to relatives in the village, raising national saving rates. Because they had good jobs and income-earning opportunities, they also delayed marriage and childbearing, lowering fertility and population growth rates. So a major factor in East Asia's economic success was the contribution of its young peasant female workforce.

It's no accident that the countries that have enjoyed an economic takeoff have been those that educated girls and then gave them the autonomy to move to the cities to find work. In contrast, it would be difficult to imagine – at least for the moment – millions of rural Pakistani or Egyptian teenage girls being fully educated and then allowed to move to the cities while still single to take up jobs and power an industrial revolution.

Leading Indian business executives have noted that one of their country's weaknesses is that it does not employ women as efficiently as China, and they are trying to rectify that. Azim Premji, chairman of Wipro Technologies, a leading technology company, notes that 26 percent of Wipro's engineers are now female. His foundation, the Azim Premji Foundation, focuses on getting more village girls in school – partly to help those individuals, but also because the result will be lower fertility and a more capable labor force to power the economy as a whole.

Implicit in what we're saying about China is something that sounds shocking to many Americans: Sweatshops have given women a boost. Americans mostly hear about the iniquities of garment factories, and they are real – the forced overtime, the sexual harassment, the dangerous conditions. Yet women and girls still stream to such factories because they're preferable to the alternative of hoeing fields all day back in a village. In most poor countries, women don't have many job options. In agriculture, for example, women typically aren't as strong as men and thus are paid less. Yet in the manufacturing world, it's the opposite. The factories prefer young women, perhaps because they're more docile and perhaps because their small fingers are more nimble for assembly or sewing. So the rise of manufacturing has generally raised the opportunities and status of women.

The implication is that instead of denouncing sweatshops, we in the West should be encouraging manufacturing in poor countries, particularly in Africa and the Muslim world. There is virtually no manufacturing for export in Africa (aside from Mauritius and small amounts in Lesotho and Namibia), and one of the ways we could help women in Egypt and Ethiopia would be to encourage factories for the export of cheap shoes or shirts. Labor-intensive factories would create large numbers of jobs for women, and they would bring in more capital – and gender equality.

The United States has established a terrific program to promote African exports by reducing tariffs on them. It's called the African Growth and Opportunity Act, or AGOA, and it's an effective aid program that never gets adequate attention or support. If Western countries wanted to do something simple that would benefit African women, they would merge AGOA with the European equivalent, called Everything But Arms. As the Oxford University economist Paul Collier has noted, that merger of standards and bureaucracies would create a larger common market for tariff-free import of African manufactured goods. That would constitute a significant incentive to locate factories in Africa, boosting employment and giving Africans a new channel to help themselves.

Almost halfway around the world, a country very different from China is also emerging as a model on gender issues. Rwanda is an impoverished, landlocked, patriarchal society that still lives in the shadow of the 1994 genocide in which 800,000 people were slaughtered in one hundred days. Most of the killers were from the Hutu tribe and most of the victims from the minority Tutsi tribe, and tribal tensions remain a challenge to the country's stability. Yet somehow from this infertile, chauvinistic soil has emerged a country in which women now play an important economic, political, and social role – in a way that hugely benefits Rwanda as a whole. Rwanda is consciously implementing policies that empower and promote women – and, perhaps partly as a result, it is one of the fastest-growing economies in Africa. In some respects, in everything but size, Rwanda is now the China of Africa.

In the aftermath of the genocide, 70 percent of Rwanda's population was female, and so the country was obliged to utilize women. But it was more than necessity. Men had discredited themselves during the genocide. Women were just minor players in the slaughter, so that only 2.3 percent of those jailed for the killings were female. As a result, there was a broad sense afterward that females were more responsible and less inclined to savagery. The country was thus mentally prepared to give women a larger role.

Paul Kagame, the rebel leader who defeated the *genocidaires* and became Rwanda's president, wanted to revive his country's economy and saw that he needed women to do that. 'You shut that population out of economic activity at your peril,' he told us, as his press secretary – a woman – looked on approvingly. 'The decision to involve women, we did not leave it to chance,' he added. 'In the constitution, we said that women have to make up 30 percent of the parliament.'

Kagame speaks fluent English, meets regularly with Americans, and perhaps realized that it would be helpful to brand Rwanda as an equal-opportunity country. Rwanda's cabinet room, which is more high-tech than its equivalent in the White House, frequently echoes with women's voices. Kagame regularly has appointed strong women to cabinet posts and other top positions. Women now hold the positions of president of the supreme court, minister of education, mayor of Kigali, and director of Rwanda television, while at the grassroots level many women played major roles in village reconstruction. By 2007 Rwanda surpassed Sweden to become the nation with the highest share of women members of any parliament in the world – 48.8 percent of its seats in the lower house. Then, in September 2008, a new election left Rwanda the first country with a majority of female legislators – 55 percent in the lower house. In contrast, 17 percent of members of the United States House of Representatives were women in 2008, leaving the United States ranked sixty-eighth among countries of the world in the share of women holding national political office.

Rwanda is one of a number of poor countries – others include Costa Rica and Mozambique – that have at least one third female total representation in parliament. Rwanda is also one of the least corrupt, fastest-growing, and best-governed countries in Africa.

Countries like Rwanda and China have shown that governments can nurture women and girls in ways that boost economic development. In such countries with good governance and equal opportunities, Western help is often particularly effective.

Murvelene Clarke was a forty-one-year-old woman in Brooklyn who felt a vague desire to be more civic-minded and to devote more of her income to charity. She was earning $52,000 a year working at a bank and thought she had plenty to meet her own needs. 'I heard about tithing, where you give ten percent of your income to the church,' Murvelene explained. 'I'm not a member of a church, but I thought I, too, should give ten percent of my income to charity.'

One priority for Murvelene was a charity that spent little on administrative expenses. So she went online and spent several hours browsing the charities that received the top rating – four stars – from Charity Navigator, a Web site that evaluates charities on their efficiency. Charity Navigator is not a perfect guide, because its focus is on overhead rather than impact, but it's a useful starting point. Murvelene came across an organization called Women for Women International, and she liked what she saw. It's a sponsorship organization that enables an American to support a particular woman in a needy country abroad. Murvelene, a black woman of Jamaican ancestry, liked the idea of sponsoring an African woman. So she signed up, agreeing to pay $27 a month for a year, and asked to be connected to a woman in Rwanda.

Murvelene was paired with Claudine Mukakarisa, a twenty-seven-year-old genocide survivor from Butare, Rwanda. Extremist Hutus had targeted her family, which was Tutsi, and she was the only survivor. Claudine had been kidnapped at the age of thirteen, along with her older sister, and had been taken to a Hutu rape house. 'They started sexually violating both of us,' Claudine explained in a shy, pained monotone when we talked with her, 'and then they started beating us.'

Large numbers of militia members came to the house, patiently lining up to rape the women. This went on for days, and of course there was no medical attention. 'We had started rotting in our reproductive organs, and maggots were coming out of our bodies,' Claudine said. 'Walking was almost impossible. So we crawled on our knees.' When Kagame's army defeated the *genocidaires,* the Hutu militia fled to Congo – but took Claudine and her sister along as well. Militia members killed her sister but finally let Claudine go.

'I don't know why I was released and my sister killed,' she said, shrugging. Probably it was because she was pregnant. Claudine was puzzled by her swelling belly, as she still had no idea about the facts of life. 'I had thought I could not get pregnant, because I had been told that a girl becomes pregnant only if she is kissed on the cheek. And I had never been kissed.'

Still only thirteen years old and very pregnant, Claudine trekked around the country trying to find help. She gave birth by herself in a parking lot. Unable to see how she would ever feed the baby, and hating its unknown father for having raped her, Claudine abandoned it to die.

'But my heart wouldn't allow me to do that,' she said. 'So I went back and picked up my baby.' Claudine begged for food in the streets, and she and the baby barely survived. 'Many people would chase me away,' she said, 'because I was stinking.' Claudine is quiet, demure, soft-spoken; her lip quivers occasionally as she tells her story in flat tones, but she is not obviously emotional. Her overriding characteristic is the determination to survive with her child.

After several years of this, an uncle took Claudine in, but he demanded sex from her in exchange for shelter. When she became pregnant again, he kicked her out. Over time, Claudine found that she could get jobs gardening or washing clothes, typically earning about $1 for a day's work. She managed to send her two children to school, but only barely: The fees were $7 per child per term, and so she and her children lived from day to day.

Murvelene's sponsorship gave new hope to Claudine and her children. Of Murvelene's $27 monthly payment, $12 goes to training programs and other support efforts, and $15 is given directly to Claudine. The managers coach the women to save – partly to build a habit of microsavings, and partly to have a cushion when they graduate from the program in a year's time – and so Claudine saves $5 each month and spends $10. Some of the $10 goes to paying her children's school fees and buying food, but Claudine devotes some to buying a large bag of charcoal, used for cooking. She sells it bit by bit at a retail markup to other poor families.

In addition, Claudine goes to the Women for Women compound each morning for classes. Mondays, Wednesdays, and Fridays are devoted to vocational training, to teach the women skills that will bring them an income for the rest of their lives. Claudine is learning beadwork, so that she can make embroidery

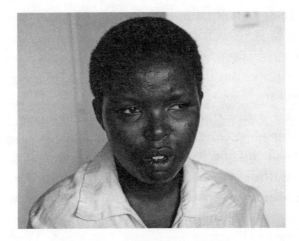

Claudine at a Women for Women meeting in Rwanda (Nicholas D. Kristof)

to sell either on her own or through Women for Women (the aim is for the embroidery to be sold in posh New York department stores). Other women learn how to use reeds to weave baskets or placemats, or, if they are really talented, they study sewing so that they can work as tailors. A tailor can earn $4 a day, a respectable income in Rwanda; those with other skills earn somewhat less. On Tuesdays and Thursdays, the women attend classes on health, literacy, or human rights. One aim is to make the women more assertive and less accepting of injustices.

Claudine and Murvelene write each other letters, and Murvelene sent Claudine pictures of New York City, to show her where she lived. Claudine and her children studied these pictures with fascination, as if they were viewing another planet.

Nine months after sponsoring Claudine, Murvelene was laid off. She laughed when we asked her if she had second thoughts about her sponsorship commitment to Claudine. 'I never regretted it for a moment,' she said. 'If I'm lucky enough to be able to help her, and she can lift herself out of the position she's in, and lift up her family members or other people around her, to me that's really important. And for me, it was a way to get out of myself. A lot of times, you forget how fortunate you are here, never really needing anything.'

237

Since being laid off, Murvelene has had freelance jobs, and she continues to allocate 10 percent of her income to charity. 'Any freelance money I get, or if somebody gives me a gift, I keep a running total in my head and think, "Okay, I've got to give so much." It's not so hard.'

Claudine is also thriving, and she feels immense gratitude toward Murvelene for giving her and her children this opportunity. It helps that the Rwandan economy is booming, creating more opportunities for Women for Women graduates. But Rwanda is flourishing precisely because it has figured out how to turn people like Claudine into economic assets.

Tears over Time Magazine

Zainab Salbi is thin with olive skin and close-cropped black hair framing large, luminous eyes. She looks like central casting's idea of a free-spirited Middle Eastern princess, and she speaks English with a tinge of a foreign accent reflecting her childhood in Iraq. Zainab grew up in Baghdad in the period shaped by the long Iran-Iraq war, always fearful of attacks, raised by a father who was a pilot and a mother who was an unusually emancipated woman trained in biology. But the crucial factor for Zainab's family was that both parents were close to Saddam Hussein. Her father was Saddam's personal pilot, and Zainab grew up calling Saddam uncle and spending weekends at his house, playing with his children.

That meant privileges and gifts, including a new car from Saddam each year, but also constant, gnawing fear. Proximity did not equal protection, and any slip could mean disaster for the entire family. One of Zainab's friends at school was the daughter of a senior official who was dragged out of a meeting on television and then executed; the daughter became a pariah. Zainab heard whispered stories of Saddam and his sons raping girls and of intelligence agents videotaping women as they were being raped and then blackmailing the victims afterward.

'He was a poison gas,' Zainab told Sheryl in a long conversation in Zainab's office in Washington, D.C. 'We breathed him slowly, sometimes dying slowly.' Yet Saddam was always courtly and helpful to Zainab, even squiring her around and giving her tours of his property. One time, when she didn't have a bathing suit and everyone else was swimming, he offered her his dishdasha, or robe, to wear so she could join in the fun. She demurred, thinking it might be too transparent when wet. He insisted. She kept refusing.

Then, when Zainab was a university student, her mother abruptly and bizarrely pushed Zainab into a marriage with an Iraqi man living in America. 'All of a sudden, when I'm age twenty, my mother begs me to accept a marriage proposal from the United States,' Zainab recalled. 'She begged and cried and said, "Please listen to me!" I wanted to be a good daughter and so I came to the United States.'

Zainab barely knew her husband, who was much older, and who soon proved abusive and distant. After three months of marriage, he became violent, threw her facedown on the bed, and raped her. That's when Zainab walked out on him. The first Gulf War had erupted in the meantime, however, so she couldn't go home. Instead, Zainab remained in the United States, bitterly resenting her mother for having pushed her into a failed marriage and terrified that the American authorities would figure out how close her family was to Saddam. 'I decided that I would never tell anyone I knew Saddam Hussein,' she said, and she kept her secret.

Slowly, life improved. Zainab met and married a gentle Palestinian doctoral student named Amjad. They planned a delayed honeymoon in Spain and saved up for it. Iraq receded from her life. Then, in 1993, when Zainab was twenty-four and had been married to Amjad for six months, they were visiting a friend. While Amjad and the friend were in the kitchen, preparing dinner, Zainab idly picked up a *Time* magazine and read an article about rape camps in Bosnia. Serbian soldiers were gang-raping women as part of a military strategy to terrorize the population. The article was accompanied by a photo of some of the women, and it struck such a chord inside Zainab that she burst into tears. Amjad came running in, alarmed. Zainab shoved the article in his face. 'We have to do something!' she said. 'I have to do something to help these women.'

Zainab called around to humanitarian organizations to see if she could volunteer to help women in Bosnia, but she couldn't find a single group working with the rape victims. She started telephoning around again, offering to set up a program. A Unitarian church

Zainab Salbi visiting the Women for Women staff in Rwanda (Trish Tobin)

agreed to hear her proposal. She walked into the church's board meeting with her father-in-law's briefcase, thinking it would make her look older. With the support of the church, Zainab and Amjad turned their basement into the operations center for a new group that they called Women for Women in Bosnia. They frantically began networking and fund-raising, donating the money they had set aside for a delayed honeymoon to Spain. The women in Bosnia needed it more.

Soon Zainab flew to the Balkans and began meeting women who had been raped by Serb soldiers. Her first meeting was with a woman named Ajsa, who had been released from a rape camp when she was eight months pregnant – too late to get an abortion.

For three years, Zainab and Amjad struggled to build their organization while taking university courses. Every dime they raised went to the four hundred women in their organization, leaving them barely anything to pay bills or to feed themselves. Zainab was just about to give up and look for a paying job when a check – for $67,000 – arrived in the mail. Working Assets, a phone company that donates 1 percent of its sales to charity, had chosen Zainab to receive the gift, and it rescued the organization. Over time the group evolved into Women for Women International, working with survivors not only in Bosnia but in war-torn countries all over the world.

Zainab's next break came in 2000, when Oprah Winfrey put her on her show for the first of seven interviews. Women for Women International began to thrive, building up a major international network of supporters and a $20 million budget. But Zainab still kept secret her association with Saddam.

One day in the spring of 2004, Zainab was in Bukavu in eastern Congo. She was talking to a woman named Nabito, who described how rebels had raped her and her three daughters, the youngest of them just nine years old. The rebels even ordered one of Nabito's teenage sons to rape her. When he didn't, they shot him in the feet. She told all this to Zainab and then said: 'I never told anybody but you this story.'

Zainab was horrified. 'What should I do?' she asked. 'Should I keep it a secret or tell the whole world?'

'If you can tell the whole world and prevent it from happening again, then do so,' Nabito said. Later that day, on the drive back to Rwanda, Zainab cried. She wept all five hours as her driver navigated the bumpy dirty roads. She cried again back at her room in the guest house. That night, in her room, she resolved that if Nabito could tell embarrassing secrets, then so could she. Zainab decided to reveal her own rape by her former husband, her family's relationship with Saddam, and another secret she had absorbed only recently.

Zainab's mother, in failing health, had come to America for a checkup, and Zainab had finally dared talk about the anger she had nursed since her first marriage. Zainab spoke of how betrayed she had felt when her supposedly liberated mother rushed her into an ultimately abusive marriage with an older man she barely knew. Why, she asked her mother, had she urged that marriage?

Zainab's mother had lost her voice by then and could communicate only by writing notes. Through tears, she scribbled her response: 'He wanted you, Zainab. I didn't see any other way.' The 'he' was Saddam Hussein. He had lusted after Zainab, and her parents had been terrified that Saddam would seize Zainab and keep her as a mistress until he found a new toy.

So, inspired by Nabito, Zainab began telling her full story, every seedy part of it. 'The irony was that I run a program that encourages women to communicate, but I didn't communicate for a long time,' Zainab said. 'Now, I do.'

Women for Women International is effective because it touches people at the grassroots level. This kind of bottom-up approach in development work has repeatedly shown its superiority in bringing about economic and social change. Meanwhile, far away in West Africa, someone else was using a similar grassroots approach to defeat one of the most ghastly and deeply embedded traditions that harms girls, genital cutting.

CHAPTER THIRTEEN

Grassroots vs. Treetops

Are women human yet? If women were human, would we
be a cash crop shipped from Thailand in containers into New
York's brothels . . .? Would our genitals be sliced out to
'cleanse' us . . .? When will women be human? When?

– CATHERINE A. MACKINNON, *Are Women Human?*

Approximately once every ten seconds, a girl somewhere in
the world is pinned down. Her legs are pulled apart, and a
local woman with no medical training pulls out a knife or razor
blade and slices off some or all of the girl's genitals. In most cases,
there is no anesthetic.

Well-meaning Westerners and Africans alike have worked for
decades to end this practice. Yet a growing number of mothers
were still arranging for their daughters to be cut. Now, finally, in
just the last few years, groups of grassroots activists have cracked
the code. Led by an Illinois woman who has lived more than half
her life in Senegal, these activists seem to have figured out how
cutting can be ended, and their movement is snowballing.
Incredibly, it looks as if they will make female genital cutting in
West Africa go the way of foot-binding in China. That makes the
campaign against genital cutting a model for a larger global movement for women in the developing world. If we want to move
beyond slogans, we would do well to learn the lessons of the long
struggle against genital cutting.

Today, female genital cutting is practiced mostly by Muslims in
Africa, though it is also found in many Christian families in Africa.

It is not found in most Arab or Islamic cultures outside Africa. The custom goes back to ancient times, and some female mummies in ancient Egypt have cut genitals. Soranos of Ephesus, a Greek physician who wrote a pioneering book on gynecology in the second century, stipulated:

> A large clitoris is a symptom of turpitude; in fact, [such women] strive to have their own flesh stimulated just like men and to obtain sexual intercourse, as it were. Now, you will perform the surgical operation on her in the following way. Placing her lying on her back with the feet closed, one should hold in place in a small forceps that which protrudes and appears to be larger and cut it back with a scalpel.

A German textbook on surgery from 1666 includes illustrations on how to amputate the clitoris, and the practice occurred regularly in England until the 1860s – even occasionally after that in Europe and America. Across a broad swath of northern Africa, the practice is still nearly universal. Worldwide, some 130 million women have been cut, and after new research, the UN now estimates that 3 million girls are cut annually in Africa alone (the previous estimate had been 2 million globally). The custom occurs on a smaller scale in Yemen, Oman, Indonesia, and Malaysia; among some Bedouin Arabs in Saudi Arabia and Israel; and among Bohra Muslims in India and Pakistan. The practice varies greatly. In Yemen, girls are typically cut within two weeks of birth, while in Egypt it can occur in the early teenage years.

The aim is to minimize a woman's sexual pleasure and hence make her less likely to be promiscuous. The most common form of cutting involves snipping the clitoris or clitoral hood (sometimes leaving the clitoris intact and more exposed, an incompetent approach that increases opportunities for orgasm). In Malaysia, the ritual sometimes involves no more than a pinprick, or simply the waving of a razor blade near the genitals. But in Sudan, Ethiopia, and Somalia, it is common to see the most extreme kind, in which the entire genital area is 'cleaned up' by snipping away the clitoris, labia, and all external genitalia. This creates a large raw wound, and the vaginal opening is then typically sewn up with a wild thistle (leaving a small opening for menstrual blood), with the legs tied together so that the wound can heal. This is called infibulation, and when the woman is married, her husband or a midwife uses a knife to reopen the sealed part so that she can have intercourse. Edna Adan, the midwife in Somaliland who runs her own maternity hospital, has been surveying all the women who have come to deliver over the years: 97 percent of them were cut, and virtually all of them infibulated. Edna showed us a video she took of an eight-year-old girl undergoing infibulation; it is excruciating to watch.

Traditional birth attendants do the genital cutting in some countries, while in Senegal and Mali it is often a woman who belongs to the blacksmith caste. Cutters mostly have learned the technique from their mothers or grandmothers, and often they don't use clean blades or can't stop the bleeding. Some girls die or suffer lifelong injuries, but there is no data; a girl who dies after being cut is usually said to have succumbed to malaria. A World Health Organization study found that cutting leads to scar tissue that makes childbirth more dangerous, particularly with the more extreme forms of cutting.

Beginning in the late 1970s there was a Western-led campaign against cutting. Previously the practice had been referred to as female circumcision, but that was considered euphemistic, so critics branded it female genital mutilation, or FGM. The United Nations took up that terminology, and international conferences were convened to denounce FGM. Laws against FGM were passed in fifteen African countries, articles were written, meetings were held – and not much changed on the ground. Guinea passed a law in the 1960s that punishes female genital cutting with a life sentence of hard labor – or, if the girl dies within forty days of being cut, a death sentence. Yet no case has ever come to trial, and 99 percent of Guinean women have been cut. In Sudan, the British first passed a law against infibulation in 1925 and extended that to all cutting in 1946. Today, more than 90 percent of Sudanese girls are cut.

'This is our culture!' a Sudanese midwife declared angrily when we asked about cutting. 'We all want it. Why is it America's business?' The midwife said that she regularly cut girls at the request of their mothers, and that the girls themselves later thanked her. And that's probably true. Mahabouba, the Ethiopian fistula patient who battled hyenas and crawled to a missionary for help, remembers how much she looked forward to her own cutting as a rite of passage.

Edna Adan deplores the cutting and says that international campaigns are ineffective, never reaching ordinary Somali women. As we were driving through the Somaliland capital of Hargeisa, she pointed suddenly to a banner across the road that denounced cutting. 'So the UN comes and puts up banners in the capital,' she said. 'What does that do? It doesn't make a bit of difference. The women can't even read the signs.' Indeed, the international denunciations of FGM prompted a defensive backlash in some countries, leading tribal groups to rally around cutting as a tradition under attack by outsiders. Opponents eventually became smarter and backed off a bit, often using the more neutral term 'female genital cutting,' or FGC. At least that didn't imply that the women they were reaching out to were mutilated, which made it awkward to continue the conversation. More important, leadership passed to African women like Edna, since they can speak with far more authority and persuasiveness than foreigners.

Perhaps the most successful effort to end cutting is that of Tostan, a West African group that takes a very respectful approach and places FGC within a larger framework of community development. Rather than lecturing the women, the program's representatives encourage villagers to discuss the human rights and health issues related to cutting and then make their own choices. The program's soft sell has worked far better than the hard sell.

Tostan was founded by Molly Melching, a hearty woman from Danville, Illinois, who still looks and sounds like the solid Midwesterner she is. Molly's high school French class led her to a fascination with all things French. She studied in France and worked in a slum largely inhabited by North Africans outside

*Molly Melching with women in a Tostan program in Senegal
who have given up genital cutting (Tostan)*

Paris. Eventually she traveled to Senegal in 1974 on a scholarly
exchange program that was supposed to last six months. Molly is
still there.

A born linguist, Molly began to learn a Senegalese local language, Wolof, and then signed up for the Peace Corps in Senegal.
Molly ran a radio program in Wolof. Later, from 1982 to 1985,
she found herself living in a village working on education and
empowerment efforts with a small grant from the U.S. Agency for
International Development.

'Not one person in the village had been to school,' Molly
recalled. 'There was no school. This was a village of wonderful
people who were as smart as could be but just had never been to
school, and who very much needed information.' The experience – plus a stint as an independent evaluator of aid programs –
fed in Molly a suspicion of big aid projects. She was living as
Senegalese do and flinched as she saw foreign aid workers squired
around in SUVs. She also observed aid programs that spent primarily on expatriate staff and didn't know what they were doing.
Without local buy-in, a well-meaning group would build a clinic
and outfit it with drugs – and then the villagers would divide the
clinic's beds among themselves, and the doctor would sell the

medicines in the market. 'Senegal seemed like a cemetery of aid projects that weren't working,' she says bluntly.

Molly evaluated literacy programs by going to 240 literacy centers – and found them mostly failures. 'What I found were classes where there were supposed to be fifty students, but nobody would be there,' she said. 'Or everybody would be falling asleep.' Likewise, she saw Westerners thundering against genital cutting and trying to pass laws against it, without actually going out in the countryside to understand why mothers cut their daughters.

'Law is a quick-fix solution, and then people think you don't have to do anything else,' Molly said. 'The real thing that will make a difference is education.' When Senegal debated a law to ban cutting, Molly initially opposed it, for fear that it would inflame ethnic politics and stir a backlash (the majority ethnic group does not cut girls, so minorities would feel imposed upon). These days she is ambivalent about the law: While passage did create a backlash, it also signaled to villagers the severity of the health concerns about cutting.

In her own family, Molly saw how peer pressure for cutting was more powerful than any law. Molly had married a Senegalese man, and they had a daughter named Zoé – who made a startling demand.

'I want to be cut,' Zoé told her mother. 'I promise I won't cry.' All of Zoé's friends were being cut, and she didn't want to be left out. Molly wasn't that indulgent a mom, and the girl changed her mind when she was told what the procedure entailed. The incident convinced Molly that the key to ending cutting would be changing village attitudes as a whole.

In 1991, she formally launched Tostan to focus on education in poor villages. Typically, Tostan will send a local trainer into a village to begin a major educational program that includes units on democracy, human rights, problem-solving, hygiene, health, and management skills. The village has to actively participate by providing a teaching space, tables and chairs, students, and room and board for the teacher. Men and women alike participate in the classes, which last for three years and involve a significant commitment of time: three sessions a week of two or three hours each. The program also includes training for village leaders, formation of community management committees, and a microcredit system to encourage small businesses. Following the lead of local women, Tostan is very careful to avoid antagonizing village men.

'We did a segment on women's rights for a while, and that just built opposition,' Molly said. 'Some of the men closed our centers, they were so angry. So we sat down and rewrote the whole module and did "people's rights" instead – democracy and people's rights. Then we had the men behind us, too. The men just want to be included; they don't want to be seen as the enemy.'

Tostan sometimes angers feminists for its cautious approach and for its reluctance to use the word 'mutilation' or even say that it is fighting against genital cutting. Instead, it relentlessly tries to stay positive, preparing people to make their own decisions. The curriculum includes a nonjudgmental discussion of human rights and health issues related to cutting, but it never advises parents to stop cutting their daughters. Still, the program broke a taboo by discussing cutting, and once women thought about it and realized that cutting wasn't universal, they began to worry about the health risks. In 1997, a group of thirty-five women attending a class in a village called Malicounda Bambara took a historic step: They announced that they would stop cutting their daughters.

From the outside, it looked like a breakthrough, and it was hailed as such. Close up, it was a disaster. Other villagers excoriated the women who made the announcement as unfeminine and un-African and accused them of taking money from white people to betray their Bambara ethnic group. The women were in tears for months and worried that they were sentencing their daughters to be spinsters. Molly decided that Tostan had erred in allowing a single village to make the announcement. After consulting a local religious leader, she came to see that cutting is a social convention linked to marriage, so that no one family can stop cutting on its own without harming its daughters' marriage prospects.

'Everybody has to change together, or you will never be able to marry your daughter,' Molly says. 'My mother put me in braces, and I bled and I cried for two years, and an African woman could have come over and said: "How can you do this to your daughter?" And my mother would have said, "I saved from my little salary to straighten my daughter's teeth, so she can get married. How dare you say I am cruel!"'

The entire marrying group must make the decision to drop cutting collectively. So Tostan began helping groups identify the other villages that commonly supply their marriage partners and then organizing intervillage discussions of cutting. Tostan also helps women organize joint declarations that they have abandoned the practice, and this approach has worked stunningly well. Between 2002 and 2007, more than 2,600 villages announced that they had ceased cutting. 'It's accelerating,' Molly said, adding that Tostan's goal is to end all cutting in Senegal by 2012.

In 2008, Senegal's government reviewed all the country's efforts to end genital cutting, and it concluded that Tostan was the only program achieving significant results. It then adopted Tostan's approach as a national model. A few days later, health officials from across that region in West Africa also embraced the Tostan model as part of a regional strategy to end cutting.

Tostan has already moved on to work in Gambia, Guinea, and Mauritania, and it has also opened up programs in Somalia and Djibouti in East Africa. Molly says it is finding a receptive audience to its bottom-up approach in each country. Tostan's work has gained praise from a host of international agencies, and in 2007 it won the Conrad N. Hilton Humanitarian Prize and a UNESCO Prize. The recognition has helped win Tostan financial support from private donors as well as from UNICEF and American Jewish World Service, allowing it to expand at a steady pace. To encourage donors, Tostan has developed its own sponsorship plan: Donors can 'adopt' a particular village of about eight hundred people and pay $12,000 for the three-year program there.

Molly is the only Westerner on staff for Tostan in Africa, although there are two Americans working in a Washington, D.C., office to raise funds and publicize the organization. The emphasis on local staff in Africa has also enabled Tostan to become unusually cost-effective, partly because Molly pays herself just $48,000 annually. Now the test is whether her model will succeed as well in Somalia, Sudan, Chad, Ethiopia, and Central African Republic – some of which are wracked by conflict that makes work in these countries dangerous. There is a long history of projects that work well on a small scale but falter when introduced across Africa. Early signs, in Somalia at least, are encouraging, and Molly is already wondering aloud whether the Tostan model could be used to help end other pernicious social customs such as honor killings.

Elsewhere in Africa, other groups are also gaining momentum against genital cutting. Leading Egyptians are increasingly speaking out against the practice, and other aid groups, including CARE, are doing pathbreaking work. Some local grassroots groups in Ethiopia and Ghana have been particularly impressive. Bill Foege, a legendary figure in public health who helped eradicate smallpox, believes that genital cutting is finally on its way out, largely because of the work of Molly and the staff at Tostan.

'They have done what UN conferences, endless resolutions, and government statements have failed to do,' Foege told us. 'When the history of African development is written, it will be clear that a turning point involved the empowerment of women. Tostan has demonstrated that empowerment is contagious, accomplished person by person and spreading village by village.'

Painstakingly, the world is learning some important lessons from the fieldwork of groups like Tostan. One is that progress really is possible; challenges are insurmountable only until the moment that they're surmounted. And we're gaining a much better tactical sense of how to do the surmounting. Big efforts that failed – the campaign in the 1970s and 1980s against FGM and the missions by Westerners to Afghanistan with the lofty goal of empowering women – fell short because they were decreed by foreigners high up in the treetops. Local people were consulted only in a perfunctory manner. The impulse of Westerners to hold conferences and change laws has, on one issue after another, proved remarkably ineffective.* As Mary Robinson, the former Irish president who later served as a terrific UN High Commissioner for Human Rights, has said: 'Count up the results of fifty years of human rights mechanisms, thirty years of multi-billion-dollar development programs and endless high-level rhetoric, and the global impact is quite underwhelming. This is a failure of implementation on a scale which shames us all.'

In contrast, look at some of the projects that have made a stunning difference: Tostan, Kashf, Grameen, the CARE project in Burundi, BRAC, the Self Employed Women's Association in India, Apne Aap. The common thread is that they are grassroots projects with local ownership, sometimes resembling social or religious movements more than traditional aid projects. Often they have been propelled by exceptionally bright and driven social entrepreneurs who had encountered the 'treetops' efforts and modified them to create far more effective bottom-up models. That is a crucial way forward for a new international movement focusing on women in the developing world.

* One exception: Successful public health initiatives have sometimes been directed from the treetops. Examples include the eradication of smallpox, vaccination campaigns, and battles against river blindness and guinea worm disease. They are exceptional because they depend on research, materials, and knowledge that do not exist at the grassroots.

Girls Helping Girls

The frontline in the grassroots war against the abuse of women may be in Africa and Asia, but Jordana Confino has figured out how to make a contribution while attending high school in Westfield, New Jersey, a suburb of New York City. With her long, dirty-blond hair, Jordana could have just alighted from a prom queen's throne. She enjoyed an upper-middle-class upbringing, oozes self-confidence, expects equal rights as her birthright – and was deeply troubled when she appreciated how unusual her privileged status is.

Jordana and the high school students she works with are reminders that the rise of social entrepreneurship has also facilitated the rise of the part-time aid worker – even one sitting in a high school classroom. In Jordana's case, her initiative started when she was about ten years old and her mother, Lisa Alter, tried to expose her daughters to problems in the rest of the world. Lisa would point out news articles or tell them about challenges faced by girls abroad: *See how lucky you have it here in New Jersey.* Lisa discovered that Jordana was far more moved by the horrors than she had expected.

'We talked about the articles, and especially those that were about girls,' Jordana remembered. 'Some of the topics were very upsetting, including female genital mutilation, the abandonment of baby girls in China, child labor. Around this time there were also a number of public stories about the Taliban ban on girls' education in Afghanistan. We talked as a family about how hard it must be for girls to escape abuse if they could not even read or write. I have to admit that the problems seemed too big for us to do

Jordana Confino at a conference on girls' education (Lisa Alter)

anything about, but we began to brainstorm about what we might do if we got a group of girls together.'

The idea fermented in the back of Jordana's mind. In the eighth grade, she teamed up with a girlfriend and began to talk seriously about starting a club focusing on these issues. Lisa and the friend's mother helped them make plans, and they all attended a United Nations conference on women and girls. Jordana was moved by the stories she heard and switched into high gear. She and her friend soon started Girls Learn International (www.girlslearninternational.org) to raise money for girls' education abroad. They made calls, put up posters, sent out letters. Jordana started visiting other schools to drum up volunteers. By the time she was in high school, she was a crusader for Girls Learn International, and the group was gathering chapters around the country.

Jordana gave the keynote address during an end-of-year assembly at the Young Women's Leadership School in the Bronx, reminding members of the audience that while they might have encountered their own difficulties, girls in other countries were struggling for food and shelter, let alone the luxury of attending school. Jordana was practically the only white girl in the room. But she had become a role model for many girls her age, as she talked about the challenges around the globe.

'In 2007, nearly sixty-six million girls do not have access to education in communities across the world,' she said. As these girls grow up, she continued, 'they join the ranks of illiterate girls, increasing the gender gap between men and women . . . Girls who are denied access to education are more likely to be trapped in a cycle of poverty and disease, forced into child marriage and prostitution, become victims of sex trafficking, domestic violence, and so-called honor killings.'

Girls Learn now has more than twenty chapters in high schools and middle schools around the country and is working on an affiliated college program as well. Some of the girls start out just trying to polish their activities lists for college applications, but many of them become moved by the foreign students they learn about and ultimately are passionate about the cause.

Each chapter of Girls Learn is paired with a partner class in a poor country where girls traditionally do not get much education: Afghanistan, Colombia, Costa Rica, El Salvador, India, Kenya, Pakistan, Uganda, Vietnam. The American girls raise money to help their partners and upgrade the foreign schools. Jordana, for instance, helped improve the office of Mukhtar Mai, the anti-rape campaigner in rural Pakistan. When Mukhtar Mai e-mails us to inform us of the latest threats against her, she does it with a computer and Internet hookup that Girls Learn paid for.

Girls Learn partners are chosen mostly by the connections cultivated by Jordana, her mother, and a professional staff of two in an office in Manhattan. Each chapter is supposed to raise at least $500 a year, and the kids have raised a cumulative total of about $50,000, which goes exclusively to partner classrooms abroad. Supporting grown-ups separately raise more than $100,000 annually to cover administrative expenses. That means that Girls Learn isn't the most efficient charity around to support girls' education abroad, since far more money goes to administrative costs in Manhattan than to keep Pakistani girls in school. Still, the purpose of Girls Learn isn't just to support girls' education abroad but also to create exchanges and build the basis for a movement at home. As an educational venture for the American girls, it's a bargain.

American high school students who might otherwise be obsessed with designer bags are sending their spending money abroad so that girls in India can have notebooks.

'Talk about getting girls involved in the process,' said Cassidy DuRant-Green, a staff member of Girls Learn. 'What better way to start than in middle school? We're building leaders, women we could be working for in twenty years.' So while the ostensible aim is to empower girls in countries like Pakistan, some of the major beneficiaries are the American girls. You see that in Jordana, and the polish and passion she has found in her cause. In her speech in the Bronx, Jordana exuded maturity and empathy as she exhorted the students to support the Girls Learn chapter, noting that girls the same age as those in the audience are being trafficked or killed for 'honor,' and she ended with a ringing crescendo: 'Girls' rights are human rights!'

CHAPTER FOURTEEN

What You Can Do

You must be the change you wish to see in the world.

— MAHATMA GANDHI

Americans knew for decades about the unfairness of segrega-tion. But racial discrimination seemed a complex problem deeply rooted in the South's history and culture, and most good-hearted people didn't see what they could do about such injustices. Then along came Rosa Parks and Martin Luther King Jr. and the Freedom Riders, along with eye-opening books like John Howard Griffin's *Black Like Me*. Suddenly the injustices were impossible to look away from, at the same time that economic change was also undermining Jim Crow. One result was a broad civil rights move-ment that built coalitions, spotlighted the suffering, and tore away the blinders that allowed good people to acquiesce in racism.

Likewise, skies were hazy, rivers oily, and animals endangered for much of the twentieth century, but environmental destruction unfolded without much comment or opposition. It seemed the sad but inevitable price of progress. And then Rachel Carson published *Silent Spring* in 1962, and the environmental movement was born.

In the same way, the challenge today is to prod the world to face up to women locked in brothels and teenage girls with fistulas curled up on the floor of isolated huts. We hope to see a broad movement emerge to battle gender inequality around the world and to push for education and opportunities for girls around the world. The American civil rights movement is one model, and so is the environmental movement, but both of those were different because they involved domestic challenges close to home. And we're wary of taking the American women's movement as a model, because if the international effort is dubbed a 'women's issue,' then it will already have failed. The unfortunate reality is that women's issues are marginalized, and in any case sex trafficking and mass rape should no more be seen as women's issues than slavery was a black issue or the Holocaust was a Jewish issue. These are all humanitarian concerns, transcending any one race, gender, or creed.

The ideal model for a new movement is one we evoked earlier: the British drive to end the slave trade at the end of the eighteenth and beginning of the nineteenth centuries. That is a singular, shining example of a people who accepted a substantial, sustained sacrifice of blood and treasure to improve the lives of fellow human beings living far away. Winston Churchill suggested that the British people's 'finest hour' was their resistance to the Nazis in the 1940s, but at least as noble an hour was the moral quickening in Britain that led to the abolition of slavery.

For most of history, slavery had been accepted as sad but inevitable. The Athenians were brilliant philosophers and abounded in empathy that made them wonderful writers and philosophers, yet they did not even debate their reliance on slavery. Jesus did not address slavery at all in the Gospels; Saint Paul and Aristotle accepted it; and Jewish and Islamic theologians believed in mercy toward slaves but did not question slavery itself. In the 1700s, a few Quakers vigorously denounced slavery, but they were dismissed as crackpots and had no influence. In the early 1780s, slavery was an unquestioned part of the global landscape – and then, astonishingly, within a decade, slavery was at the top of the British national agenda. The tide turned, and Britain banned the slave trade in 1807 and in 1833 became one of the first nations to emancipate its own slaves.

For more than half a century, the British public bore tremendous costs for their moral leadership. On the eve of the British abolition of slave-trading, British ships carried 52 percent of the slaves transported across the Atlantic, and British colonies produced 55 percent of the world's sugar. Without new slaves, the British colonies in the

New World were devastated, and Britain's great enemy, France, benefited enormously. So did the United States. Sugar production in the British West Indies fell 25 percent in the first thirty-five years after Britain's abolition of the slave trade, while production in competing slave economies rose by 210 percent.

The British navy led the way in trying to suppress the slave trade, both in the Atlantic and within Africa itself. This led to the loss of some five thousand British lives, plus higher taxes for the British people. And such unilateral action was costly diplomatically, enraging other countries and putting Britain in open conflict with rival military powers. The British antislavery efforts led to a brief war with Brazil in 1850 and to war scares with the United States in 1841 and with Spain in 1853, as well as to sustained tense relations with France. Yet Britain did not flinch. Its example ultimately prompted France to abolish slavery in 1848, inspired the American abolitionists and the Emancipation Proclamation, and pushed Cuba to enforce a ban on slave imports in 1867, in effect ending the transatlantic slave trade.

Two scholars, Chaim Kaufmann and Robert Pape, calculate that for sixty years Britain sacrificed an annual average of 1.8 percentage points of its GNP because of its moral commitment to ending slavery. That is an astonishing total, cumulatively amounting to more than an entire year's GNP for Great Britain (for the United States today, it would be the equivalent of sacrificing more than $14 trillion), a significant and sustained sacrifice in the British standard of living. It was a heroic example of a nation placing its values above its interests.

Credit for the abolitionist movement usually goes to William Wilberforce, and indeed he was one of the foremost leaders of the movement and the one who turned the tide. But Wilberforce joined after abolitionism was well under way, and the public wasn't stirred solely by Wilberforce's eloquence. A central part of the campaign – and one worth learning from today – was a meticulous effort to explain to the English exactly what conditions were like on slave ships and plantations.

Slavery did not exist in Britain itself, only in British territories abroad, so for the average English family slavery was out of sight. As with sex trafficking in India today, it was easy to cluck about the brutality of it all and then move on. The abolitionist who overcame that challenge was Thomas Clarkson, who had first become interested in the issue as a student at Cambridge when he wrote about slaves for a Latin contest. His research so horrified him that he became an ardent abolitionist for life. Clarkson became the driving force behind the Society for Effecting the Abolition of the Slave Trade. 'If anyone was the founder of the modern human-rights movement,' *The Economist* has observed, 'it was Clarkson.'

After leaving university, Clarkson undertook enormous risks to move clandestinely through ports in Liverpool and Bristol where slaving ships docked, to talk to seamen and to gather evidence about the trade. Clarkson acquired manacles, branding irons, thumbscrews, leg shackles, and gruesome implements that were used to force a slave's jaws open. He found a former captain of slave ships who came forward and described their holds. And Clarkson obtained a diagram of a Liverpool slave ship, the *Brookes*, and made posters showing how it was loaded with 482 slaves. That image became the icon of the abolitionist movement, and it underscored an important point: Clarkson and the abolitionists were scrupulous about not exaggerating. The *Brookes*, in fact, had carried up to 600 slaves on some journeys, but Clarkson thought it best to use the most carefully documented and conservative figures to guarantee credibility.

Apologists for slavery at the time often described benevolent farming operations in the West Indies, indulgently caring for slaves' every need, but Clarkson's evidence proved that conditions were often revolting. The slavers were furious and paid a group of sailors to assassinate Clarkson; they nearly beat him to death.

Clarkson and Wilberforce seemed to be fighting a hopeless campaign: Britain had a huge economic stake in the continuation of the slave trade, and the suffering was endured by distant peoples whom many Britons considered inferior savages. Yet when British public opinion confronted what it meant to pack human beings into the hold of a ship – the stink, the disease, the corpses, those bloody manacles — citizens recoiled and turned against slavery. It's a useful lesson that what ultimately mattered wasn't just the abolitionists' passion and moral conviction but also the meticulously amassed evidence of barbarity.

Likewise, success came not only from making politicians see the 'truth' but also from putting relentless domestic political pressure on them. Clarkson traveled thirty-five thousand miles on horseback, and a former slave, Olaudah Equiano, lectured all over Britain on a five-year book tour. In 1792, 300,000 people boycotted sugar from the West Indies – the greatest consumer boycott in history until that point. That year, more people signed a petition against slavery than were eligible to vote in British elections. And in Parliament, Wilberforce bargained furiously to build a voting bloc to overcome the shipping and slavery lobby. Then, as now, government leaders found ethical arguments most persuasive when they were backed by the raw insistence of voters.

In the 1790s, it was common to dismiss the abolitionists as idealistic moralizers who didn't appreciate economics or understand geopolitical complexities such as the threat from France. In the same way, these days, the 'serious issues' are typically assumed to be terrorism or the economy. But the moral issue of the subjugation of women isn't frivolous today any more than slavery was in the 1790s. Decades from now, people will look back and wonder how societies could have acquiesced in a sex slave trade in the twenty-first century that, as we've seen, is bigger than the transatlantic slave trade was in the nineteenth. They will be perplexed that we shrugged as a lack of investment in maternal health caused half a million women to perish in childbirth each year.

Leadership must come from the developing world itself, and that is beginning to happen. In India, Africa, and the Middle East, men and women alike are pushing for greater equality. These people need our support. In the 1960s, blacks like Dr. King led the civil rights movement, but they received crucial backing from Freedom Riders and other white supporters. Today, the international movement for women needs 'freedom riders' as well — writing letters, sending money, or volunteering their time.

Moreover, emancipation of women offers another dimension in which to tackle geopolitical challenges such as terrorism. In the aftermath of 9/11, the United States tried to address terrorism concerns in Pakistan by transferring $10 billion in helicopters, guns, and military and economic support; in that same period, the United States became steadily more unpopular in Pakistan, the Musharraf government less stable and extremists more popular. Imagine if we had used the money instead to promote education and microfinance in rural Pakistan, through Pakistani organizations. The result would likely have been greater popularity for the United States and greater involvement of women in society. And, as we've argued, when women gain a voice in society, there's evidence of less violence. Swanee Hunt, a former U.S. ambassador to Austria now at Harvard, recalled the reaction of a Pentagon official in 2003 in the aftermath of the 'shock and awe' invasion of Iraq: 'When I urged him to broaden his search for the future leaders of Iraq, which had yielded hundreds of men and only seven women, he responded, "Ambassador Hunt, we'll address women's issues after we get the place secure." I wondered what "women's issues" he meant. I was talking about security.'

Think about the major issues confronting us in this century. These include war, insecurity, and terrorism; population pressures, environmental strains, and climate change; poverty and income gaps. For all these diverse problems, empowering women is part of the answer. Most obviously, educating girls and bringing them into the formal economy will yield economic dividends and help address global poverty. Environmental pressures arise almost inevitably from surging population growth, and the best way to reduce fertility in a society is to educate girls and give them job opportunities. Likewise, we've argued that one way to soothe some conflict-ridden societies is to bring women and girls into schools, the workplace, government, and business, partly to boost the economy and partly to ease the testosterone-laden values of these countries. We would never argue that the empowerment of women is a silver bullet, but it is an approach that offers a range of rewards that go far beyond simple justice.

Consider Bangladesh for a moment. It is poor, often politically dysfunctional, with tremendous uncertainties ahead of it. Yet it is also incomparably more stable than Pakistan, of which it was a part until 1971 (Bangladesh was called East Pakistan until then). After the country split, Bangladesh was initially presumed to be hopeless, and Henry Kissinger famously dubbed it a 'basket case.' It suffered from the same political violence and poor leadership as Pakistan, and yet today its future looks more assured. There are many reasons for the different outcomes, including the cancer of violence that spread from Afghanistan to Pakistan and the Bengali intellectual tradition that has moderated extremism in Bangladesh. Yet surely one reason Bangladesh is more stable today is that it invested enormously in women and girls, so that a girl in Bangladesh is far more likely to go to school than a Pakistani girl, and afterward far more likely to hold a job. The upshot is that Bangladesh today has a significant civil society and a huge garment industry full of women workers who power a dynamic export sector.

Nearly everyone who works in poor countries recognizes that women are the third world's greatest underutilized resource. 'The first thing we learned is that men are often untrainable,' said Bunker Roy, who runs Barefoot College, an India-based aid organization that operates in Asia, Africa, and Latin America. 'So now we work only with women. We pick a woman from Afghanistan, from Mauritania, from Bolivia, from Timbuktu, and in six months we train her to be a barefoot engineer' working on water supplies or other issues.

Almost invariably around the globe, countries and companies that have deployed women according to their talents have prospered. 'Encouraging more women into the labor force has been the single biggest driver of Euro-zone's labor market success, much more so than "conventional" labor market reforms,' Goldman Sachs wrote in a research report in 2007. Likewise, public companies that have more women executives consistently perform better than those with fewer women. One study of America's Fortune 500 companies found that the one quarter with the most female executives had a return on equity 35 percent higher than the quarter with the fewest female executives. On the Japanese stock exchange, the companies with the highest proportion of female employees performed nearly 50 percent better than those with the lowest. In each case, the most likely reason isn't that female executives are geniuses. Rather, it is that companies that are innovative enough to promote women are also ahead of the curve in reacting to business opportunities. That is the essence of a sustainable economic model. Moving women into more productive roles helps curb population growth and nurtures a sustainable society.

Consider the costs of allowing half a country's human resources to go untapped. Women and girls cloistered in huts, uneducated, unemployed, and unable to contribute significantly to the world represent a vast seam of human gold that is never mined. The consequence of failing to educate girls is a capacity gap not only in billions of dollars of GNP but also in billions of IQ points.

Psychologists have long noted that intelligence as measured by IQ tests has risen sharply over the years, a phenomenon known as the Flynn Effect, after a New Zealand intelligence researcher named James Flynn. The average American IQ, for example, rose by eighteen points from 1947 to 2002. Over thirty years, the IQ of Dutch conscripts rose twenty-one points and those of Spanish schoolchildren by ten points. One scholar estimated that if American children of 1932 had taken an IQ test in 1997, then half of them would have been classified as at least borderline mentally retarded.

The cause of the Flynn Effect isn't fully understood, but it affects primarily those with lower scores, who may not have received adequate nutrition, education, or stimulation. Iodine deficiency is a factor in some countries. As people become better nourished and better educated, they perform better on intelligence tests. Thus it's no surprise that a particularly large Flynn Effect has been detected in developing countries such as Brazil and Kenya. The IQ of rural Kenyan children rose eleven points in just fourteen years, a pace greater than any Flynn Effect reported in the West.

Tererai Trent in front of the hut in which she was born, in Zimbabwe
(Tererai Trent)

Girls in poor countries are particularly undernourished, physically and intellectually. If we educate and feed those girls and give them employment opportunities, then the world as a whole will gain a new infusion of human intelligence – and poor countries will garner citizens and leaders who are better equipped to address those countries' challenges. The strongest argument we can make to leaders of poor countries is not a moral one but a pragmatic one: If they wish to enliven their economies, they had better not leave those seams of human gold buried and unexploited.

One of the groups that has increasingly focused on women for these pragmatic reasons is Heifer International, an aid organization based in Arkansas that gives cows, goats, chickens, or other animals to farmers in poor countries. Its head is Jo Luck, a former state cabinet official in Arkansas under then-governor Bill Clinton. On assuming the presidency of Heifer in 1992, Jo traveled to Africa, where one day she found herself sitting on the ground with a group of young women in a Zimbabwe village. One of them was Tererai Trent.

Tererai is a long-faced woman with high cheekbones and a medium brown complexion; she has a high forehead and tight cornrows. Like many women around the world, she doesn't know when she was born and has no documentation of her birth. She thinks it may have been 1965, but it's possible that it was a couple of years later. As a child, Tererai didn't get much formal education, partly because she was a girl and was expected to do household chores. She herded cattle and looked after her younger siblings. Her father would say: *Let's send our sons to school, because they will be the breadwinners.* 'My father and every other man realized that they did not have social security and hence they invested in male children,' Tererai says. Tererai's brother, Tinashe, was forced to go to school, where he was an indifferent student. Tererai pleaded to be allowed to attend, but wasn't permitted to do so. Tinashe brought his books home each afternoon, and Tererai pored over them and taught herself to read and write. Soon she was doing her brother's homework every evening.

The teacher grew puzzled, since Tinashe was a poor student in class but always handed in perfect homework. Finally, the teacher noticed that the handwriting was different for homework and for class assignments, and whipped Tinashe until he confessed the truth. Then the teacher went to the children's father, told him that Tererai was a prodigy, and begged for her to be allowed to attend school. After much argument, the father allowed Tererai to attend school for a couple of terms, but then he married her off at about age eleven.

Tererai's husband barred her from attending school, resented her literacy, and beat her whenever she tried to practice by reading a scrap of old newspaper. Indeed, he beat her for plenty more as well. She hated her marriage but had no way out. 'If you're a woman and you are not educated, what else?' she asks.

Yet when Jo Luck came and talked to Tererai and the other young women, Jo kept insisting that things did not have to be this way. She kept saying that they could achieve their goals, repeatedly using the word 'achievable.' The women caught the repetition and asked the interpreter to explain in detail what 'achievable' meant. That gave Jo a chance to push forward. 'What are your hopes?' she asked the women, through the interpreter. Tererai and the others were puzzled by the question, because they didn't really have any hopes. Frankly, they were suspicious of this white woman who couldn't speak their language, who kept making bewildering inquiries. But Jo pushed them to think about their dreams, and, reluctantly, they began to think about what they wanted. Tererai timidly voiced her hope of getting an education. Jo pounced and told her that she could do it, that she should write down her goals and methodically pursue them. At first, this didn't make any sense to Tererai, for she was a married woman in her mid-twenties.

There are many metaphors for the role of foreign assistance. We like to think of aid as a kind of lubricant, a few drops of oil in the crankcase of the developing world, so that gears move freely again on their own. That is what Heifer International's help amounted to in this village: Tererai started gliding along freely on her own. After Jo Luck and her entourage disappeared, Tererai began to study frantically, while raising her five children. She went away to her mother's village to escape her husband's beatings. Painstakingly, with the help of friends, she wrote down her goals on a piece of paper: 'One day I will go to the United States of America,' she began, for goal one. She added that she would earn a college degree, a master's degree, and a PhD – all exquisitely absurd dreams for a married cattleherder in Zimbabwe who had less than one year's formal education. But Tererai took the piece of paper and folded it inside three layers of plastic to protect it, then placed it in an old can. She buried the can under a rock where she herded cattle.

Then Tererai took correspondence classes and began saving money. Her self-confidence grew as she did brilliantly in her studies, and she became a community organizer for Heifer. She stunned everyone with superb schoolwork, and the Heifer aid workers encouraged her to think that she could study in America. One day, in 1998, she received notice that she had been admitted to Oklahoma State University.

Some of the neighbors thought that a woman in her thirties should focus on educating her children, not herself 'I can't talk about my children's education when I'm not educated myself,' Tererai responded. 'If I educate myself, then I can educate my children.' So she climbed into an airplane and flew to America.

At Oklahoma State, Tererai took as many credits as she possibly could and worked nights to make money. She earned her degree and then returned to her village. She dug up the tin can under the rock and took out the paper on which she had scribbled her goals. She put checkmarks beside the goals she had fulfilled, and buried the tin can again.

Heifer International offered Tererai a job, and she began work in Arkansas – while simultaneously earning a master's degree part-time. When she earned her MA, Tererai again returned to her village. After embracing her family members and relatives, she dug up her tin can and checked off her most recently achieved goal. Now she is working on her PhD at Western Michigan University, and she has brought her five children to America. Tererai has finished her course work and is completing a dissertation about AIDS programs among the poor in Africa. She will become a productive economic asset for Africa, all because of a little push and helping hand from Heifer International. And when she has her doctorate, Tererai will go back to her village and, after hugging her loved ones, go out to the field and dig up her can again.

There is a broad scholarly literature about social movements, and experts have noted that one of the most striking changes in recent years has been a surge in female leadership. The civil rights and anti-Vietnam War movements may have been the last such major efforts in the United States that were overwhelmingly male in their top ranks. Since then, women have led such diverse efforts as Mothers Against Drunk Driving and the pro- and anti-feminist movements. While women still lag in political, corporate, and government positions, they dominate the civil sector in much of the world. In the United States, women now lead Harvard, Princeton, and MIT, as well as the Ford Foundation and the Rockefeller Foundation. The groups in the National Council of Women's Organizations represent 10 million women. The same pattern is evident abroad. In South Korea, women hold 14 percent of the seats in the National Assembly but lead 80 percent of the country's NGOs. In Kyrgyzstan, women don't hold a single seat in parliament but run 90 percent of the NGOs.

In the nineteenth century, wealthy American women disdained the women's suffrage movement, instead contributing generously to men's colleges and schools, and to churches and charities. Often, rich women were strikingly generous to institutions that openly discriminated against women. The women's suffrage movement was thus forced to raise money mostly from sympathetic men. Likewise, in recent decades, wealthy American women haven't been particularly generous toward international women's causes, but there are signs that that may be beginning to change. American women are now playing an increasingly important role in the philanthropic world, and 'women's funds' that support women and girls are booming. There are now more than ninety in the United States alone.

So the time is ripe for a new emancipation movement to empower women and girls around the world. Politicians should take heed: In the United States, a 2006 poll found that 60 percent of respondents said that 'improving the treatment of women in other countries' was 'very important' for American foreign policy (another 30 percent said it was 'somewhat important'). The movement should adhere to these principles:

- Strive to build broad coalitions across liberal and conservative lines. This makes practical results far easier to achieve.
- Resist the temptation to oversell. The humanitarian community has undermined its credibility with its exaggerated predictions (journalists joke that aid groups have predicted ten of the last three famines). Research about women tends to come from people who care passionately about justice and gender, and who have convictions before they begin their studies. So be cautious about the findings. There's nothing to be gained by exaggeration.
- Helping women doesn't mean ignoring men. For example, it's crucial to fund the development of vaginal microbicides, creams that women could apply to protect themselves from HIV without their partners knowing. But it may help women just as much if boys and men are circumcised, for that slows the spread of

AIDS and reduces the chance that men will infect their partners.

- American feminism must become less parochial, so that it is every bit as concerned with sex slavery in Asia as with Title IX sports programs in Illinois. It is already making good progress in this respect. Likewise, Americans of faith should try as hard to save the lives of African women as the lives of unborn fetuses. In short, all of us need to become more cosmopolitan and aware of global repression based on gender.

If there were a fifth principle, it would be: Don't pay too much attention to the first four. Any movement needs to be flexible; it should be relentlessly empirical and open to different strategies in different places. For example, we've repeatedly described educating girls as the single best way to lower fertility, improve children's health, and create a more just and dynamic society. But as we were writing this book, two new studies pointed to another approach to revolutionize fertility and gender in the villages: television.

One study, by an Italian development economist, Eliana La Ferrara, examined the impact of a television network, Rede Globo, as it expanded in Brazil. Globo is known for its soap operas, which have huge and passionate followings and whose main characters are women with few children. It turns out that when the Globo network reached a new area in Brazil, in the following years there were fewer births there – particularly among women of lower socioeconomic status and women already well along in their reproductive years. That suggested that they had decided to stop having children, emulating the soap opera characters they admired.

A second study focused on television's impact on rural India. Two scholars, Robert Jensen of Brown University and Emily Oster of the University of Chicago, found that after cable television arrived in a village, women gained more autonomy – such as the ability to leave the house without permission and the right to participate in household decisions. There was a drop in the number of births, and women were less likely to say they preferred a son over a daughter. Wife-beating became less acceptable, and families were more likely to send daughters to school.

These changes occurred because TV brought new ideas into isolated villages that tended to be very conservative and traditional. Before TV arrived, 62 percent of women in the villages surveyed thought it was acceptable for husbands to beat wives, and 55 percent of women wanted their next child to be a son (most of the rest did not want a daughter; they just didn't care). And fully two thirds of the women said they needed their husband's permission to visit friends.

Then, with television, new ideas infiltrated the villages. Most of the popular cable television programs in India are soap operas set among middle-class families in the cities, where women hold jobs and come and go freely. Rural viewers came to recognize that the 'modern' way is for women to be treated as human beings. The effect was huge: 'introducing cable television is equivalent to roughly five years of female education,' the professors report. This doesn't mean that we should drop programs to send girls to school and instead settle for introducing cable television to villages full of wife beaters, for these findings are tentative and need to be replicated elsewhere. But as we have argued, a movement for women must be creative and willing to learn and incorporate new approaches and technologies.

The movement's agenda should be broad and enveloping, while focusing on four appalling realities of daily life: maternal mortality, human trafficking, sexual violence, and the routine daily discrimination that causes girls to die at far higher rates than boys. The tools to address these challenges include girls' education, family planning, microfinance, and 'empowerment' in every sense. One useful measure to help foster these is CEDAW, the Convention on the Elimination of All Forms of Discrimination. It was adopted by the UN General Assembly in 1979, and so far 185 countries have become a party to it; the United States continues to refuse to ratify it, because of Republicans' concerns that CEDAW could nibble away at American sovereignty by surrendering authority to an international convention. Those concerns are absurd. In addition, the UN should have a prominent agency to support gender equality (there is one in theory, UNIFEM, but it is minuscule). The United States should have a separate cabinet department that oversees all foreign aid and development issues, as Britain does, and this department should emphasize the role of women.

Yet ultimately, as we've shown, what will change the patterns of life in an African village is less likely to be CEDAW or a new American cabinet position, and more likely a new school or health center in that village. It's fine to hold UN conferences on education, but sometimes it does more good to allocate the money to projects on the ground. We would like to see a grassroots campaign bringing together feminist organizations and evangelical churches and everyone in between, calling on the president and Congress to pass three specific initiatives. Ideally these would be coordinated with similar efforts from Europe, Japan, and other donor countries, but if necessary they could start as American projects.

The first would be a $10 billion effort over five years to educate girls around the world and reduce the gender gap in education. This initiative would focus on Africa but would also support – and prod – Asian countries such as Afghanistan and Pakistan to do better. The aim would be not just to fund new schools, with DONATED BY THE AMERICAN PEOPLE written on the sides, but to experiment with finding the most cost-effective ways to support education. In some countries that may be providing school uniforms to girls from poor families, or deworming communities, or providing scholarships to the best-performing girls, or helping girls manage menstruation, or supporting school lunches, or extending Mexico's Oportunidades program to Africa. These approaches should be rigorously tried on a randomized basis, and assessed by outside evaluators, so that we can determine which are most cost-effective.

The second initiative would be for the United States to sponsor a global drive to iodize salt in poor countries, to prevent tens of millions of children from losing approximately ten I.Q. points each as a result of iodine deficiency while their brains are still being formed in the uterus. As we discussed in the chapter on girls' education, female fetuses are particularly prone to impaired brain development when the mother's body lacks enough iodine, and so girls would be the major beneficiaries. Canada already sponsors the Micronutrient Initiative, which supports iodization of salt, but there is far more work to be done – and it is appalling that so many girls will suffer irreversible brain damage when by one estimate a mere $19 million would pay for salt iodization in the countries that still desperately need it. This iodization campaign would thus cost very little, and it would underscore that for all the criticisms of foreign aid, there are still some methods that are cheap, simple, and highly cost-effective. Iodizing salt may not be glamorous, but it gets more bang for the buck than almost any form of foreign aid.

The third initiative would be a twelve-year, $1.6 billion project to eradicate obstetric fistula, while laying the groundwork for a major international assault on maternal mortality. Dr. L. Lewis Wall, the president and managing director of the Worldwide Fistula Fund, has drafted with Michael Horowitz, a conservative agitator on humanitarian issues, a detailed proposal for a campaign to end fistulas. The plan includes the construction of forty fistula centers around Africa, as well a new institute to coordinate the campaign. This is one of the few areas in reproductive health that unites Democrats and Republicans, and it would cast a spotlight on the need for better maternal care generally. The campaign would showcase the opportunity to help some of the world's most forlorn young women, deepen obstetric skills in Africa, and generate the energy to take subsequent steps to tackle maternal mortality.

These three steps – campaigns to fund girls' education, to iodize salt to prevent mental retardation, and to eradicate fistula – would not solve the problems of the world's women. But action on these three measures would raise the underlying issues higher on the international affairs agenda, and would illustrate solutions to the problems. Once people see that there *are* solutions, they will be more willing to help in myriad other ways.

*

The more Westerners the movement reaches, the better. But the most effective supporters will donate not only their money but also their time, by volunteering on the front lines. If you care about poverty you must understand it, not just oppose it. And understanding poverty comes from spending time observing it directly.

In talking about sex trafficking, we mentioned Urmi Basu, who runs the New Light shelter for trafficked women in Kolkata. Over the years we've steered several Americans to volunteer at New Light, teaching English to the children of prostitutes, and they find it pretty overwhelming at first. One of those we introduced to Urmi was Sydnee Woods, an assistant city attorney in Minneapolis who wasn't finding everything she wanted in life from her job. She asked her boss for a ninety-day unpaid leave to go to India to work at New Light, and he flatly said no. So Sydnee quit, sold her home, and moved to Kolkata. She found it a very rough adjustment, as she put it in an e-mail to us:

> It took me about 6 months to actually admit to myself that I hate India (well, Kolkata, at least). Truly I absolutely loved New Light – the children, the mothers, the staff, the other volunteers, Urmi. But I hated everything else about being in Kolkata. I found it extremely difficult being a single, black American woman there. I was constantly met with suspicion – not so much due to my color, but because I was not married and was often by myself (in restaurants, at the mall, etc.). The staring was emotionally exhausting and I don't think I ever truly got used to it.

Chastened that our advice had produced such a painful experience, we asked Sydnee if that meant that she regretted having gone. Would she recommend such an immersion to others? Moments later a very different e-mail arrived:

> I am so glad I went! I am considering going back to New Light next year. I fell in love with all of the children, but two of them, siblings Joya and Raoul (they are 4 and 6, I think),

truly touched my heart and I am totally committed to making sure they get an education and get out of Kalighat [the red-light district]. I know that I did some good there, which is satisfying. The experience (good and bad) changed me forever. I have become incredibly laid back and able to deal with setbacks and hardships much more easily. I had never traveled out of the country (other than touristy trips to Bermuda, Mexico and the Bahamas) and now I can't imagine not traveling abroad as often as possible. I made lifelong friends in India. It's difficult to put into words – but I am a different, better person. I would definitely recommend it – especially to other single, black women. It was difficult – but necessary. India changes you – it makes you confront things about yourself that you may have chosen not to confront. As far as I'm concerned that can only be good. It was good for me.

Indeed, while the main motivation for joining this global movement is to help others, the result is often to help oneself. As Sir John Templeton said, 'Self-improvement comes mainly from trying to help others.' Social psychologists have learned a great deal about happiness in recent years, and one of the surprises is that the things we believe will make us happy won't. People who win the lottery, for example, enjoy an initial spike of happiness but then adjust and a year later are not significantly happier than those who haven't won. Our happiness levels seem to be mostly innate, and not markedly affected by what happens to us, good or bad. People in end-stage dialysis, for example, turn out to be no different in their moods through the day than a comparison group of healthy people. And while those who suffer a crippling disability are initially deeply unhappy, they adjust quickly. One study found that just a month after becoming paraplegics, accident victims were in fairly good moods a majority of the time. Other research found that within two years of suffering a moderate disability, life satisfaction fully recovers to the predisability level. So Jonathan Haidt, a psychologist at the University of Virginia who has studied happiness, advises that if you are hit by a truck and end up a paraplegic, or if you win the lottery, remember that a year from now, it won't make much difference to your happiness level.

Yet Professor Haidt and others advise that there are a few factors that *can* affect our happiness levels in a sustained way. One is 'a connection to something larger' – a greater cause or a humanitarian purpose. Traditionally, this was what brought people to churches or other religious institutions, but any movement or humanitarian initiative can provide a sense of purpose that boosts one's happiness quotient. We are neurologically constructed so that we gain huge personal dividends from altruism.

Thus we hope you will join this growing crowd and back it in whatever way you can – volunteering at Mukhtar Mai's school in Pakistan, writing letters as part of Equality Now campaigns, or sponsoring Tostan to educate a village about genital cutting. Browse the aid groups in the appendix of this book, or go to www.charitynavigator.org. Then find a group or two that you want to commit to. Philanthropists and donors traditionally haven't been sufficiently interested in women's rights abroad, giving money instead to higher-brow causes such as the ballet or art museums. There could be a powerful international women's rights movement if only philanthropists would donate as much to real women as to paintings and sculptures of women.

We don't presume to say that all of your giving should be targeted to the needs of women abroad, any more than all of ours is. But we hope that some of your giving will go to these causes, and that you will give your time as well as your dollars. A portion of the income from this book will go to some of these organizations.

If you're a student, find out whether your school or college has classes or study abroad programs that address these issues. Consider volunteering for a summer internship at one of the organizations we've talked about. Or take a 'gap year' before or after university for travel or an internship. If you're a parent, take your kids not just to London but also to India or Africa. At a town meeting, ask a candidate about maternal health. Write a letter to the editor of your local paper calling for a big push for girls' education.

Four Steps You Can Take in the Next Ten Minutes

The first step is the hardest, so here are several things you can do right now:

1. Go to www.globalgiving.org or www.kiva.org and open an account. Both sites are people-to-people (P2P), meaning that they link you directly to a person in need overseas, and this makes them an excellent way to dip your toe in. Global Giving lets you choose a grassroots project to which to give money in education, health, disaster relief, or more than a dozen other areas around the developing world. Kiva lets you do the same for microlending to entrepreneurs. Browse the sites to get a sense of the needs and donate or lend money to those that appeal to you, perhaps as a gift to a family member or a friend. Or try a third site, www.givology.com, started by students at the University of Pennsylvania to help children in developing countries pay for primary school. The site initially focused on China but has since expanded to India and Africa. On Global Giving, for example, we have supported a program to keep runaway girls in Mumbai from entering prostitution, while on Kiva we lent money to a woman making furniture in Paraguay.
2. Sponsor a girl or a woman through Plan International, Women for Women International, World Vision, or American Jewish World Service. We ourselves are sponsors through Plan, and we exchange letters and have visited our children in the Phillippines, Sudan, and Dominican Republic. Sponsorship is also a way to teach your children that not all kids have iPods.
3. Sign up for e-mail updates on www.womensenews.org and a

similar service, www.worldpulse.com. Both distribute information about abuses of women and sometimes advise on actions
that readers can take.

4. Join the CARE Action Network at www.can.care.org. This
   will assist you in speaking out, educating policy makers, and
   underscoring that the public wants action against poverty
   and injustice. This kind of citizen advocacy is essential to create
   change. As we've said, this movement won't be led by the
   president or by members of Congress, any more than their
   historical counterparts led the civil fights or abolitionist
   movements – but if leaders smell votes, they will follow. The
   government will act where our national interests are at stake;
   however, history has repeatedly shown that where our values
   are at stake, leadership must come from ordinary citizens
   like you.

These four steps are simply a way to break the ice. After you have
done that, browse the organizations listed in the appendix, find
one that seems particularly meaningful – and dive in. Join forces
with some friends or form a giving club to multiply the impact.
Now let's get on with it and speed up the day when women truly
hold up half the sky.

APPENDIX

ORGANIZATIONS SUPPORTING WOMEN

Here are some of the groups that specialize in supporting women in developing countries. In addition, there are many outstanding aid groups, such as International Rescue Committee, UNICEF, Save the Children, and Mercy Corps, that are not listed below because women and girls are not their only focus. This list is not a rating, screening, or exhaustive list; it is a quirky compendium of groups both small and large that we've seen in action. Consider it a starting point for further research. Two useful Web sites to consult for more information about aid groups are **www.charitynavigator.org** and **www.givewell.net**.

Afghan Institute of Learning, **www.creatinghope.org**, operates schools and other programs for women and girls in Afghanistan and in the border areas of Pakistan.

American Assistance for Cambodia, **www.cambodiaschools.com**, has fought trafficking and now has a program to subsidize poor girls so that they remain in school.

Americans for UNFPA, **www.americansforunfpa.org**, supports the work of the UN Population Fund. It is similar to 34 Million Friends of UNFPA, **www.34millionfriends.org**.

Apne Aap, **www.apneaap.org**, battles sex slavery in India, including in remote areas in Bihar that get little attention. Apne Aap welcomes American volunteers.

Ashoka, **www.ashoka.org**, is an organization that identifies and invests in social entrepreneurs around the world, many of them women.

Averting Maternal Death and Disability, **www.amddprogram.org**, is a leading organization focused on maternal health.

BRAC, **www.brac.net**, is a terrific Bangladesh-based aid group that is now expanding in Africa and Asia. It has an office in New York City and accepts interns.

Campaign for Female Education (CAMFED), **www.camfed.org**, supports schooling for girls in Africa.

CARE, **www.care.org**, increasingly has focused on women and girls.

Center for Development and Population Activities (CEDPA), **www.cedpa.org**, works on issues related to women and development.

Center for Reproductive Rights, **www.reproductiverights.org**, based in New York, focuses on reproductive.health worldwide.

ECPAT, **www.ecpat.net**, is a network of groups fighting child prostitution, particularly in Southeast Asia.

Edna Adan Maternity Hospital, **www.ednahospital.org**, provides maternity care in Somaliland. It welcomes volunteers.

Engender Health, **www.engenderhealth.org**, focuses on reproductive health issues in the developing world.

Equality Now, **www.equalitynow.org**, lobbies against the sex trade and gender oppression around the world.

Family Care International, **www.familycareintl.org**, works to improve maternal health, primarily in Africa, Latin America, and the Caribbean.

Fistula Foundation, **www.fistulafoundation.org**, supports the Addis Ababa Fistula Hospital in Ethiopia, established by Reg and Catherine Hamlin.

Global Fund for Women, **www.globalfundforwomen.org**, operates like a venture capital fund for women's groups in poor countries.

Global Grassroots, **www.globalgrassroots.org**, is a young organization focused on women in poor countries, particularly Sudan.

Grameen Bank, **www.grameen-info.org**, pioneered microfinance in Bangladesh and has now branched into an array of development programs.

Heal Africa, **www.healafrica.org**, runs a hospital in Goma, Congo, that repairs fistulas and tends to rape victims. It welcomes volunteers.

Hunger Project, **www.thp.org**, focuses on empowerment of women and girls to end hunger.

International Center for Research on Women, **www.icrw.org**, emphasizes gender as the key to economic development.

International Justice Mission, **www.ijm.org**, is a Christian-based organization that fights sex trafficking.

International Women's Health Coalition, **www.iwhc.org**, based in New York, has been a leader in the struggle for reproductive health rights around the globe.

Marie Stopes International, **www.mariestopes.org**, based in the

United Kingdom, focuses on reproductive health care around the world.

New Light, **www.newlightindia.org**, is Urmi Basu's organization to help prostitutes and their children in Kolkata, India. It welcomes volunteers.

Pathfinder International, **www.pathfind.org**, supports reproductive health in more than twenty-five countries.

Pennies for Peace, **www.penniesforpeace.org**, run by Greg Mortenson (author of *Three Cups of Tea*), provides education in Pakistan and Afghanistan, for girls in particular.

Population Services International, **www.psi.org**, is based in Washington, D.C., and makes fine use of the private sector in reproductive health.

Pro Mujer, **www.promujer.org**, supports women in Latin America through microfinance and business training.

Self Employed Women's Association (SEWA), **www.sewa.org**, is a huge union for poor, self-employed women in India. It accepts volunteers.

Shared Hope International, **www.sharedhope.org**, fights sex trafficking around the world.

Somaly Mam Foundation, **www.somaly.org**, led by a woman who as a child was trafficked herself, fights sex slavery in Cambodia.

Tostan, **www.tostan.org**, is one of the most successful organizations in overcoming female genital cutting in Africa. It accepts interns.

Vital Voices, **www.vitalvoices.org**, supports women's rights in many countries and has been particularly active in fighting trafficking.

White Ribbon Alliance for Safe Motherhood, **www.whiteribbonalliance .org**, campaigns against maternal mortality around the world.

Women for Women International, **www.womenforwomen.org**, connects women sponsors with needy women in conflict or postconflict countries.

Women's Campaign International, **www.womenscampaigninterna-tional.org**, is dedicated to increasing the participation of women in political and democratic processes worldwide.

Women's Dignity Project, **www.womensdignity.org**, cofounded by an American woman, facilitates the repair of obstetric fistulas in Tanzania.

Women's Learning Partnership, **www.learningpartnership.org**, emphasizes women's leadership and empowerment in the developing world.

Women's Refugee Commission, **www.womensrefugeecommission.org**, is linked to the International Rescue Committee and focuses on refugee women and children.

Women's World Banking, **www.womensworldbanking.org**, supports microfinance institutions around the world that assist women.

Women Thrive Worldwide, **www.womenthrive.org**, is an international advocacy group focused on the needs of women in poor countries.

Worldwide Fistula Fund, **www.worldwidefistulafund.org**, works to improve maternal health and is building a fistula hospital in Niger.

ACKNOWLEDGEMENTS

This book arose in large part from our years of reporting together for *The New York Times*, and so we owe a huge debt to those who made that reporting possible. That group includes Arthur Sulzberger Jr., who gave Nick the column and who with his family has supported the *Times*'s vision of covering important news all over the world despite the cost. When we watched other news organizations pull back from covering international news in recent years, we were enormously relieved and proud to be part of a family-owned newspaper with the backing of the Sulzbergers. They show a steadfast commitment to a mission greater than quarterly profits, and all consumers of news owe them a huge debt of gratitude.

Among others at *The Times* to whom we owe special thanks are Bill Keller, Gail Collins, and Nick's current editor, Andrew Rosenthal. It was Andy who approved the book leave that made this work possible and who puts up with Nick periodically disappearing into jungles and conflict zones. Naka Nathaniel, a former *Times* videographer, regularly accompanied Nick on trips for five years, beginning during the Iraq war, and was the perfect companion when they were arrested together in one country after another. David Sanger, the chief Washington correspondent of *The Times*, has been a pal since we were in college together and a terrific sounding board ever since. And a special thanks to the many foreign correspondents of *The Times* from Kabul to Johannesburg who opened their homes, offices, and Rolodexes to us when we dropped into town.

Many years ago Bill Safire introduced us to the best of literary agents: Anne Sibbald and Mort Janklow. They have been enormously helpful ever since and have played midwife to each of our books. Jonathan Segal, our editor at Knopf, is an editorial alchemist who was an early believer in this project and greatly shaped it at every stage. Meticulous editing is a dying art in much of the publishing industry, but not with Jon and not at Knopf.

A handful of people read the entire manuscript and offered detailed suggestions. These include Esther Duflo of MIT; Josh Ruxin of Columbia University; Helene Gayle of CARE; Sara Seims of the Hewlett

Suad Ahmed, telling her story in a refuge camp in Chad
(Nicholas D. Kristof)

Foundation; and Jason DeParle, Courtney Sullivan, and Natasha Yefimov of *The Times*.

A special group of people has worked tirelessly to spread the message of *Half the Sky* throughout the multimedia world, including film, television, and cyberspace. Mikaela Beardsley has brought together an extraordinary group, including a fellow film producer, Jamie Gordon, along with Lisa Witter of Fenton Communications and Ashley Maddox and Dee Poku of The Bridge. They are passionately committed to sparking a new movement on behalf of the world's women. In addition, Suzanne Seggerman at Games for Change and Alan Gershenfeld at E-line Ventures have contributed their energy and expertise to create a video game of *Half the Sky*.

We dedicated our first book to our parents, Ladis and Jane Kristof and David and Alice WuDunn, and we could dedicate every book and article we have ever written to our parents without coming close to requiting our debts to them. Then there are our children – Gregory, Geoffrey, and Caroline – who endured a measure of negligence because of our reporting and writing. Our dinner table has often been the sounding board for ideas expressed here, and they helpfully pointed out when our ideas were inane.

The heart of this book is the reporting we undertook over many years in Asia, Africa, and Latin America. We intruded by asking women to describe intimate, terrifying, or stigmatizing experiences, and stunningly often they agreed. Sometimes they risked punishment from the authorities

ACKNOWLEDGEMENTS

or the ostracism of their communities, yet they still cooperated because they wanted to help battle oppression. We'll never forget Suad Ahmed, a twenty-five-year-old Darfuri woman whom we met in a Chadian refugee camp encircled by Janjaweed militias. Suad had ventured out with her beloved younger sister, Halima, to get firewood to cook food, when she saw the Janjaweed racing toward them. Suad told Halima to run back to the camp and then boldly made a diversion of herself by jumping up and running in the opposite direction so that Halima could escape. The Janjaweed saw Suad and ran after her; then they beat her, and eight of them gang-raped her. She allowed us to tell her story, using her name. When we asked why, she answered: *That's the only way I can fight back against the Janjaweed, by telling what happened to me and giving my name.*

We owe so much to women like Suad, not only for their assistance but also for inspiring us with their courage and dedication to a cause larger than themselves. That is one reason we are dedicating our book in part to them. Many of these women are illiterate, impoverished, and live in remote villages — and they taught us so much. We have been honored to sit at their feet.

Most of the quotations and reporting in this book derive from our own interviews. Where we heard quotations secondhand and can't be sure the wording is exactly right (such as statements by Akku Yadav when he was terrorizing the inhabitants of Kasturba Nagar), we use italics rather than quotation marks. When we give an age, it's typically the age at the time of the interview. Another convention: We often use the royal 'we' even if only one of us was present at a scene.

This is not a complete bibliography of the books and papers we consulted, but in these notes, we try to provide citations for quotations or information that came from sources other than interviews. Most of the academic papers are available online at no charge through a quick search of the Web.

INTRODUCTION *The Girl Effect*

xiv **This study found that thirty-nine thousand baby girls die:** Sten Johansson and Ola Nygren, 'The Missing Girls of China: A New Demographic Account,' *Population and Development Review* 17, no. 1 (March 1991): 35–51.

xv **to punish a woman for an inadequate dowry:** The dowry system itself may reflect the degree of female empowerment in society. Some anthropologists believe that where women are permitted to work more outside the house they have greater economic value, and thus dowries matter less or are replaced by a bride price, in which money is paid to the bride's family rather than the other way around. An overview of the dowry and bride price, and an explanation for why they often exist side by side, is in Nathan Nunn, 'A Model Explaining Simultaneous Payments of a Dowry and Bride-Price,' manuscript, March 4, 2005. He examined 186 societies around the world and found a dowry system alone in 11 of these societies, a bride price alone in 98 societies, a combination of both dowry and bride price in 33 societies, and neither dowry nor bride price in 44 societies.

xvi **Amartya Sen:** The landmark report that launched this field of inquiry was Amartya Sen, 'More Than 100 Million Women Are Missing,' *The New York Review of Books*, December 20, 1990. That was followed by Ansley J. Coale, 'Excess Female Mortality and the Balance of the Sexes in the Population: An Estimate of the Number of "Missing Females,"' *Population and Development Review*, September 17, 1991. The third estimate is Stephan Klasen and Claudia Wink, '"Missing Women": Revisiting the Debate,' *Feminist Economics* 9 (January 2003): 263–99.

xvi **50 percent more likely to die:** That estimate of excess female mortality among Indian infants comes from the United Nations Development Programme but may be an understatement. Professor Oster cites data indicating that between the ages of one and four years, girls in India die at a rate 71 percent higher than if they were treated the same as boys. Emily Oster, 'Proximate Sources of Population Sex Imbalance in India,' manuscript, October 1, 2007. The 71 percent is derived from Oster's figures of 1.4 percent expected mortality for Indian girls between the ages of one and four, compared to actual mortality of 2.4 percent.

xvii **quantified the wrenching trade-off:** Nancy Qian, 'More Women Missing, Fewer Girls Dying: The Impact of Abortion on Sex Ratios at Birth and Excess Female Mortality in Taiwan,' CEPR Discussion Paper No. 6667, January 2008.

xxi **In 2001 the World Bank:** *Engendering Development Through Gender Equality in Rights, Resources, and Voice*, World Bank Policy Research Report (Washington, D.C.: World Bank, 2001); also, *The State of the World's Children 2007: Women and Children, the Double Dividend of Gender Equality* (New York: UNICEF, 2006).

xxi **The United Nations Development Programme:** *United Nations Development Programme: Global Partnership for Development, United Nations Development Programme Annual Report 2006* (New York: UNDP, 2006), p. 20.

xxii **'Women are the key':** Hunger Project, 'Call for Nominations for the 2008 Africa Prize,' statement, June 3, 2008, New York.

xxii **French foreign minister Bernard Kouchner:** Bernard Kouchner, speech to International Women's Health Coalition, New York City, January 2008.

xxii The Center for Global Development: *Girls Count: A Global Investment & Action Agenda* (Washington, D.C.: Center for Global Development, 2008).

xxii 'Gender inequality hurts economic growth': Sandra Lawson, 'Women Hold Up Half the Sky,' *Global Economics Paper No. 164*, Goldman Sachs, March 4, 2008, p. 9.

CHAPTER ONE *Emancipating Twenty-First-Century Slaves*

6 There are 2 to 3 million prostitutes in India: That estimate comes from Moni Nag, *Sex Workers of India: Diversity in Practice of Prostitution and Ways of Life* (Mumbai: Allied Publishers, 2006), p. 6. It is generally in accord with other estimates. An estimate in the same range comes from an NGO in Delhi, Bharatiya Patita Uddhar Sabha, which calculated that there are 2.4 million sex workers across India. A 2004 journal article asserted that India has 3.5 million commercial sex workers, a quarter of them seventeen or younger: Amit Chattopadhyay and Rosemary G. McKaig, 'Social Development of Commercial Sex Workers in India: An Essential Step in HIV/AIDS Prevention,' *AIDS Patient Care and STDs* 18, no. 3 (2004): 162.

6 One 2008 study of Indian brothels: Kamalesh Sarkar, Baishali Bal, Rita Mukherjee, Sekhar Chakraborty, Suman Saha, Arundhuti Ghosh, and Scott Parsons, 'Sex-trafficking, Violence, Negotiating Skill and HIV Infection in Brothel-based Sex Workers of Eastern India, Adjoining Nepal, Bhutan and Bangladesh,' *Journal of Health, Population and Nutrition* 26, no. 2 (June 2008): 223–31. These self-reported estimates of the proportion of prostitutes in India who entered brothels voluntarily may be high, because of the prostitutes' fear of punishment from pimps for telling the truth.

6 China has more prostitutes: In the early 1990s, a common estimate for the number of prostitutes in China was 1 million, and that had increased to 3 million by about 2000. In recent years, higher figures have often been used. Qiu Haitao, author of a Chinese-language work on China's sexual revolution, estimates that there are 7 million sex workers in China. A scholar, Zhou Jinghao, who has written about the history of prostitution, has estimated that there are 20 million prostitutes in China. Another, Zhong Wei, offers an estimate of 10 million. The higher numbers include *er-nai*, who are more like concubines or mistresses in other countries. One reason to give credence to the high estimates is that the authorities have periodically released figures suggesting that more than 200,000 women a year are arrested annually in the standard spring crackdown on vice. There is some forced sex trafficking in China's southwest of girls from ethnic minorities who do not speak Mandarin Chinese well, and some of those girls end up in the brothels of Thailand or Southeast Asia.

China's larger problem with trafficking concerns not prostitution but women who are to be wives of peasants in remote areas. This phenomenon, called *guimai funu*, exists on a vast scale; researchers have estimated that there are many tens of thousands of cases each year. Typically the young woman is promised a job in a factory or restaurant in a coastal area and then is taken to a remote village and sold to a man for the equivalent of a few hundred dollars. She may be tied up for the first few months, or at least closely watched so that she does not escape. After the woman has a baby, she usually resigns herself to her fate and decides to stay in the village.

10 **And *The Lancet*:** Brian M. Willis and Barry S. Levy, 'Child Prostitution: Global Health Burden, Research Needs, and Interventions,' *The Lancet* 359 (April 20, 2002).

11 **27 million modern slaves:** The figure of 27 million slaves appears, for example, in the opening line of *Not for Sale*, a commendable call to arms against trafficking by David Batstone (New York: HarperCollins, 2007). The figure is widely cited in the growing literature about human trafficking. Two of the more scholarly works are by Louise Brown, a British sociologist who conducted research among the brothels of Lahore, Pakistan. Her books include *The Dancing Girls of Lahore* (New York: HarperCollins, 2005) and *Sex Slaves: The Trafficking of Women in Asia* (New York: Vintage, 2000). Somewhat more popular is Kevin Bales, *Ending Slavery: How We Free Today's Slaves* (Berkeley: University of California Press, 2007). An impressionistic anthology is Jesse Sage and Liora Kasten, eds., *Enslaved: True Stories of Modern Day Slavery* (New York: Palgrave Macmillan, 2006), with chapters about individuals from all over the world. Igor David Gaon and Nancy Forbord, *For Sale: Women and Children* (Victoria, B.C.: Trafford Publishing, 2005), provides a focus on the problem

in southeastern Europe. Human Rights Watch has also published excellent studies of trafficking in Japan, Thailand, Togo, Bosnia, and India. Gary Haugen, an evangelical Christian who founded International Justice Mission, an antitrafficking organization with a large Christian following and a global network, has written *Terrify No More: Young Girls Held Captive and the Daring Undercover Operation to Win Their Freedom* (Nashville, Tenn.: Thomas Nelson Publishers, 2005).

11 **and a very small number of boys:** We focus on female sex slaves because they far outnumber the males. There are male prostitutes in the developing world, but they are more likely to be freelancers who are not forced into the business or locked up in brothels. One careful sociological study of male sex workers is Mark Padilla's *Caribbean Pleasure Industry: Tourism, Sexuality, and AIDS in the Dominican Republic* (Chicago: University of Chicago Press, 2007).

12 **As the journal *Foreign Affairs* observed:** The quotation comes from Ethan B. Kapstein, 'The New Global Slave Trade,' *Foreign Affairs* 85, no. 6 (November/December 2006): 105.

12 **In 1791, North Carolina decreed:** Rodney Stark, *For the Glory of God: How Monotheism Led to Reformations, Science, Witch-Hunts, and the End of Slavery* (Princeton, N.J.: Princeton University Press, 2003), pp. 320–22.

CHAPTER TWO *Prohibition and Prostitution*

30 **HIV prevalence was inexplicably high:** Kamalesh Sarkar et al., 'Epidemiology of HIV Infection Among Brothel-Based Sex Workers in Kolkata, India,' *Journal of Health, Population and Nutrition* 23, no. 3 (September 2005): 231–35.

31 **Harvard School of Public Health:** The MAP Network, which monitors AIDS, found that sex-worker HIV prevalence in Kolkata was 1 percent until 1994, and that it reached 51 percent in Mumbai in 1993. *MAP Network Regional Report*, October 1997.

31 **Another is Urmi Basu:** One of the most creative efforts to help Indian children in the brothels is the Kalam creative writing project, through Urmi's program in Kolkata. It conducted poetry workshops to teach the children how to write poems, and then published some of those poems – in English and Bengali – in *Poetic*

Spaces, a privately printed booklet. The idea is that Bengalis revere culture and poetry, and so if they see that prostitutes and their children write poetry, they will feel more empathy for trafficking victims. We don't know if the project succeeded in building empathy, but it did produce moving poetry. The Kalam project was conducted with the Daywalka Foundation, a small American foundation that focuses on trafficking in India and Nepal.

32 **But Anup Patel:** The statement from Anup Patel is from a manuscript, 'Funding a Red-Light Fire,' prepared for publication in the *Yale Journal of Public Health*. Anup, a Yale medical student, used his extra scholarship funds to form a group to help trafficking victims: Cents of Relief (www.centsofrelief.org).

34 **Mumbai's brothels historically were worse:** The crackdown approach was also applied in Goa, India, but there hasn't been much serious follow-up to determine if it worked. A bitterly critical comment on that crackdown, favoring instead the Sonagachi model, is Maryam Shahmanesh and Sonali Wayal, 'Targeting Commercial Sex-Workers in Goa, India: Time for a Strategic Rethink?' *The Lancet* 364 (October 9, 2004): 1297–99. Likewise, sympathetic accounts of a model like DMSC's can be found in Geetanjali Misra and Radhika Chandiramani, *Sexuality, Gender and Rights: Exploring Theory and Practice in South and Southeast Asia* (New Delhi: Sage Publications, 2005), especially chapter 112. Those sympathetic to the Sonagachi model sometimes argue that while sex work is unpleasant and dangerous, so are scavenging at garbage dumps and other jobs that the poor typically perform. Melissa Farley is among those who counter that while there are many unpleasant jobs, prostitution is uniquely degrading. She is editor of *Prostitution, Trafficking, and Traumatic Stress* (Binghamton, N.Y.: Haworth Maltreatment & Trauma Press, 2003).

35 **A decade later, Sweden's crackdown:** Norway looked at both the Swedish and Dutch models and produced an excellent report about the two approaches. Most of the data come from that report: 'Purchasing Sexual Services in Sweden and the Netherlands, a Report by a Working Group on the Legal Regulation of the Purchase of Sexual Services,' Oslo, 2004. Likewise Scotland examined the Dutch and Swedish approaches, along with that of New South Wales in Australia, and preferred Sweden's strategy: Scottish Parliament, Local Government and

Transport Committee, 'Evidence Received for Prostitution Tolerance Zones (Scotland) Bill Stage One,' February 4, 2004.

CHAPTER THREE *Learning to Speak Up*

57 A retired high court judge, Bhau Vahane: Raekha Prasad, 'Arrest Us All,' *The Guardian*, September 16, 2005.

The New Abolitionists

61 'The agricultural revolution': Bill Drayton, 'Everyone a Changemaker: Social Entrepreneurship's Ultimate Goal,' *Innovations* 1, no. 1 (Winter 2006): 80–96.

CHAPTER FOUR *Rule by Rape*

68 Women aged fifteen through forty-four: The calculation that more women die or are maimed from male violence than from the other causes comes from Marie Vlachova and Lea Biason, eds., *Women in an Insecure World: Violence Against Women, Facts, Figures and Analysis* (Geneva: Centre for the Democratic Control of Armed Forces, 2005), p. vii. The discussion of acid attacks comes from the same work, pp. 31–33.

69 21 percent of Ghanaian women reported in one survey: Ruth Levine, Cynthia Lloyd, Margaret Greene, and Caren Grown, *Girls Count: A Global Investment & Action Agenda* (Washington, D.C.: Center for Global Development, 2008), p. 53.

69 political office in Kenya: Swanee Hunt, 'Let Women Rule,' *Foreign Affairs* (May/June 2007): 116.

69 Woineshet: Emily Wax, a superb reporter, published an excellent article about Woineshet's case from which we also gained details: 'Ethiopian Rape Victim Pits Law Against Culture,' *The Washington Post*, June 7, 2004, p. A1.

75 Namely: sexism and misogyny: The late Jack Holland wrote a fine book a few years ago titled *Misogyny: The World's Oldest Prejudice* (New York: Carroll & Graf, 2006). He wrote that he often encountered surprise that a book about misogyny would be written by a man, and his response was always: 'Why not? It was invented by men.'

76 **One study suggests that women perpetrators were involved:** Dara Kay Cohen, 'The Role of Female Combatants in Armed Groups: Women and Wartime Rape in Sierra Leone (1991–2002),' unpublished essay, Stanford University, Palo Alto, Calif, 2008.

76 **As for wife beating:** Robert Jensen and Emily Oster, 'The Power of TV: Cable Television and Women's Status in India,' manuscript, July 30, 2007, p. 38.

Mukhtar's School

79 **Mukhtar Mai:** For more information about Mukhtar Mai, read her autobiography (full disclosure: Nick wrote the foreword). It's Mukhtar Mai, *In the Name of Honor* (New York: Atria, 2006). See also Asma Jahangir and Hilna Jilani, *The Hudood Ordinances: A Divine Sanction?* (Lahore: Sange-Meel Publications, 2003).

CHAPTER FIVE *The Shame of 'Honor'*

93 **Half of the women in Sierra Leone:** Rape figures in Liberia, Sierra Leone, and parts of the Kivus come from Anne-Marie Goetz, 'Women Targeted or Affected by Armed Conflict: What Role for Military Peacekeepers,' UNIFEM presentation, May 27, 2008, Sussex, U.K.

95 **John Holmes:** The quotation about Congo comes from an excellent article: Jeffrey Gettleman, 'Rape Epidemic Raises Trauma of Congo War,' *The New York Times*, October 7, 2007, p. A1.

97 **The hospital is called HEAL Africa:** In this chapter we focus on the HEAL Africa hospital in North Kivu. In South Kivu there is another hospital, Panzi Hospital, with a similar story of heroism as it treats rape victims and repairs fistulas.

CHAPTER SIX *Maternal Mortality — One Woman a Minute*

104 **Fistulas like hers are common:** For a medical review of issues related to obstetric fistulas, see 'The Obstetric Vesicovaginal Fistula in the Developing World,' supplement to *Obstetric & Gynecological Survey*, July 2005. Catherine Hamlin wrote an autobiography that was published in her native Australia: Dr. Catherine

Hamlin, with John Little, *The Hospital by the River: A Story of Hope* (Sydney: Macmillan, 2001).

109 L. Lewis Wall: L. Lewis Wall, 'Obstetric Vesicovaginal Fistula as an International Public-Health Problem,' *The Lancet* 368 (September 30, 2006): 1201.

109 Eleven percent of the world's inhabitants: 'Of Markets and Medicines,' *The Economist*, December 19, 2007.

110 maternal mortality ratio (MMR): The figures are not terribly reliable, largely because the death of a pregnant woman in the villages isn't considered significant – and so nobody counts all of them. The numbers we use are principally drawn from a major UN study, *Maternal Mortality in 2005: Estimates Developed by WHO, UNICEF, UNFPA, and the World Bank* (Geneva: World Health Organization, 2007). It's an excellent overview of the statistics. The statistical approach has been tweaked somewhat since the previous study: *Maternal Mortality in 2000: Estimates Developed by WHO, UNICEF, UNFPA* (Geneva: World Health Organization, 2004).

111 psychological studies show that statistics: The research by psychologists on how we are moved by individual cases and not by large-scale suffering raises important issues for anyone trying to galvanize a public response to suffering. It certainly shapes the way we approach our work. See Paul Slovic, '"If I Look at the Mass, I Will Never Act": Psychic Numbing and Genocide,' *Judgment and Decision Making* 2, no. 2 (April 2007): 79–95. Remarkably, the human interest in helping victims seems to taper as soon as the number of victims rises above one.

A Doctor Who Treats Countries, Not Patients

116 Allan Rosenfield: Some of the quotes come from a brochure, *Taking a Stand: A Tribute to Allan Rosenfield, a Legacy of Leadership in Public Health*, published by Columbia University's Mailman School of Public Health, 2006.

CHAPTER SEVEN *Why Do Women Die in Childbirth?*

125 two basic evolutionary trade-offs: The discussion of evolution borrows from a wonderful book about the history of childbirth: Tina Cassidy. *Birth: The Surprising History of How We Are Born* (New York: Atlantic Monthly Press, 2006).

128 **In one careful study:** Nazmul Chaudhury, Jeffrey Hammer, Michael Kremer, Karthik Muralidharan, and F. Halsey Rogers, 'Missing in Action: Teacher and Health Worker Absence in Developing Countries,' *Journal of Economic Perspectives* 20, no. 1 (Winter 2006): 91-116.

129 **'Maternal deaths in developing countries':** Mahmoud F. Fathalla, 'Human Rights Aspects of Safe Motherhood,' *Best Practice & Research: Clinical Obstetrics & Gynaecology* 20, no. 3 (June 2006): 409-19. Dr. Fathalla is an Egyptian obstetrician who has championed maternal health issues.

129 **As *The Lancet* noted:** The quote about the lack of interest in women's issues reflecting an unconscious bias comes from Jeremy Shiffman and Stephanie Smith, 'Generation of Political Priority for Global Health Initiatives: A Framework and Case Study of Maternal Mortality,' *The Lancet* 370 (October 13, 2007): 1375.

129 **Exhibit A is Sri Lanka:** An excellent discussion of Sri Lanka's success in curbing maternal mortality is found in Ruth Levine, *Millions Saved: Proven Successes in Global Health* (Washington, D.C.: Center for Global Development, 2004), especially chapter 5. Honduras is often touted as another example of how even poor countries can achieve astounding reductions in maternal mortality. In the early 1990s, the Honduran government targeted maternal health and the reported MMR in Honduras dropped by 40 percent in seven years. But nothing is as simple as it seems. In 2007, the UN used a new methodology to calculate a maternal mortality ratio for Honduras that was actually higher than it had been back in 1990. Were the improvements in Honduras real? The only lesson seems to be that reliable maternal death figures are exceptionally elusive in poor countries. The success – or possible success – in Honduras is discussed in Levine's *Millions Saved*, and also in Jeremy Shiffman, Cynthia Stanton, and Ana Patricia Salazar, 'The Emergence of Political Priority for Safe Motherhood in Honduras,' *Health Policy and Planning* 19, no. 6 (2004): 380-90. Kerala, India, is also often cited as an example of a place where political will reduced maternal mortality, and that is probably right. Kerala's MMR is variously estimated as anywhere between 87 and 262, compared to a figure of 450 for India as a whole.

133 **study of a fundamentalist Christian church:** The MMR of the fundamentalist Christian sect that eschews medical care is discussed in 'Perinatal and Maternal Mortality in a Religious Group – Indiana,' *MMWR Weekly*, June 1, 1984, pp. 297–98.

133 **'keystone in the arch':** 'Emergency Obstetric Care: The Keystone of Safe Motherhood,' editorial, *International Journal of Gynecology & Obstetrics* 74 (2001): 95–97.

135 **'Investing in better health for women':** Activists who argue that fighting maternal mortality is highly cost-effective cite various estimates about the productivity cost from maternal mortality and morbidity. USAID once claimed that the global impact of maternal deaths and neonatal deaths was about $15 billion in lost productivity, half for mothers and half for newborns. But that methodology was suspect, and we think it's a mistake to try to justify maternal health expenses based on productivity. Men typically work in the formal economy, contributing to GNP, so their productivity is typically higher than that of women or children. So if you try to justify health interventions based on reducing lost productivity caused by sickness, you would prioritize middle-aged men over women or children.

Edna's Hospital

137 **Edna Adan:** Edna's name follows the convention in many Muslim countries. The pattern is for each person to get one name, then to tack on the father's name afterward. If further clarification is needed, the paternal grandfather's name can be added after that. So Edna herself was given only the one name. But since her father was named Adan, she calls herself Edna Adan. When needed for clarity, she adds her grandfather's name and becomes Edna Adan Ismail.

140 **That's when Ian Fisher wrote an article:** The article about Edna that led Anne Gilhuly to try to help was Ian Fisher, 'Hargeisa Journal; A Woman of Firsts and Her Latest Feat: A Hospital,' *The New York Times*, November 29, 1999, p. A4.

CHAPTER EIGHT FAMILY *Planning and the 'God Gulf'*

146 **'contrary to its stated intentions':** The quote from Dr. Eunice Brookman-Amissah comes from 'Breaking the Silence: The

Global Gag Rule's Impact on Unsafe Abortion,' a report from the Center for Reproductive Rights, New York, 2007, p. 4.

148 **Indeed, UNFPA achieved a major breakthrough:** Li Yong Ping, Katherine L. Bourne, Patrick J. Rowe, Zhang De Wei, Wang Shao Xian, Zhen Hao Yin, and Wu Zhen, 'The Demographic Impact of Conversion from Steel to Copper IUDs in China,' *International Family Planning Perspective* 20, no. 4 (December 1994): 124. See also Edwin A. Winckler, 'Maximizing the Impact of Cairo on China,' in Wendy Chavkin and Ellen Chesler, eds., *Where Human Rights Begin: Health, Sexuality and Women in the New Millennium* (New Brunswick, N.J.: Rutgers University Press, 2005).

148 **For every 150 unsafe abortions:** Hailemichael Gebreselassie, Maria F. Gallo, Anthony Monyo, and Brooke R. Johnson, 'The Magnitude of Abortion Complications in Kenya,' *BJOG: An International Journal of Obstet*rics and *Gynaecology* 112, no. 9 (2005): 1129–35. See also David A. Grimes, Janie Benson, Susheela Singh, Mariana Romero, Bela Ganatra, Friday E. Okonofua, and Iqbal H. Shah, 'Unsafe Abortion: The Preventable Pandemic,' *The Lancet* 368 (November 25, 2006): 1908–19; and Gilda Sedgh, Stanley Henshaw, Susheela Singh, Elisabeth Ahman, and Iqbal H. Shah, 'Induced Abortion: Estimated Rates and Trends Worldwide,' *The Lancet* 370 (October 13, 2007): 1338–45.

149 **'We've lost a decade':** *Return of the Population Growth Factor: Its Impact Upon the Millennium Development Goals,* Report of Hearings by the All Party Parliamentary Group on Population, Development and Reproductive Health, House of Commons, U.K., January 2007.

149 **one pioneering family planning project:** Matthew Connelly, *Fatal Misconception: The Struggle to Control World Population* (Cambridge, Mass.: Harvard University Press, 2007), pp. 171–72.

149 **One carefully conducted experiment in Matlab:** Wayne S. Stinson, James F. Phillips, Makhlisur Rahman, and J. Chakraborty, 'The Demographic Impact of the Contraceptive Distribution Project in Matlab, Bangladesh,' *Studies in Family Planning* 13, no. 5 (May 1982): 141–48.

150 **Education Act of 1870:** Mukesh Eswaran, 'Fertility in Developing Countries,' in Abhijit Vinayak Banerjee, Roland

Benabou, and Dilip Mookherjee, *Understanding Poverty* (New York: Oxford University Press, 2006), p. 145. See also T. Paul Schultz, 'Fertility and Income,' in the same volume, p. 125.

150 **crucial these days in fighting AIDS:** A comprehensive article on the genetic origins of AIDS and the timeline of its spread is M. Thomas, P. Gilbert, Andrew Rambaut, Gabriela Wlasiuk, Thomas J. Spira, Arthur E. Pitchenik, and Michael Worobey, 'The Emergence of HIV/AIDS in the Americas and Beyond,' *Proceedings of the National Academy of Sciences* 104 (November 2007): 18566–70.

150 **Women are about twice as likely:** Ann E. Biddlecom, Beth Fredrick, and Susheela Singh, 'Women, Gender and HIV/AIDS,' *Countdown 2015 Magazine*, p. 66; available online at www.populationaction.org/2015/magazine/sect6_HIVAIDS.php.

150 **AIDS to spread around the globe:** An excellent resource on foreign aid efforts against HIV/AIDS is Helen Epstein, *The Invisible Cure: Africa, the West, and the Fight Against AIDS* (New York: Farrar, Straus and Giroux, 2007).

151 **A University of California study:** Nada Chaya and Kali-Ahset Amen with Michael Fox, *Condoms Count: Meeting the Need in the Era of HIV/AIDS* (Washington, D.C.: Population Action International, 2002), p. 5. Much of the information about condoms comes from this booklet. More detail about the long history of condoms, and religious opposition to them, is in Aine Collier, *The Humble Little Condom: A History* (New York: Prometheus Books, 2007).

151 **began spreading the junk science:** The evidence of the effectiveness of condoms against HIV and various STDs is discussed in 'Workshop Summary: Scientific Evidence on Condom Effectiveness for Sexually Transmitted Disease (STD) Prevention,' National Institutes of Health, June 12–13, 2000; available online at www.ccv.org/downloads/pdf/CDC_Condom_Study.pdf.

152 **'Your body is a wrapped lollipop':** Camille Hahn, 'Virgin Territory,' *Ms.* (Fall 2004). The lollipop formulation is widely used by abstinence enthusiasts, and abstinence lollipops are sold on www.abstinence.net.

156 **Poverty Action Lab:** Esther Duflo, Pascaline Dupas, Michael Kremer, and Samuel Sinei, 'Education and HIV/AIDS Prevention: Evidence from a Randomized Evaluation in Western

Kenya,' manuscript, June 2006; and Pascaline Dupas, 'Relative Risks and the Market for Sex: Teenage Pregnancy, HIV, and Partner Selection in Kenya,' manuscript, October 2007, www.dartmouth.edu/~pascaline/.

159 **Pentecostal megachurch in Kiev, Ukraine:** Information about Christianity in the developing world comes from Mark Noll, professor at Wheaton College, in an unpublished presentation to the Council on Foreign Relations, New York, March 2, 2005. See also the good discussion of Christianity's role in nurturing women in the developing world in Philip Jenkins, *The New Faces of Christianity: Believing the Bible in the Global South* (New York: Oxford University Press, 2006), especially chapter 7.

160 **Arthur Brooks:** There's also a discussion of religious giving to the developing world in *The Index of Global Philanthropy 2007*, especially pp. 22–23 and pp. 62–65.

Jane Roberts and Her 34 Million Friends

162 **But Jane Roberts:** The story of the founding of 34 Million Friends is told in Jane Roberts, *34 Million Friends of the Women of the World* (Sonora, Calif: Ladybug Books, 2005).

CHAPTER NINE *Is Islam Misogynistic?*

166 **a very large proportion are predominantly Muslim:** Two books that give an excellent introduction to women in the Islamic world are Jan Goodwin, *Price of Honor: Muslim Women Lift the Veil of Silence on the Islamic World* (New York: Penguin, 2003), and Geraldine Brooks, *Nine Parts of Desire: The Hidden World of Islamic Women* (New York: Anchor, 1995).

167 **In contrast, opinion polls underscore:** *Arab Human Development Report 2005: Towards the Rise of Women in the Arab World* (New York: UNDP, 2006), Annex II, pp. 249 *et seq.*

167 **Grand Mufti Sheikh Abdulaziz:** 'Saudi Arabia's Top Cleric Condemns Calls for Women's Rights,' *The New York Times*, January 22, 2004, p. A 13.

167 **After the Taliban was ousted:** *Afghanistan in 2007: A Survey of the Afghan People* (Kabul: The Asia Foundation, 2007).

169 **Amina Wadud, an Islamic scholar:** Amina Wadud, *Qur'an*

and Woman: Rereading the Sacred Text from a Woman's Perspective (New York: Oxford University Press, 1999).

169 A useful analogy is slavery: Rodney Stark, *For the Glory of God: How Monotheism Led to Reformations, Science, Witch-Hunts and the End of Slavery* (Princeton, N.J.: Princeton University Press, 2003), pp. 301–4. See also Bernard Lewis, *Race and Slavery in the Middle East: An Historical Enquiry* (New York: Oxford University Press, 1992), and Murray Gordon, *Slavery in the Arab World* (New York: New Amsterdam Books, 1990). For examples of how slaves were treated in different Islamic societies, see Shaun E. Marmon, ed., *Slavery in the Islamic Middle East* (Princeton, N.J.: Markus Wiener Publishers, 1999).

170 a longtime adversary, Ali: The followers of Ali are the Shiites, and so even today Aisha is distinctly unloved by Shiites. Aisha is a common name for Sunni girls; it is almost unknown among Shiites.

171 some Islamic feminists: Fatima Mernissi, *The Veil and the Male Elite: A Feminist Interpretation of Women's Rights in Islam*, trans. Mary Jo Lakeland (New York: Basic Books, 1991). See also Fatima Mernissi's other books, including *Beyond the Veil: Male-Female Dynamics in Modern Muslim Society*, rev. ed. (Bloomington: Indiana University Press, 1987). A pioneer within the Arab world in fighting for women's rights was Nawal el Saadawi, author of *The Hidden Face of Eve: Women in the Arab World* (Boston: Beacon Press, 1980).

171 Another dispute about the Koran: Christoph Luxenberg, *The Syro-Aramaic Reading of the Koran: A Contribution to the Decoding of the Language of the Koran* (Berlin: Hans Schiler Publishers, 2007). We corresponded with Luxenberg by e-mail but don't know his true identity; he uses the pseudonym for safety, since fundamentalists might try to kill him.

172 the complexity of gender roles: One way to understand the nuances of Islam in the West is to take a look at *Muslim Girl* magazine. Founded in 2006 by a Pakistani-American, Ausma Khan, it is unapologetic about Islam while also supporting human rights and projecting models of smart and assertive young women.

172 'I'm a Nobel Peace Prize-winner': Shirin Ebadi also explores these issues in her book, *Iran Awakening: A Memoir of Revolution and Hope* (New York: Random House, 2006).

176 'For each percentage-point increase': Henrik Urdal, 'The Demographics of Political Violence: Youth Bulges, Insecurity and

Conflict,' mimeograph, 2007. There is a rich and controversial literature about the tendency of all-male cohorts to be particularly violent. See David T. Courtwright, *Violent Land: Single Men and Social Disorder from the Frontier to the Inner City* (Cambridge, Mass.: Harvard University Press, 1998). For a biological take, see Dale Peterson and Richard Wrangham, *Demonic Males: Apes and the Origins of Human Violence* (New York: Mariner Books, 1997).

177 **In Yemen, women make up only 6 percent:** Ricardo Hausmann, Laura D. Tyson, and Saadia Zahidi, *The Global Gender Gap Report 2006* (Geneva: World Economic Forum, 2006), and *Arab Human Development Report 2005*, p. 88.

177 **As a UN Arab Human Development Report put it:** *Arab Human Development Report 2005*, p. 24.

178 **'The status of women':** M. Steven Fish, 'Islam and Authoritarianism,' *World Politics* 55 (October 2002): 4–37; quotations from p. 37 and pp. 30–31.

178 **'The economic implications of gender discrimination':** David S. Landes, *The Wealth and Poverty of Nations: Why Some Are So Rich and Some So Poor* (New York: W. W. Norton, 1998), pp. 412–13.

CHAPTER TEN *Investing in Education*

187 **'The evidence, in most cases':** Esther Duflo, 'Gender Equality in Development,' BREAD Policy Paper No. 011, December 2006.

188 **the state of Kerala:** Amartya Sen and others have often held up Kerala as an example of what is possible for women in development. We share the enthusiasm for what Kerala has achieved in education, health, and gender but are deeply disappointed with its economic mismanagement and market-unfriendly investment climate. Kerala's economy has stagnated and depends on remittances from Kerala natives who work in the Gulf. More information on Kerala is in K. P. Kannan, K. R. Thanappan, V. Raman Kutty, and K. P. Aravindan, *Health and Development in Rural Kerala* (Trivandrum, India: Integrated Rural Technology Center, 1991).

188 **the case for investing in girls' education:** See Barbara Herz and Gene B. Sperling, *What Works in Girls' Education: Evidence and Policies from the Developing World* (New York: Council on Foreign

Relations, 2004). There are many, many other studies and reports on the impact of girls' education, but this is a useful summary of the findings. See also *Girls Education: Designing for Success* (Washington, D.C.: World Bank, 2007), and Dina Abu-Ghaida and Stephan Klasen, *The Economic and Human Development Costs of Missing the Millennium Development Goal on Gender Equity* (Washington, D.C.: World Bank, 2004).

188 **Indonesia vastly increased school attendance:** Lucia Breierova and Esther Duflo, 'The Impact of Education on Fertility and Child Mortality: Do Fathers Really Matter Less Than Mothers?' unpublished manuscript, March 2002.

188 **Similarly, Una Osili:** Una Okonkwo Osili and Bridget Terry Long, 'Does Female Schooling Reduce Fertility? Evidence from Nigeria,' manuscript, June 2007.

190 **FemCare:** Claudia H. Deutsch, 'A Not-So-Simple Plan to Keep African Girls in School,' *The New York Times*, November 12, 2007, Special Section on Philanthropy, p. 6.

190 **Fetuses need iodine:** Erica Field, Omar Robles, and Maximo Torero, 'The Cognitive Link Between Geography and Development: Iodine Deficiency and Schooling Attainment in Tanzania,' manuscript, October 2007, www.economics.harvard.edu/faculty/field/files/Field IDD_ Tanzania.pdf

191 **One of the pioneers is Mexico:** Tina Rosenberg discusses Santiago Levy's launch of Progresa, later renamed Oportunidades, in 'How to Fight Poverty: Eight Programs That Work,' Talking Points memo for www.nytimes.com, November 16, 2006. See also World Bank, 'Shanghai Poverty Conference Case Summary: Mexico's Oportunidades Program,' 2004; Emmanuel Skoufias, 'PROGRESA and Its Impacts upon the Welfare of Rural Households in Mexico,' International Food Policy Research Institute, Research Report 139, 2005; Alan B. Krueger, 'Putting Development Dollars to Use, South of the Border,' *The New York Times*, May 2, 2002.

192 **the UN's school feeding program:** *Food for Education Works: A Review of WFP FFE Programme Monitoring and Evaluation, 2002–2006* (Washington, D.C.: World Food Programme, 2007).

192 **A study in Kenya by Michael Kremer:** Michael Kremer, Edward Miguel, and Rebecca Thornton, 'Incentives to Learn,' manuscript, updated January 2007.

194 **'We find little robust evidence':** Raghuram G. Rajan and Arvind Subramanian, 'Aid and Growth: What Does the Cross-Country Evidence Really Show?' *The Review of Economics and Statistics* 90, no. 4 (November 2008): 643.

194 **Yet when Bono spoke:** TED International Conference, June 2007. Mwenda and Bono had a widely discussed run-in over aid effectiveness there. See also Nicholas D. Kristof, 'Bono, Foreign Aid and Skeptics,' *The New York Times*, August 9, 2007, p. A19.

Ann and Angeline

198 **Angeline Mugwendere's parents:** Some material here comes from a pamphlet, *I Have a Story to Tell* (Cambridge, U.K.: Camfed, 2004), p. 11.

202 **Half of Tanzanian women:** Figures for abuse by teachers in South Africa, Tanzania, and Uganda come from Ruth Levine, Cynthia Lloyd, Margaret Greene, and Caren Grown, *Girls Count: A Global Investment & Action Agenda* (Washington, D.C.: Center for Global Development, 2008), p. 54.

CHAPTER ELEVEN *Microcredit: The Financial Revolution*

208 **Muhammad Yunus:** See Muhammad Yunus, *Banker to the Poor: Micro-Lending and the Battle Against World Poverty* (New York: Public Affairs, 2003); David Bornstein, *The Price of a Dream: The Story of the Grameen Bank* (New York: Oxford University Press, 1996); Phil Smith and Eric Thurman, *A Billion Bootstraps: Microcredit, Barefoot Banking, and the Business Solution for Ending Poverty* (New York: McGraw-Hill, 2007).

212 **A remarkable study:** Edward Miguel, 'Poverty and Witch Killing,' *Review of Economic Studies* 72 (2005): 1153.

213 **The economists Abhijit Banerjee and Esther DuHo:** Abhijit V. Banerjee and Esther Duflo, 'The Economic Lives of the Poor,' *Journal of Economic Perspectives* 21, no. 1 (Winter 2007): 141.

214 **In Ivory Coast:** Esther Duflo and Christopher Udry, 'Intra-household Resource Allocation in Côte d'Ivoire: Social Norms, Separate Accounts and Consumption Choices,' Yale University Economic Growth Center Discussion Paper No. 857.

214 **In South Africa:** Esther Duflo, 'Grandmothers and Grand-daughters: Old-Age Pension and Intra-Household Allocation in South Africa,' *World Bank Economic Review* 17, no. 1 (2003): 1–25. Cash transfers to grandmothers did not improve the height and weight of their grandsons, only of their granddaughters. Another study found an inconsistent result: When these new pensions went to South African men, children looked after by those men increased their schooling more than when the new pension went to women. The author himself was startled by his result, and it is an outlier. Eric V. Edmonds, 'Does Illiquidity Alter Child Labor and Schooling Decisions? Evidence from Household Responses to Anticipated Cash Transfers in South Africa,' National Bureau of Economic Research, Working Paper 10265.

215 **'When women command greater power':** Esther Duflo, 'Gender Equality in Development,' BREAD Policy Paper No. 011, December 2006, p. 14.

215 **To its credit the U.S. government:** A similar project is the Women's Legal Rights Initiative, backed by the U.S. Agency for International Development. See *The Women's Legal Rights Initiative: Final Report, January 2007* (Washington, D.C.: USAID, 2007).

217 **the conventional wisdom in development circles:** One study found that the more women in a country's parliament, the less corruption. But that may say more about the countries that elect women than about the women MPs themselves. Europe is not very corrupt and elects many women, but those facts aren't necessarily related; rather, they may both be functions of a well-educated postindustrial society.

217 **One fascinating experiment:** Esther Duflo and Petia Topalova, 'Unappreciated Service: Performance, Perceptions, and Women Leaders in India,' and 'Why Political Reservation?' *Journal of the European Economic Association* 3, nos. 2–3 (May 2005): 668–78, http://econ-www.mit.edu/files/794. Another paper looked at the spending of female village leaders in India and found that they were more likely to elicit participation from women and to spend money on issues of concern to women, such as drinking water. Raghabendhra Chattopadhyay and Esther Duflo, 'Women as Policy Makers: Evidence from a Randomized Policy Experiment in India,' *Econometrica*, 72, no. 5 (September 2004): 1409–43.

218 Whatever the impact: Grant Miller, 'Women's Suffrage, Political Responsiveness, and Child Survival in American History,' *The Quarterly Journal of Economics* 123, no. 3 (August 2008): 1287.

CHAPTER TWELVE *The Axis of Equality*

226 'A woman has so many parts': Lu Xun, 'Anxious Thoughts on "Natural Breasts,"' September 4, 1927, in Lu Xun: *Selected Works*, trans. Yang Xianyi and Gladys Yang, vol. 2 (Beijing: Foreign Languages Press, 1980), p. 355. Lu Xun is among the greatest of modern Chinese writers, a brilliant polemicist for human rights and the equality of women.

226 Zhang Yin: David Barboza, 'Blazing a Paper Trail in China,' *The New York Times*, January 16, 2007, p. C1. Another quote came from a Bloomberg article that appeared in *China Daily*: 'U.S. Trash Helps Zhang Become Richest in China,' January 16, 2007. Information also came from 'Paper Queen,' *The Economist*, June 9, 2007. Zhang Yin is sometimes also known as Cheong Yan, which is the Cantonese version of her name. Zhang Yin was edged out as China's richest person in 2007 by another woman, though not a self-made one. Yang Huiyan was given ownership by her family of its real estate company, Country Garden, and its public offering left her worth $16 billion. That made her richer than Rupert Murdoch, George Soros, and Steve Jobs. David Barboza, 'Shy of Publicity, but Not of Money,' *The New York Times*, November 7, 2007, p. C1. The economic crisis beginning in 2008 has undoubtedly changed all of these wealth figures.

229 The sex ratio of newborns: Some evidence suggests that the rising incomes of women will lead to a self-correction of the sex-selective abortion that has produced a shortfall of girls. For example, one of the cash crops that has been booming in coastal China is tea, and women are generally perceived as having an advantage in harvesting it because they are shorter and have smaller hands. The number of 'missing girls' dropped significantly in the tea-growing areas compared to areas producing other crops. One scholar found that increasing incomes overall had no effect on sex ratios, but that rising female incomes reduced the sex ratio disparity. Each increase in women's income amounting to 10 percent of family income led to an increase in the survival rate of girls of 1 percentage point. Nancy Qian, 'Missing Women and the Price of Tea in China: The Effect of Sex-Specific Income on Sex Imbalance,' manuscript, December 2006. See also Valerie M. Hudson and Andrea M. den Boer, *Bare Branches: The Security Implications of Asia's Surplus Male Population* (Cambridge, Mass.: MIT Press, 2004).

231 **Leading Indian business executives:** In one respect, neglect can benefit girls in India. One study found that in Mumbai, low-caste boys continue to follow traditional routes by attending Marathi-language schools and then finding employment through the caste network. The boys were helped by these social networks but also were locked into low-level jobs. Because girls didn't matter and traditionally were outside the networks, they were allowed to choose English-language schools. Once the girls learned English, they were able to compete for well-paying jobs. Kaivan Munshi and Mark Rosenzweig, 'Traditional Institutions Meet the Modern World: Caste, Gender, and Schooling Choice in a Globalizing Economy,' *The American Economic Review* 96, no. 4 (September 2006): 1225–52.

232 **Sweatshops have given women a boost:** A feminist critique of trade has emerged that disputes our arguments; it asserts that young women are often exploited and preyed upon in sweatshops. There is an element of truth to such charges. Trade-based factories are grim and exploitative, but they are still better than the alternative of life in the village – and that's why women seek the factory jobs. The feminist critique argues that globalization led to an erosion of traditional socialist ideas about equality. All that is true, but socialist ideology was too divorced from economic reality to be more than a fragile foundation for gender equality. We can't do justice to the feminist critique here, but see *The Feminist Economics of Trade*, ed. Irene Van Staveren, Diane Elson, Caren Grown, and Nilüfer Çağatay (New York: Routledge, 2007); *Feminist Economics* (July/October 2007), a special issue about China; Stephanie Seguino and Caren Grown, 'Gender Equity and Globalization: Macroeconomic Policy for Developing Countries,' *Journal of International Development* 18 (2006): 1081–1104; Yana van der Meulen Rodgers and Nidhiya Menon, 'Trade Policy Liberalization and Gender Equality in the Labor Market: New Evidence for India,' manuscript, May 2007. Additional

resources reflecting this approach – much more skeptical about the benefits to women of trade than we are – are to be found at the International Gender and Trade Network, www.igtn.org. Our own view is that this critique is sound about the shortcomings of trade but greatly undervalues the benefits.

233 **As the Oxford University economist Paul Collier has noted:** Paul Collier, *The Bottom Billion: Why the Poorest Countries Are Failing and What Can Be Done About It* (New York: Oxford University Press, 2007), pp. 168–70.

233 **Rwanda is an impoverished, landlocked, patriarchal society:** For a discussion of gender in Rwanda, see *Rwanda's Progress Towards a Gender Equitable Society* (Kigali: Rwanda Women Parliamentary Forum, 2007). Rwanda also empowers women sexually, through two little-known practices that are almost unique in their emphasis on female sexual pleasure. One is the custom among Rwandan women (along with some Baganda women in Uganda) of stretching their genitals as children, in a manner intended to enhance their sexual pleasure as adults. The second practice is called *kunyaza*, and involves sex that focuses on clitoral stimulation, without penetration. Again, the main purpose is to give the woman sexual pleasure. Leana S. Wen, *Thoughts on Rwandan Culture, Sex and HIV/AIDS*, manuscript dated February 2007; and Sylvia Tamale, 'Eroticism, Sensuality, and "Women's Secrets" Among the Baganda: A Critical Analysis,' 2005, www.feministafrica.org.

241 **Zainab Salbi:** See Zainab Salbi and Laurie Becklund, *Between Two Worlds: Escape from Tyranny, Growing up in the Shadow of Saddam* (New York: Gotham Books, 2005).

CHAPTER THIRTEEN *Grassroots vs. Treetops*

245 **Soranos of Ephesus:** Soranos's original textbook on gynecology is lost, but two Latin translations survive. The quotation on performing a clitoridectomy comes from the seventh-century Latin translation of Paulus of Aegina, as found in Bernadette J. Brooten, *Love Between Women: Early Christian Responses to Female Homoeroticism* (Chicago: University of Chicago Press, 1996), p. 164 n. 58; the illustration from a 1666 German textbook is reproduced in Brooten's book as figure 12.

245 **3 million girls are cut annually:** *Changing a Harmful Social Convention: Female Genital Mutilation / Cutting*, Innocenti Digest no. 12 (New York: UNICEF, 2005, 2007). This is also a useful source of data about the geographic reach and incidence of FGC. The person who has written about cutting the longest, ever since 1978, and the most comprehensively, is Fran P. Hosken, author of *The Hosken Report: Genital and Sexual Mutilation of Females*, 4th rev. ed. (Lexington, Mass.: Women's International Network News, 1993). Hosken has estimated that a total of 149 million women are cut. See also *Agency for International Development: Abandoning Female Genital Mutilation / Cutting: An In-Depth Look at Promising Practices* (Washington, D.C.: U.S. Agency for International Development, 2006), especially pp. 29–38.

 A much more limited practice of disfigurement also designed to keep girls chaste is breast ironing. In Cameroon, weights, bands, or belts are used to flatten the breasts so that girls will be less likely to end up raped or seduced. Cameroonian parents calculate that in a world in which girls are prone to abuse, the best way to protect a daughter is to disfigure her.

CHAPTER FOURTEEN *What You Can Do*

260 **Two scholars:** Chaim D. Kaufmann and Robert A. Pape, 'Explaining Costly International Moral Action: Britain's Sixty-Year Campaign Against the Atlantic Slave Trade,' International Organization 53 (Autumn 1999): 637. This is an outstanding article, and the figures we cite for the price Britain paid in confronting the slave trade draw from it.

260 **William Wilberforce:** William Hague, William Wilberforce: *The Life of the Great Anti-Slave Trade Campaigner* (London: Harcourt, 2007). Hague and Senator Brownback are among the modern politicians who say they have been inspired by Wilberforce.

261 **'If anyone was the founder':** 'Slavery: Breaking the Chains,' *The Economist*, February 24, 2007, p. 72.

263 **Swanee Hunt:** Swanee Hunt, 'Let Women Rule,' *Foreign Affairs* (May/June 2007): 120.

264 **'Encouraging more women':** Kevin Daly, *Gender Inequality, Growth and Global Ageing*, Global Economics Paper No. 154, Goldman Sachs, April 3, 2007, p. 3.

264 **One study of America's Fortune 500 companies:** 'The Bottom Line on Women at the Top,' *Business Week*, January 26, 2004. This particular study was conducted by Catalyst, but similar studies have often been conducted over the years with the same results. Parallel research on the Japanese economy has been conducted by Kathy Matsui of Goldman Sachs; see her path-breaking report, *Womenomics: Buy the Female Economy*, Goldman Sachs Investment Research, Japan, August 13, 1999. Since then, Matsui has written a series of follow-ups and helped coin the term 'womenomics.'

265 **developing countries such as Brazil and Kenya:** R. Colom, C. E. Flores-Mendoza, and F. J. Abad, 'Generational Changes on the Draw-a-Man Test: A Comparison of Brazilian Urban and Rural Children Tested in 1930, 2002 and 2004,' *Journal of Biosocial Science* 39, no. 1 (January 2007): 79–89.

265 **The IQ of rural Kenyan children:** B. Bower, 'I.Q. Gains May Reach Rural Kenya's Kids,' *Science News*, May 10, 2003; Tamara C. Daley, Shannon E. Whaley, Marian D. Sigman, Michael P. Espinosa, and Charlotte Neumann, 'I.Q. on the Rise: The Flynn Effect in Rural Kenyan Children,' *Psychological Science* 14, no. 3 (May 2003): 2115–19.

269 **The civil rights and anti-Vietnam War movements:** Sidney Tarrow, *Power in Movement: Social Movements and Contentious Politics*, 2nd ed. (Cambridge, U.K.: Cambridge University Press, 1998), especially p. 204. See also David A. Snow, Sarah A. Soule, and Hanspeter Kriesi, The Blackwell Companion to Social Movements (New York: Wiley, 2007).

269 **In South Korea:** Hunt, 'Let Women Rule,' is the source for information about South Korea and Kyrgyzstan.

270 **In the nineteenth century:** Stephanie Clohesy and Stacy Van Gorp, *The Powerful Intersection of Margins & Mainstream: Mapping the Social Change Work of Women's Funds* (San Francisco: Women's Funding Network, 2007).

270 **In the United States, a 2006 poll found:** Scott Bittle, Ana Maria Arumi, and Jean Johnson, 'Anxious Public Sees Growing Dangers, Few Solutions: A Report from Public Agenda,' *Public Agenda Confidence in U.S. Foreign Policy Index*, Fall 2006.

271 **two new studies:** The Brazil study is Eliana La Ferrara, Alberto Chong, and Suzanne Duryea, 'Soap Operas and Fertility: Evidence

from Brazil,' manuscript, March 2008. The India study is Robert
Jensen and Emily Oster 'The Power of TV: Cable Television and
Women's Status in India,' manuscript, July 30, 2007, p. 38.

273 **the UN should have a prominent agency:** Nobody has been
more articulate than Stephen Lewis in calling for a UN agency to
focus on women. See Stephen Lewis, *Race Against Time: Searching
for Hope in AIDS-Ravaged Africa* (Berkeley, Calif.: Publishers Group
West, 2005).

276 **Social psychologists have learned a great deal:** Jonathan
Haidt, *The Happiness Hypothesis: Finding Modern Truth in Ancient
Wisdom* (New York: Basic Books, 2006). See also Alan B. Krueger,
Daniel Kahneman, David Schkade, Norbert Schwarz, and Arthur
Stone, 'National Time Accounting: The Currency of Life,' draft
paper, March 31, 2008.

INDEX

Page numbers in *italics* refer to illustrations

Ababiya, Ummi, xvii
Ababiya, Zahra, xvii
Abdulaziz, Grand Mufti Sheikh, 167,
   302*n*
Abid, Sadaffe, 209–10
abortions, 145–9
  forced, 116, 147
  reduction of, 148, 271
  sex-selective, xvii, 148, 229
  unsafe, 111, 121, 148, 300*n*
Abraham, Lois, 163–5
abstinence-only programs, 152–3, 156,
   157, 301*n*
acid attacks, 55, 58, 75
  maiming and blinding with, xv, *xv*, 69, 85
  see also bride burning
Adan, Edna, 137–44, *141, 143*, 246, 247,
   299*n*
Addis Ababa, 70, *70*, 72–4, 105–9,
   112–14, 134
Addis Ababa Fistula Hospital, 106–9, *108*,
   112–14, *113, 133*, 134–5
Adelaja, Sunday, 159
adultery, 159, 170
Affleck, Ben, 101
Afghan Institute of Learning, 181, 182
Afghanistan, xxii, 76–7, 166, 179–83
  oppression of women in, 167, *168*,
   173–6, 179–83, 254
  Taliban ousted in, 167, 179, 181–2, 302*n*
Africa, xvi, xxii, 68–75
  HIV/AIDS in, 153–7
  hunger and poverty in, *xvii*, xxii, 111,
   113, 198–201
  maternal mortality in, 110–11, 121–5
  slave trade from, 12, 259–62, 311*n*
  sub-Saharan, 10, 110–11, 148
African Growth and Opportunity Act
   (AGOA), 232

Agency for International Development
   (US), 248, 307*n*
agricultural revolution, 61, 295*n*
aid workers, 29, 30, 38, 45–6, 60, 65–6,
   67, 83–4, 85, 92–3, 99–100, 145–6,
   179–83, 248–9
  church sponsored, 98, *99*, 100–3, 106,
   145, 158–61
  government, 160, 191–4
  private, 98–103, *99*, 140, 145–6,
   160–1, 162–5, 179, 209–10
Aisha (wife of Prophet Muhammad),
   170–1
Akhtar, Naseem, 87
alcohol, 159, 213, 214, 220
  prohibition of, 29
Al-Tirmidhi, 171
America Chung Nam, 227
American Assistance for Cambodia, xviii,
   20, 22, 42, 43, 45–6, 47
American Jewish World Service, 251, 279
Amir, Halima, 84–5
Amnesty International, 167
Amsterdam City Council, 35
anesthesia, 119, 120, 129, 133
Annan, Kofi, 204
antiabortion activism, 145–9
antibiotics, 125, 127, 131
anti-immigrant laws, xiii
antipoverty programs, xxi, 191–7, 202
antitrafficking activism, xxiii, 5, 10–12, 16,
   17–18, 19, 25–30, 35–7
  financial support of, 60, 62, 67
  first world/third world alliance, 67
  new abolitionists of, 60–7
  political action in, 27–8, 28–30, 34–7
  political will lacking in, 25–6, 28, 36
"Anxious Thoughts on 'Natural Breasts'"
   (Lu Xun), 226

Apne Aap Women Worldwide, 6, 16, 17–18, 28, 36, 253
Aquino, Corazón, 217
Arab Human Development Report, 177
Are Women Human? (MacKinnon), 244
Aristotle, 259
Ashoka, 61–2
Ashoka Fellows, 61, 63, 67, 183, 210
Asian Development Bank, 20
Aswad, Du'a, 91–2
Atta, Muhammad, 171
Averting Maternal Death and Disability (AMDD), 118, 145
Awiti, Cyprian, 146
Awona, Alain, 123
Azar, Naeema, *xv*
Azim Premji Foundation, 231–2

Bales, Kevin, 11
Banerjee, Abhijit, 213
Bangladesh, xxi, 6, 19, 31, 69, 149, 208–9, 264
Ban Ki-moon, 96
Barefoot College, 264
Basu, Urmi, 31, 275, 293–4*n*
Battle of the Camel, 170
Be, Abbas, 66–7, 67
Be the Change: Your Guide to Ending Slavery and Changing the World (Hunter), 60
Bhagat, Asho, 54, 58
Bhutto, Benazir, 217
Bibi, Muktaran *see* Mai, Mukhtar
Bible, 90, 169
Biden, Joseph, 75
Bill & Melinda Gates Foundation, 30, 118
birth attendants, 121, 127, 132
Black Like Me (Griffin), 258
blood, 123–4, 189–90
blood feuds, 72
Bok, Derek, 184
Bono, 194, 306*n*
Bornstein, David, 62
Boston University, 199
BRAC, xxi, 253
brains, 126, 274
Brazil, 10, 271, 312*n*
breast-feeding, 7
    HIV infection and, 47, 195
Breierova, Lucia, 188, 305*n*

bride burning, xv, *xv*, xvi, 75
bride price, 70, 289*n*
Brokaw, Tom, 179
Brookes (slave ship), 261
Brookings Institute, 231
Brookman-Amissah, Eunice, 146
Brooks, Arthur, 160, 302*n*
brothels, xii-xiii, 167, 258
    banning and closing of, 29–30, 44, 49, 64, 65
    children held hostage in, 7, 9–10, 13–17, 32
    clandestine, 34–5, 37
    discouraging return of prostitutes to, 38, 40, 66
    enslavement of girls in, xxiii, xxiv, 3–20, *12, 17,* 25–6, 29–34
    escape and rescue from, xviii, xxiii, 15–16, *17,* 19, 25, 38–46, *39,* 49, 51, 65, 66
    legal, 28–9, 30–6
    price negotiation in, 32, 41
    profits of, 29, 35, 44
    raids on, 16, 29, 38, 65, 66
    tours of, 30–3
    women managers of, 43–4, 75
    see also prostitutes, prostitution
Brownback, Sam, 159, 311*n*
Brown University, xvii, 271
Buchanan, Patrick, 150
Buckley, Christopher, 3
Buddhism, 43
Burundi, 151, 220–5, 253
Bush, George H.W., 146, 147, 151
Bush, George W., 28, 82, 110, 151–2
    AIDS program of, 152, 159–60
    family planning funds cut by, 145–7, 162–5
Bush, Laura, 83
Buttar, Amna, 87
Byamungu, Dada, 102

California, University of, 151, 301*n*
Cambodia, xi, 100
    brothels in, *12,* 37–45, *41,* 153
    poverty in, 19–24, 45
    schools built in, 20–4, *22,* 189
Cambridge University, 261
Cameroon, 121–8, 147, 311*n*

Campaign for Female Education (Camfed), 201–3
cancer, 68, 112
capitalism, 13, 60, 207
CARE, xxii, 30, 145, 158, 221–4, 252, 253, 280
Carson, Rachel, 258
Carter, Jimmy, 197
Catholic Relief Services, 67, 157–8
cell phones, 82, 91, 175
Center for Global Development, xxii, 291n
Chakupewa, Julienne, 94
Chandara, Lor, 42
Charity Navigator, 235
Chicago, University of, 153, 271
childbirth
    breech deliveries in, *143*
    C-section deliveries in, 108, 119, 122, 123, 132, 134–5, 144
    death and injury in, 49, 104, 105–16, 117–20, 121–36, 162, 211, 213
    HIV/AIDS infection in, 47, 48, 154, 195
    hospital delivery in, 122, 126, 130–1, 222
    neglect of health care in, 105–9, 112–13, 115–16, 119, 121–3, 135–6
    obstructed labour in, 104, 105–6, 112, 121–6, 127
    removing placenta in, 144
    unattended, 236
    see also maternal mortality; pregnancy
children
    death rates of, 110, 196–7, 219
    enslavement of, 7–10, 13–17, 32
    growth and development of, 192, 214–15
    IQs of, 265, 273–4, 312n
    of prostitutes, 3, 10, 65, 275
China, xiv–xvi, 90, 132, 226–33
    economic growth of, xx, 226–7, 229, 231
    education of girls in, 184–7, 228, 230
    exports and imports of, 227, 231
    female foot-binding in, 228, 230, 244, 278
    female infanticide in, xiv, 76, 228, 229, 254, 289n
    Guangdong Province, xx, 187
    improved status of women in, 226–7, 228–32, 233
    prostitution in, 6, 10, 228, 229, 291–2n
    ratio of men to women in, xvi, 229
    sex-selected abortions, xvii, 148, 229
    women in labor force of, xx, 226–7, 229, 230–1
China Wakes (Kristof and WuDann), 229
Chinese Communist Party, 147, 229
Christianity
    conservative, 146, 157–61
    position of women in, 168
Churchill, Winston, 259
circumcision, 156, 270–1
civil rights movement, 51, 74, 258, 262, 269, 280, 312n
Civil War (US), 74
Clarke, Murvelene, 234–8
Clarkson, Thomas, 261–2
Cleland, John, 149
Clinton, Bill, 151, 217, 265
Clinton, Hillary Rodham, 28
Cohen, Dara Kay, 76, 296n
Collier, Paul, 233, 311n
colostomies, 108, 114
Columbia University, 76, 145, 194
    Center for Population and Family Health at, 117
    Mailman School of Public Health at, *116*, 117, 297n
    Medical School of, 115
Communism, collapse of, 13
community organizers, 18, 58, 63–7
concubines, 30, 228, 230
condoms, 214
    failure to make use of, 7, 31, 32, 151, 153
    HIV/AIDS transmission and, 29, 151, 157, 158
    promotion and distribution of, 29, 30, 31, 35, 151–2, 156–7, 158, 301n
Confino, Jordana, 254–6, *255*
Confucius, 90
Congo, 157–8, 235, 242
    civil war in, 93–7, 100–1, 157
    rape in, 93–6, *96*, 96–7
Congress, U.S., 36, 152, 216–17, 219, 273, 280
    see also House of Representatives, U.S.

Conrad H. Hilton Humanitarian Prize, 251
contraception,117, 131, 149
  education and, 149–50
  see also abortions; condoms; IUDs
Convention on the Elimination of All Forms
    of Discrimination (CEDAW), 272–3
Cotton, Ann, 198–201, *200*
Cotton, Catherine, 199
Council on Foreign Relations, xiv, xxiii, 302*n*
counterterrorism, xxii, 89, 183, 263
Courtwright, David, 176, 304*n*
criminal gangs, 6, 13, 37, 53–4, 55–6, 58,
  63–4, 65, 67, 85, 228

Dai Manju, 184–7, *185*
Dalits (Untouchables), 52–8
Danish Refugee Council, 142
Darfur, 92–3, 96
democracy, 162, 178, 249
Democratic Party, 28, 274
depression, 114
De Regalada, Martha Alica, 158
diarrhea, 115, 197
divorce, 44, 76, 104, 109, 138, 173, 210
doctors
  access to, 128, 133, 146, 157–8
  eschewing of, 133, 166, 298*n*
  female, 166
  indifference and absenteeism of, 125, 128
  shortage of, 127, 134
  training of, 128, 132, 134, 143
Doctors of the World, 92
Doctors Without Borders, xxii, 157
Donaldson, Peter, 149
dowries, xv, 70, 289–90*n*
Drayton, Bill, 60–1, 67, 183, 210, 295*n*
drugs, xii, 119, 120, 248
  addiction to, 17, 38, 42–3
  anti-HIV, 47
  rehabilitation from use of, 29
Dufflo, Esther, 187, 188, 213, 214–15,
  301*n*, 304*n*, 306*n*
Dungiri, Ratna, 55
DuRant-Green, Cassidy, 257
Durbar Mahila Samanwaya Committee
  (DMSC), 30–4

Easterly, William, 194
Ebadi, Shirin, 172, 303*n*

eclampsia, 119, 121
Economist, The, 261
Edna Adan Maternity Hospital, 137, 140–4,
  141, 143, 246
education
  business and job training, 29, 46, 49, 58,
    65, 102–3, 141, 173, 202–3, 210,
    236–7
  changing culture of violence through, 75,
    78, 81, 182, 183
  gender discrimination in, 13, 20, 95,
    137, 166, 181, 199–200
  of girls, xvi, xx–xxi, 14, 18, 19–24, *22,*
    52, 53, 63, 73, 76, *80,* 80–1,
    83–5, *87,* 130, 135, 138, 150,
    154, 161, 172, 182–84, 198–203,
    207, 214, 217, 230, 254–7
  investing in, 21, 58, 85, 161, 184–97,
    200–3, 213, 305*n*
  maternal mortality and, 126–7
  study-abroad programs, 98–9, 102–3, 276
  see also schools
Education Act (1870), 150, 300–1*n*
Egal, Ibrahim, 138–9
Ehlers, Sonette, 68
Emancipation Proclamation, 260
Engendering Development Through Gender Equality
    in Rights, Resources, and Voice, xxi
English language, 64, 84, 85, 99, 138, 143,
  145, 166, 174, 181, 227
Ensler, Eve, 68
environmental movement, 258
Equality Now, 73, 277
Equiano, Olaudah, 262
Ethiopia, *xvii,* 69–75, 104–9, 112–14, 217
  rape laws in, 70, 73, 74
Ethiopian Women Lawyers Association, 71,
  74
Everything But Arms, 232

faith healing, 132, 159
family planning, 115–16, 131, 145–65,
  182, 207, 222, 300*n*
  religious and government obstruction of,
    145–9, 151, 157–9, 163
  see also abortions; abstinence-only
    programs; condoms; contraception;
    United Nations Population Fund
Farmer, Paul, xxii, 118, 131

female genital mutilation (FGM), xiv, 76, 138, 162, 166, 228, 243, 244–53, 254, 311*n*
  campaign against, 245–53
  clitoral amputation in, 245
female infanticide, 168, 290*n*
  in China, xiv, 76, 228, 229, 254, 289*n*
FemCare, 190, 305*n*
femininity, 52
feminism, 29, 30, 31, 271
  Islamic, 170, 303*n*
  see also women's rights movement
Field, Erica, 190–1, 305*n*
Fish, M. Steven, 178
Fisher, Ian, 140, 299*n*
fistulas, 111, 163, 247, 258, 274, 296–7*n*
  incontinence and odor with, 95, 104, 106–7, 112–13, 114, 142
  rectovaginal, 95, 97
  surgical repair of, 97, 103, 104, 108–9, 114, *133*, 134, 143
  vesicovaginal, 95
Flannery, Jessica, 212
Flannery, Matt, 212
Florence of Arabia (Buckley), 3
Flynn, James, 265
Flynn Effect, 265
Foege, Bill, 252
food, *xvii*, 75, 214, 236
  distribution of, *xvii*, 157, 191–3, *193*, 305*n*
Ford Foundation, 269
Foreign Affairs, 12
Freedom Riders, 258, 262
Free the Slaves, 11
Friends of Edna's Hospital, 141, 142

Gandhi, Indira, 217
Gandhi, Mohandas K. "Mahatma", 62, 258
Gashe, Mamitu, *133*, 134
Gates, Bill, 177
Gayle, Helene, 158
gender discrimination
  deaths of girls and women from, xvi, *xvii*, xxiii, 121, 128–9
  economic implications of, xxii, 178, 291*n*
  education and empowerment of women as solution to, xix, xxi–xxii, xxiv, 75

  in health care, xiv, xvi, xviii, 23, 75, 108–9, 121, 123
  Muslim, xxii, 91, 156–78, 174–83
  spread of HIV/AIDS and, 150, 153
  unequal pay and, xvi, xx
genocide
  in Darfur, 92–3, 96
  in Rwanda, 96, 233–4, 235–7
Gerson, Michael, 159–60
Ghana, 21, 69, 201–2, 295*n*
Ghosh, Geeta, 31–2
Gilhuly, Anne, 140, 144
Gilhuly, Bob, 144
girls, women
  advocacy and support of, 63, 73–4
  control of economic assets by, 205–12, 215–16, 221–5
  death rates of, 212
  disappearance of, xvi, 9, 120, 290*n*
  empowerment of, 30, 35, 52, 56–8, 74, 130
  job opportunities and training for, xii, xviii–xix, *xix*, xvi, xxiii, 29, 41, 45–6, 47, 49, 58, 65–6, 71, 102–3, 141, 173, 182–3, 202, 205–12, 221–5, 226–33, 236–7, 264–5, 269–70
  life expectancy of, xvi, 212
  neglected health care of, xiv, xvi, *xvii*, xviii, 23, 75, 108–9, 121, 123
  political aspirations of, 69, 139, 144, 216–19, 233–4
  ratio of men to, xvi, 177
  as social entrepreneurs, 55–67, 179–83, 208–11, 253
Girls Be Ambitious, 22
Girls Scouts, xiv
Girls Learn International, 255–7
Glamour, 83, 84
Global Fund for Women, 62
Global Giving, 279
globalization, 13
Global Network for Neglected Tropical Disease Control, 189
Goldman Sachs, xxii, 264, 290*n*, 311*n*
Goodman, Ellen, 164–5
Graham, Billy, 159
Graham, Franklin, 159
Grameen Bank, xxi, 208, 253

Greenwich High School, 140
Griffin, John Howard, 258
Grijalva, Frank, 19–21, 23–4, 189
Gulf War, 240
Gupta, Ruchira, 16, 25, 28, 31, 63, 64

Haidt, Jonathan, 276–7, 313n
Hamlin, Catherine, 107–10, 114, 296n
Hamlin, Reg, 107, 134
Hammerquist, Natalie, 24
Harkin, Tom, 19
Harvard University, 149, 178, 188, 190–1,
    193, 263, 269
  Medical School of, 118
  School of Public Health of, 31, 131,
    293n
Hasina, Meena, 3–11, 4, 14, 15–18, 19,
    25, 64
Hasina, Naina, 7, 9–10, 13–17, 17
Hasina, Vivek 4, 7, 9, 13–17
Haugen, Gary, 29, 293n
HEAL Africa Hospital, 97, 99, 99, 100–3,
    296n
health care
  clinics and centers of, 72, 92, 95, 97, 98,
    119, 126–7, 130, 145–6, 156,
    180, 182, 192, 248
  costs of, 108, 119, 122, 123, 127, 135
  funding of, 102–3, 111–12, 118, 141–3
  gender discrimination in, xv, xvi, xviii,
    23, 75, 108–9, 121, 123
  maternal, 85, 104, 105–20, 121–36,
    137–44, 179
  medical supplies for, 93, 123, 125, 127,
    129, 131, 134, 142, 190
  of rape victims, 72, 88, 92–3
  see also doctors; nurses; public health;
    specific hospitals
Heifer International, 266–9
Helms, Jesse, 159
Hinduism, 15, 65, 166
HIV/AIDS, 10, 13, 29–30, 35, 150–60,
    269
  curbing spread of, 29, 30, 35, 93, 135,
    150–7, 158, 159, 160, 194, 195
  deaths from, 10, 13, 19, 21, 29, 40,
    154, 155, 211
  education on, 156–7, 302n
  marriage and, 66, 67, 153, 154

medical treatment of, 47, 151, 153, 156
origins of, 121, 301n
orphans of, 160
prostitution and, 6–7, 19, 30, 35, 46–9
testing and diagnosis of, 7, 34, 46–9,
    154, 156, 195, 222
transmission of, 47, 48, 150, 153–7,
    195, 223
vulnerability of women to, 150, 153–4,
    156–7, 301n
Holbrook, Tara, 140–1
Holmes, John, 95, 296n
Holocaust, 259
homosexuality, 150
honor killings, xxiii, xxiv, 24, 75, 90–3,
    228, 257, 278
  by Muslims, 91–2, 166, 167
Horowitz, Michael, 160, 274
Hotez, Peter, 189
House of Representatives, U.S., 216–17,
    234
Hou Yifan, 230
How to Change the World (Bornstein), 62
hudood laws, 207
Hudson Institute, 160
Huichol tribe, 129
human rights, xiii-xiv, 92, 248, 260
  education in, 20–4, 237
  laws, policies, and conventions of, 118
  recognition and support of, xxiii, xiv,
    19–24, 51, 58–9, 129, 253
  safe childbirth and, 118, 129, 136
hunger, xvii, xxi, 111–12, 113, 132
Hunger Project, xxii
Hunt, Swanee, 263, 296n, 311n
Hunter, Zach, 60, 63
Huron Report, 227
Hussein, Saddam, 239–40, 242
Hutu militia, 94–5, 233, 235
Hyderabad, 64–7
hymens, 84, 90
  medical inspection of, 91, 172–3, 202–3
  see also virgins

Ideal Woman in Islam (Imran), 166
Imran, Muhammad, 166
India
  Bihar state in, 3, 4, 5, 16, 18, 25, 28
  birth rate in, 149

bride burning in, *xv*, xv
caste system in, 52–8
education of girls in, xvi, 188, 232
efforts to correct gender discrimination
    in, xvi, xvii, xxi, 231–2
high death rates of women in, xv, 110,
    111, 130
HIV/AIDS in, 7, 30, 34
Kasturba Nagar slum in, 51–9, 289*n*
Kerala state in, xvi, 188, 304*n*
maternal mortality in, 130, 132
poverty and malnutrition in, 52–3
prostitution in, 3–20, *5, 12, 17*, 25–6,
    29–34, 36, 275–6, 291*n*
women leaders in, 218
Indiana University, 188
Indonesia, 188, 215, 305*n*
infant formula, 195
infants
    burning of, 144
    deaths of, 106, 110, 112, 123, 137
    diarrhea in, 115, 197
    see also childbirth; female infanticide
Injaz program, 173
International Food Policy Research
    Institute, 192
International Journal of Gynecology & Obstetrics,
    133
International Justice Mission, 28, 30, 37
International Labour Organization, 10
International Rescue Committee, 145, 281
International Violence Against Women Act,
    75
International Women's Health Coalition,
    62, 118, 152, 290*n*
Internet, 60, 91, 102, 103
    e-mail on, 21, 24, 163, 275–6, 279
iodine deficiency, 190–1, 265, 273–4, 305*n*
Iran, 6, 29, 172, 174, 178
Iran-Iraq war, 239
Iraq, 76, 91, 239–40
    U.S. invasions of, 240, 263
Ireland, 110, 111, 253
Islam
    early respect for women in, 168, 183
    head coverings and burkas required of
        women in, *80*, 81, 84, 86, 167,
        168, 168–9, 172, 173, 174, 181
    Ramadan observance in, 174

women's rights progress in, 172–3, 183
    see also Muslims
Issoufou, Ramatou, 119, 146
IUDs, 117, 158
    copper-T vs. steel-ring, 148
Ivins, Molly, 164–5

Janjaweed militias, 92
Japan, 10, 167
Jemma, Aberew, 72–4
Jensen, Robert, 271, 296*n*
Jesus Christ, 64, 159, 259
Jews, 169, 180, 259
Johnson, Lyndon B., 139

Kabul, 76–8, *168*, 173–5, 179–82
Kagame, Paul, 233–4, 235
Kashf Foundation, 205, 207–11, *209*, 253
Kaufmann, Chaim, 260, 311*n*
Kayode, Obende, 119–20
Kennedy, Ruth, 109, 112, 134
Kenya, 69, 145–6, 189, 193, 194, 312*n*
Kharas, Homi, 231
King, Martin Luther, Jr., 51, 62, 258, 262
Kissinger, Henry, 264
Kiva, 212, 279
Kolkata (Calcutta), 16, 25, 275–6
    Sonagachi red-light district of, 30–4
Koran, xxii, 169–72, 182, 303*n*
    gender discrimination in, 169, 170–1
    reinterpretation of, 169, 171
Kouchner, Bernard, xxii, 290*n*
Kremer, Michael, 193, 301*n*, 305*n*
Krisher, Bernard, 20, 43, 45–6, 49
Krishnan, Sunitha, 63–7, *63*
Kun Sokkea, 21–4, *22*

La Ferrara, Eliana, 271, 312*n*
Lancet, 10, 117, 129, 132, 292*n*, 294*n*, 298*n*
Landes, David, 178, 304*n*
League of Women Voters, 162
Lee Jong-wook, 69
legal rights, 85, 210
Leghari, Farooq, 88
Lemokouno, Prudence, 121–5, *122*, 127,
    136, 147
leprosy, 108, 109
Levy, Santiago, 191
Lewis, Stephen, 96, 134, 313*n*

Li Honggui, xiv
Lincoln, Abraham, 25
Loma Linda University, 181
Long, Bridget, 188
Long Pross, *12*
Loose Change to Loosen Chains (LC2LC), 60
Luck, Jo, 265, 267–8
Lugar, Richard, 75
Lusi, Jo and Lyn, 100–1
Luxenberg, Christoph, 171, 303*n*
Lu Xun, 226, 308*n*

Macapagal-Arroyo, Gloria, 217
MacKinnon, Catherine A., 244
Mai, Mukhtar, 79–89, *80, 87*, 256, 296*n*
  government harassment of, 81–2, 86–7, 89
  rape of, 79–80, 82, 91
  schools and organizations founded by, 80, *81*, 83–5, *87*, 99, 277
Mai, Shakur, 79
Maine, Deborah, 117
malaria, 68, 101, 121, 131, 135, 160, 194, 195, 211, 212, 220
Malaysia, xii–xiii, xxiii, 48, 245
Maloney, Carolyn, 28, 152
Mao Zedong, 229
Margolies-Mezvinsky, Marjorie, 216–17
Marie Stopes International, 145–6, 164
marriage
  child and teenage, 76–7, 84–5, 228
  delay of, 116, 131, 188, 232
  forced, 72, 105, 174–5, 240, 242, 256
  HIV/AIDS and, 66, *67, 153, 154*
  of prostitutes, xviii, 44, 66, 153–4
  after rape, 70–4, 105
  sex before, 70–4, 91, 93, 173–4
Massachusetts Institute of Technology (MIT), 156, 187, 188, 269
massage, 6, 46, 114
Mastoi clan, 79
maternal morbidity, 104–14, 119–20, 135
maternal mortality, xi, xiii, 49, 104–14, 118–20, 121–36, 148, 162, 211, 214, 217, 297*n*
  contributions to the cause of, 103, 111–12, 117–18, 134–6, 137
  factors in, 121–9, 146

  lack of attention to, 117, 134–5
  lack of education and, 126–7
  lack of rural health systems and, 127–8
  poverty and, 122, 129–30, 136
  progress in reduction of, 129–36
maternal mortality ratio (MMR), 110–11, 130, 297*n*
Mather, Cotton, 104
McConnell, Harper, 98, *99*, 100–3, 158
McGovern, George, 192
Melching, Molly, 247–53, *248*
Memory, a Monologue, a Rant, and a Prayer, A (Ensler), 68
menstruation, 171, 189
  management of, 189–90, 202
mental retardation, 274
Mercy Corps, 81, 281
Mernissi, Fatema, 171
methamphetamines, 42–3
Mexico, 22, 129, 167, 191–2, 273, 305*n*
microfinance, xxi, xxii, 202, 205–12, 264, 306–8*n*
  interest rates in, 211
  repayment in, 207, 208, 210
Micronutrient Initiative, 274
midwives, 112, 117, 126, 137, 199
  training of, 130, 132, 134, 138, 143
Migiro, Asha-Rose, 121
Miguel, Edward, 212, 307*n*
Millennium Challenge, 215–16
Miller, Grant, 219, 308*n*
Minnesota, University of, 100
misogyny, 68–78, 98, 295*n*
  Islam and, xxii, 91, 166–83, 302–4*n*
missionaries, 106, 145, 157–9, 247
mistresses, 235
  teenage, 153–4, 156–7, 223
Mogae, Festus, 216
More, Jija, 57
Morgan Guaranty Trust Company, 186
morphine, 17
Mortenson, Greg, 179
mosquito nets, 131, 195, 212, 213, 220
Mothers Against Drunk Driving, 269
mothers-in-law, 77, 204–5, 221
Mouassa, Emilienne, 123
Mount Holyoke College, 209
Mozah, Sheikha, 172
Mugwendere, Angeline, 198, 203, 306*n*

INDEX

Muhammad (Prophet), 168, 169–71, 175

Muhammad, Abdu, 192–3

Muhammad, Mahabouba, 104–9, *108*, 247

Muhammad, Saima, 204–8, *205*, 211

Muhammad VI, King of Morocco, 173

Mukakarisa, Claudine, 235–8, *237*

Mukhtar Mai School for Girls, *80*, 80–1,
83–5, 87–8, 99

Mukhtar Mai Women's Welfare
Organization, 85

Mumbai (Bombay), 30, 31, 34, 279

see also female infanticide; honor killings

Musharraf, Pervez, 80, 81–3, 87, 89, 263

Muslims, xv

177, 183

discriminatory practices of, xxii, 91,
156–78, 179–83

Shiite, 303n

Sunni, 91

see also Islam

Mwenda, Andrew, 194

Nairobi, 74, 132

Najabi, Zoya, 76–8, *77*

Narayane, Alka, 53

Narayane, Madhukar, 53

Narayane, Usha, 52–9, *52*, 63

Nathaniel, Naka, 38, 49–50, *52*, 123–4

National Association of Evangelicals, 159

National Council of Women's
Organizations, 162, 269

NATO, xxii–xxiii

Nazis, 259

Nepal, 4, 6, 25–6

Netherlands, prostitution, legalized in,
34–5, 294n

Neuwirth, Jessica, 73

New Light, 31, 275–6

New York, N.Y., xiv, 62, 73, 83, 107, 117,
192, 237, 256

New York Review of Books, xvi, 290n

New York Times, xiv, 38, 49, 140, 227

New York University, 194

Niger, 109n, 110–11, 118–20, 146

Nigeria, 13, 69, 115–16, 188

Nike Foundation, xxii

Nine Dragons Paper, 227

Nineteenth Amendment, 219

Nixon, Richard M., 147

Nkunda, Laurent, 95

Nobel Prize, xvi, xxi, 172, 208, 303n

209, 269, 291n

NoVo Foundation, xxii

Nutt clan, 3, 17

Nyabenda, Goretti, 220–5, *224*

Obama, Barack, 152, 165

Oklahoma State University, 268

Omar, Caliph, 170

Oportunidades, 191–2, 273, 305n

Osli, Una, 188, 305n

Oster, Emily, 153, 271, 290n, 296n

Overlake School (Cambodia), 20–4, *22*

Overlake School (Washington), 19–21, 23

Oxford University, 232–3, 311n

Pakistan, xv, xxii, 6, 12–13, 76, 79, 110,
263, 264

education in, *80*, 80–1, 83–5, 87–8, 99,
179, 256–7, 277

208

Pape, Robert, 260, 311n

Parks, Rosa, 258

Patel, Anup, 32–3, 294n

Paul, Saint, 168, 259

Paulos, Mahdere, 74

Peace Corps, 116, 161

Pennsylvania, University of, 279

Wharton School of, 208

Pentecostalism, 159, 302n
Peterson, Sandy, 140–1, 144
physical therapy, 108, 114
pimps, 8–9, 29, 33–4, 36, 37, 38, 40, 65, 66
Pipi, Pascal, 122–5, 127
pirated goods, 25–6, 30
Plan International, 279
plastic surgery, 85
police, 9, 36, 58–9
    bribery and corruption of, xiii, 8, 15, 16,
        29, 36, 40, 44, 53, 61–2, 64, 81
    brothels raided by, 16, 29, 38, 65, 66
    failure to act by, 8, 25–6, 53, 54–5, 75, 93
    protective custody by, 56, 73
    rape by, 54, 93
polygamy, 167, 177
Population Council, 149
Population Council of Thailand, 116
postexposure prophylaxis kits, 93
poverty, 98, 107, 196
    education and promotion of women in
        fight against, xx–xxi, 19–24, 183,
        184–7, 195, 198–203, 204–25
    maternal mortality and, 122, 129–30, 136
    spending habits and, 212–15
    see also antipoverty programs
Prajwala, 65–7
pregnancy
    delay and prevention of, 105–6, 116,
        149–50, 156, 188–9, 231
    determining gender in, xvi, 229
    HIV transmission and, 47, 48–9
    medical crises in, 115, 119, 121–5,
        132–3, 135–6
    prenatal and maternal care in, 85,
        104–20, 121–44, 145–6, 167, 190
    rape and, 235–6
    teenage, 105–6, 109
    unwanted, 148–9
    see also childbirth
Premji, Azim, 231–2
prison, xiii, 56, 93, 173–5, 183
Procter & Gamble, 190
Prohibition, 28
prostitutes, prostitution, 213, 291–5n
    abuse, rape and killing of, xii–xiii, 4–6,
        8, 11, 12, 13–16, 17, 29–37,
        39–41, 43–4, 51, 66
    arrest and imprisonment of, xiii

breaking the spirit of, 4–5, 7–8, 11, 44,
    66
child and teenage, 5–6, 10, 12, 14, 28,
    29, 32, 34, 35, 36–45
children of, 3, 7, 10, 65, 275
cracking down on, 34–7, 44, 64, 65, 294n
debts of, xii, 43, 45
ding-dong xiaojie, 6
disease risks, 6–7, 10, 13, 19, 30–1, 34,
    35, 40, 46–9, 291n
divisive politics of, 27–30
dressing and decoration of, 14, 32, 38
drugging of, xii, 4–5, 17, 38, 42–3
economic motivation of, 10, 13, 30, 64
empowerment of, 30, 34, 51–2
as entrepreneurs, 6, 10, 13
intergenerational, 3, 7, 8
interviewing of, 38–50, 64, 65
joy feigned by, xii–xiii, 11
kidnapping and enslavement of, xxiii,
    xxiv, 3–20, 12, 17, 19, 25–6,
    29–42
legalization and regulation of, 28–9,
    30–6, 294n
managerial roles of, 44, 75
marriage of, xviii, 9, 44, 66, 153–4
in massage parlors and clubs, 6, 10
men criminalized for use of, 35, 294n
paying for release of, 39–42
pregnancy of, 7
rehabilitation, counseling and training of,
    64–6, 67
returning to home and families by, 41–2,
    66
social services and health checks for, 29,
    34, 35
statistics on, 6, 10–11, 34
stigma of, 9, 38, 40
suicide of, 64
unionizing of, 30–4
as victims vs. criminals, 35
voluntary, 6, 10, 13, 28, 29, 34–5, 43
    see also brothels; sex trafficking
public health, 115–18, 120, 130, 219, 252
Purpose Driven Life, The (Warren), 160

Qian, Nancy, xvii, 290n
Qian Xinzhong, 147
Quakers, 259

racism, 258
Rajan, Raghuram, 194
Ramdas, Kavita, 62
Rangdale, Rajashri, 57
Rania, Queen of Jordan, 172
rape, 70, 239, 240
　of boys, 79
　in brothels, xii, 5, 11, 15, 32, 37
　child and teenage, 54, 70–5, 92, 93, 95,
　　104, 141, 235
　examination and treatment for, 73, 88,
　　s92, 93, 95, 97, 98
　female facilitation of, 76, 295n
　gang, 53, 54, 64, 71, 76, 79, 83, 88, 92,
　　94–5, 235, 241
　humiliation and stigma of, 53–4, 64, 68,
　　69–70, 80, 93, 94
　kidnapping and, 70–3, 79, 88, 235
　marriage after, 70–4, 105
　mass, 70, 92, 95–6, 96, 97
　mutilation and, 93–4, 95, 97, 104
　postexposure prophylaxis treatment
　　after, 93
　pregnancy and, 235–6
　prevention of, 68, 79
　prosecution of, 70, 74, 80, 89
　as punishment, 79–80, 88, 90–1, 92–3,
　　167
　reporting of, 71, 80, 88, 92, 93
　statistics on, 93
　suicide following, 80, 94
　threats of, 53, 55–6, 58, 92
　as tool of war, 76, 93–7, 96, 104, 235,
　　241
　undermining tribal and family structures
　　with, 91, 92, 94
　underreporting of, 64, 69
　of virgins, 70–3
Rapex, 68
Reagan, Ronald, 147
Rede Globo, 271
red-light districts, 3, 15, 28, 30–5, 38,
　64–5, 67
refugees, 145, 146, 181
Rendall, Sapor, 46
Republican Party, 28, 151, 273
Review of Economics and Statistics, 194
Rice, Condoleezza, 82
river blindness, 253n

Roberts, Jane, 162–5, 163, 302n
Robinson, Mary, 253
Rockefeller Foundation, 149, 269
Roman Catholic Church, 64–5, 67, 151,
　157–8
Roman Empire, fall of, 61
Rosenfield, Allan, 115–19, 116, 120,
　131–2, 134, 145, 297n
Rosenfield, Clare, 115
Roy, Bunker, 264
Rural School Project, 20
Rwabirinba, Noel, 95, 96
Rwanda, 76, 96, 118, 237, 242, 310n
　genocide in, 96, 233–4, 235–7
　promotion of women in, 233–4

Sachs, Jeffrey, xxii, 194
Saddleback Church, 160
Safe Motherhood Initiative
　conference of (1987), 132
safe motherhood programs, 145
Salbi, Zainab, 239–43, 241
salt, iodized, 190, 273–4
Salti, Soraya, 173
Samaritan's Purse, 159
Samatar, Mohamed, 140
San Bernardino Sun, 162
Saudi Arabia, 167, 168–9
Save the Children, 281
schools, 188–94
　abuse by teachers in, 202
　deworming of students in, 189
　dropping out of, 184, 189, 192
　feeding programs in, 192–3, 193, 305n
　founding and building of, 63, 64, 65–6,
　　67, 80, 80–1, 83–5, 87–8, 101,
　　179, 189
　secret, 181–2
　tuition and fees of, 184–7, 198, 200,
　　201, 203, 236
　uniforms worn in, 116
　see also education
Scruggs, Stirling, 164
Segaye, Simeesh, 112–14, 113
Self Employed Women's Association, xxi,
　253
Sen, Amartya, xvi, xxi, 290n
Senegal, 165, 249–51
sepsis, 121, 131

September 11 terrorist attacks, xxii, 20,
  25, 171
sexism, 75, 229, 295n
sex tourism, 27, 35
sex trafficking, xi–xiii, xv, xx–xxi, 3–20,
  25–6, 98, 146, 159, 217
  Atlantic slave trade compared with,
    11–13
  of boys, 11
  promises of legitimate jobs and, xi–xii,
    39, 43, 45, 66, 105
  ranking of countries on handling of, 36
  statistics on, 10–11
  see also brothels; prostitutes, prostitution
sexual harassment, xi, 23, 202
sexual honor codes, 91, 92–3
sexually transmitted diseases (STDs), 35,
  153, 156, 222, 301n
  see also HIV/AIDS
sex workers see prostitutes, prostitution
Shaw, George Bernard, 51
shelters, 76, 85
Sheppard-Towner Act, 219
Shields, Brooke, 83
Shikwati, James, 194–5
Sierra Club, 162
Sierra Leone, 76, 93, 110, 296n
Silent Spring (Carson), 258
slavery, xviii, xxiv, 25, 259–62
  abolition of, 24, 158, 170, 259–62, 280
  in antebellum America, 6, 12, 260
  modern forms of, 60–7
slaves, 26
  abuse and killing of, 12, 261
  forced labor of, 10, 60
  transatlantic trade in, 12, 259–62, 311n
smallpox, 115, 197, 252
Smith, Chris, 147
social entrepreneurs, 60–7, 179–83,
  208–11, 253
  aid workers vs., 60–1, 62, 67
  financial support of small-scale programs
    by, 60–1, 62, 67
  initiative and social tools of, 60–1, 62,
    67
  rise of, 60–1
social services, 28–9, 38, 45–6, 63
Society for Effecting the Abolition of the
  Slave Trade, 261

Sok Khorn, 44
soldiers
  child, 95, 96
  rape by, 76, 93–7, 96, 104, 235, 241
  women, 76
Solon, 90
Somalia, 137–9, 245
Somaliland, 137–44, 246, 247
Sonagachi Project, 30–4
Song Dynasty, 90
Soranos of Ephesus, 245, 310n
South Africa, 68, 69, 116, 154–5, 202,
  307n
  collapse of apartheid in, 214
  pension system in, 214, 307n
Srey Momm, 38, 40–4, 41
Srey Neth, 38–41, 39, 43, 45–50
Srey Rath, xi–xiii, xxiii-xix, xix, 4
Sri Lanka, 27, 129–32, 298n
State Department, U.S., 11, 83, 147
  antitrafficking actions of, 36, 75
Steinem, Gloria, 73
sterilization, involuntary, 147–8
Stiglitz, Joseph, xxi
Stone, Michael, 76
Streep, Meryl, 73
Subramanian, Arvind, 194
Sudan, 92, 151
sugar, 213, 260
suicide, 65, 92, 105, 113, 141, 171
  rape followed by, 80, 94
Summers, Lawrence, xxi, 187n
Swahili, 98, 102, 103
sweatshops, xx, 19, 232, 309–10n
Sweden, 34–5, 235, 294n
Syed, Shershah, 93

Taliban, 167, 179, 181–2, 254
Tanzania, 134, 191, 194, 201, 212, 306n
Teach for America, 161
Teach the World, 161
television, 271, 312n
Templeton, Sir John, 276
terrorism, 36, 89, 263
  campaign against, xxii, 89, 183, 263
  by criminals, 53–9
  Muslim, xxii, 20, 25, 171, 176–7
  rape as, 76, 92, 93–7, 96, 104, 235, 241
Tertullian, 168

Thailand, xi, xiii, xviii–xix, 20, 27, 45, 116–17, 134, 292n
34 Million Friends of UNFPA, 163–4, 302n
Three Cups of Tea (Mortenson), 179
Time, 240
Tiwari, Avinash, 54
Tobela, Gertrude, 154–5
Tobela, Thabang, 154–6, *155*
Tobela, Victor, 154–5
Tonga tribe, 200
Tostan, 248–53, *248*
Trafficking in Persons (TIP) Report, 36, 37, 75
Trafficking Victims Protection Act (2000), 27–8
Trent, Tererai, *266*, 266–9
tuberculosis, 49, 144
Tutsi tribe, 233, 235
Twain, Mark, xi
ultrasound technology, xvii, 229
UNICEF, xxi, 192, 251
UNIFEM, 273, 296n
United Kingdom, 10, 62, 100, 135, 138, 142, 149–50, 198, 200–1, 259–62, 311n
United Nations (UN), xxi, 10, 93, 94, 95, 128, 132, 139, 157, 252–3
    Millennium Development Goal of, 132, 135
United Nations Development Programme (UNDP), xxi, 290n
United Nations Population Fund (UNFPA), 92, 119, 146–8, 152, 183, 300n
    funding cuts of, 145–8, 157, 162–5
    funding restored to, 152, 162–5
United Nations Refugee Agency, 142
United States, xix–xx, 10, 27, 176
    Chinese immigration to, xix–xx
    education in, 19–24, 98–9, 100, 255–7
    healthcare spending in, 110, 135
    maternal mortality, 110, 111, 128, 133
    ratio of men to women in, xi, 176
    slavery in, 6, 12, 260
    women's issues and foreign policy of, xiv, x, 75, 135, 145–9, 151–2, 162–5, 271, 272
United States Agency for International Development (USAID), 75, 110, 142
Upper Room church, 100

Urdal, Hendrik, 176, 303n
Urdu language, 85, 86
U.S. Committee for UNFPA, 164–5
uterus rupture, 121, 125

vaccines, xvi, 62, 75, 115, 136, 142, 191, 253n
vaginal microbicides, 270
vaginas, sexual violence and, 93–4, 95
Vahane, Bhau, 57
Vetticatil, Joe, 64–5
violence against women, 68–89
    culture of sexual predation and, 69–76
    domestic, 69, 75, 77, 84, 90, 204, 206, 220, 272, 295–6n
    education and, 75, 78, 81, 182, 183
    laws in support of, 70, 91
    maiming and injury from, xvi, 68–9, 85, 92
    participation of women in, 75–8, 106
    statistics on, 69
virgins, 6, 13, 155, 170
    obsession with chastity of, 84, 90–1, 92, 173
    rape of, 70–3
    sale of, 29, 30, 37, 39–40
    testing of, 91, 173, 202
    see also hymens
Vital Voices, 28

Wadud, Amina, 169, 302–3n
Wall, L. Lewis, 109, 274, 297n
Wanjera, Rose, 145–6
Warren, Rick, 160
Wealth and Poverty of Nations, The (Landes), 178, 304n
Wellstone, Paul, 28
Wen Lok, 43
White House, 60, 82, 139, 159–60, 234
wife beating, 69, 75, 77, 84, 90, 204, 206, 220, 272, 295–6n
Wilberforce, William, xxi, 60, 62, 260–1, 311n
Wilde, Oscar, 145
Winfrey, Oprah, 109, 242
witch killing, 75, 212, 306n
Women for Women in Bosnia, 241, *241*
Women for Women International, 235, 236, 237, *237*, 241, 243, 279

Women's Campaign International, 217
Women's Detention Center (Kabul), 173–6
women's rights movement, 62, 71, 73–4,
    158–9, 182, 259, 263–80
  in Middle East, 172–3, 228
  see also feminism; women's suffrage
women's solidarity groups, 207, 221–5
women's suffrage, 128, 218–19, 268,
    308n
Woods, Syndee, 275–6
Working Assets, 241
World Bank, xxi, 20, 127, 131, 135, 151,
    192, 194, 208, 231, 290n
World Economic Forum, 167
World Food Programme (WFP), 192
World Health Organization (WHO), 30,
    69, 110, 111, 132, 139, 142, 213,
    246
World Vision, 279
World War I, 128
World War II, 176, 259

Worldwide Fistula Fund, 109n, 274
worms, 189, 197, 253n

Xie Jun, 230
Xu Yuhua, 230

Yacoobi, Sakena, *180*, 181–3
Yadav, Akku, 53–9
Yale University, 32, 208
Yemen, 167, 177, 304n
Yokadouma Hospital, 121–8
Young Women's Leadership School, 255
Yunus, Muhammad, xxi, 208, 306n

Zafar, Roshaneh, 208–11, *209*
Zebene (father of Woineshet), 70, 70–2
Zebene, Woineshet, 69–74, *70*, 295n
Zedillo, Ernesto, 191
Zhang Yin, 226–7, 308n
Zhu Chen, 230
Zimbabwe, 198–201, 202–3, 265–8